Postnationalist Ireland

'This is a work of vision, a suggestion for new ways of thinking about ourselves and our post-Troubles world, which should be required reading for all those involved in the Northern Ireland peace process.'

Marianne Elliott, *University of Liverpool*

The encroachment of globalization and demands for greater regional autonomy have had a profound effect on the way we picture Ireland. This challenging new look at the key question of sovereignty asks us how we should think about the identity of a 'postnationalist' Ireland. Richard Kearney goes to the heart of the conflict over demand for communal identity, traditionally expressed by nationalism, and the demand for a universal model of citizenship, traditionally expressed by republicanism. In so doing, he asks us to question whether the sacrosanct concept of absolute national sovereignty is becoming a luxury ill-afforded in the emerging new Europe.

Kearney then takes us beyond the political with chapters on the influence of such philosophers as George Berkeley, John Toland and John Tyndall and looks at some of the myths in Irish poetry and nationhood.

Postnationalist Ireland provides a recasting of contemporary Irish politics, culture, literature and philosophy and will appeal to students of these subjects and Irish studies in general.

Richard Kearney is Professor of Philosophy at University College, Dublin, and lectures regularly at Boston College. He has presented cultural and literary features on Irish and European television and has recently published his first novel, *Sam's Fall*.

'Whatever is given / can always be reimagined, however four-square, /
. . . it happens to be'

(Seamus Heaney)

Postnationalist Ireland

Politics, culture, philosophy

Richard Kearney

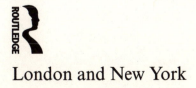

London and New York

First published 1997
by Routledge
11 New Fetter Lane, London EC4P 4EE

Simultaneously published in the USA and Canada
by Routledge
29 West 35th Street, New York, NY 10001

Typeset in Times by RefineCatch Limited, Bungay, Suffolk
Printed and bound in Great Britain by
TJ Press (Padstow) Ltd, Padstow, Cornwall

British Library Cataloguing in Publication Data
A catalogue record for this book is available from the British Library

Library of Congress Cataloguing in Publication Data
Kearney, Richard.
    Postnationalist Ireland: politics, culture, philosophy /
    Richard Kearney.
            p.   cm.
    Includes bibliographical references and index.
    1. Ireland—Politics and government—1949– .
    2. English literature, Irish authors—History and criticism.
    3. National characteristics, Irish, in literature.
    4. Ireland—Civilization—20th century.   5. National characteristics, Irish.
    6. Ireland—In literature.   7. Nationalism—Ireland.
    8. Philosophy—Ireland.   I. Title.
    DA963.K34   1996
    941.60824—dc20   96–5492
                            CIP

ISBN 0–415–11502–7 (hbk)
ISBN 0–415–11503–5 (pbk)

For John McNamara
In memoriam

Contents

viii   *Contents*

Acknowledgements

Most of the material in the present volume is original to it, though some sections of the chapters have appeared over the years in earlier, less developed versions. Portions of 'Postnationalism and Postmodernity' appeared as 'Postmodernity and Politics' (in *History of European Ideas*, 1993) and as an *Irish Times* series, 'Postmodern Ireland' (1987). Parts of 'Ideas of a Republic' were first formulated in another *Irish Times* series of that name (August 1989) and in more developed form as 'The Irish Heritage of the French Revolution: The Rights of the People and the Rights of Man' (in *Ireland and France*, 1992). Earlier and shorter versions of Chapters 5, 6 and 7 appeared, respectively, as 'The Fifth Province: Between the Local and the Global' (in *Migrations*, 1990); 'Myth and Motherland' (in the Field Day series, 1984); and 'Myth and Modernity in Irish Poetry' (in *Contemporary Irish Poetry*, 1992). The final part of this volume comprises three lectures on three Irish thinkers who straddle the national–international divide, given at three conferences: The International George Berkeley Conference at the Sorbonne, 1985; The John Toland Conference of Eighteenth-Century Studies at University College Cork, 1992; and The International John Tyndall Conference at Carlow, 1993. Chapter 3, 'Genealogy of the Republic', was first delivered as a series of lectures as Visiting European Professor at Boston College in 1991.

My thanks to the various universities and publishers who solicited this material in its initial drafts; to my colleagues in the philosophy departments of University College Dublin and Boston College, and the following individuals who kindly read the manuscript and offered helpful advice: Simon Partridge of the European Regionalist Movement, Seamus Deane of Notre Dame University, Marianne Elliott of Liverpool University, Luke Gibbons of Dublin City University, Kevin Whelan of Boston College, and Tom Garvin and Attracta Ingram of the Politics Department at University College Dublin. The extent of my debt to these and other colleagues is evident, I hope, in the detailed endnotes to the chapters below – endnotes where I have chosen to develop the more philosophical, technical and infrastructural issues underlying my general presentation. These extensive annotations, glosses and commentaries comprise a parallel subtext to the main text which argues more in terms of principles than of details. My gratitude also goes to Adrian Driscoll at Routledge for his encouragements and assistance, and to my wife, Anne, and daughters, Simone and Sarah, for being so helpful in ways estimable and inestimable.

The studies in this volume may be read as a critical continuation of my earlier volume of Irish essays, *Transitions: Narratives in Modern Irish Culture* (Wolfhound Press / Manchester University Press), first published in 1987 and reprinted in paperback in 1996, and more generally of the two 'collective' volumes of essays, *The Crane Bag Book of Irish Studies* (vols 1 and 2, Blackwater Press / Wolfhound Press, Dublin, 1981, 1985), frequently cited throughout this work.

Introduction
Beyond the nation-state

This is a book about separations. To separate, here, does not mean to repudiate; it means to step back in order to rethink some of the prevailing ideas and images that have shaped the political understanding of most modern Irish citizens. My aim is not to denounce nationalism – Irish or British – out of hand, but to reinterrogate its critical implications. Hence my endeavours, in what follows, to evaluate the origins and ends of the main ideologies informing the Irish–British syndrome and to suggest how they might be critically redeployed in a new configuration. My own tentative itinerary on this path is charted, for what it is worth, in three joint-submissions to political Forums published below as Chapter 5 – Forum for a New Ireland (1983), Opsahl Commission (1993), Forum for Peace and Reconciliation (1995). These represent three stages in a transition from what might broadly be called a nationalist to a postnationalist position. I include them not out of self-regard, but because I consider it unwise for anyone today to speak *about* the 'national question' without also stating where he/she is speaking *from*.

At a more theoretical level, this volume attempts to *separate out* a number of elided terms which have conditioned the political culture of these islands. I am thinking, for example, about the separation of region from state, state from nation, nation from republic, republicanism from nationalism, nationality from sovereignty, absolute sovereignty from shared sovereignty, internationalism from supranationalism, federation from centralization. And I am thinking, further, about the disentangling of these separated terms into their various kinds and qualifications – e.g. nationalism into 'civic', 'ethnic', 'romantic', 'economic', 'separatist', 'sectarian' and 'cultural'; republicanism into 'classical', 'modern' and 'postmodern'. In each case, it is a question of unpacking wholes in favour of parts; of differentiating in order to better apprehend; of disassembling the ideologies which have undergirded the parallel constructs of a United Kingdom and a United Ireland out of fidelity to their constituent participants and peoples.

This labour of critical demarcation is intended as a modest exercise in intellectual democracy, seeking to match people's responsibilities with rights and to interrogate the vexed issue of people's identity. For surely democracy is, in the first and final analysis, about *people* more than about land, law or ideology. But here, precisely, we confront the fundamental question of *popular sovereignty*: Who exactly are the people? Are they *a* people, *the* people, or peoples? Are 'people' to be understood primarily as persons or nations? citizens or communities? regions or states? In short, how are we to respond to Cicero's inaugural (and still unresolved) question about the nature and origin of the *civitas*?

Each of the chapters in this volume attempts some kind of critical response. The first endeavours to tease out the notion of sovereignty, the second and third republicanism, the fourth nationalism, the fifth the nation-state. The ensuing parts on 'Culture' and 'Philosophy' pursue further interrogations regarding myths of motherland and the rapport between national and cosmopolitan identities. We cannot, I believe, expect to transform the political *reality* of the nation-state without a corresponding revision of its political *imaginary*.[1]

In every study, it must be said at the outset, the attempt to advance a postnationalist paradigm is equally, in the Irish–British context, an effort to adumbrate a postunionist one. (Unionism being understood as a variant of British nationalism.) The overriding aim of this inquiry is, at bottom, to point to possibilities of loosening up the nationalist–unionist logjam.

CONCEPTS OF THE NATION

By way of introduction, it may be useful to briefly anticipate here some of the different meanings of the term *nation* – the most pivotal and recurring concept in our eleven chapters below.

In current usage, a nation is often assumed to be a *state*, or a group of people aspiring in common towards the condition of a state. As a state, the modern nation is generally, in fact or in aspiration, a sovereign entity with significant control over its government – and recognized as such by those resident within the nation and by other nations in the world (e.g. the assembly of nation-states known as the United Nations). As a *legal* entity, the nation-state usually endorses what might be called 'civic' nationalism: the claim that the nation is composed of all those – regardless of colour, language, creed or race – who subscribe to the nation's political principles or constitution. The nation is thus defined as 'civic' to the extent that it recognizes the nation as a community of 'equal, rights-bearing citizens, united in patriotic attachment to a shared set of political practices and values'.[2] Britain is frequently cited as an example of civic nationalism in its efforts, from the mid-eighteenth century onwards, to forge a nation-state composed of four different nations (Irish, Scots, Welsh and English), under a civic rather than ethnic definition – that is, a shared allegiance to a common Parliament, Crown, rule of law. Whether Britain actually succeeded in this, or simply masked 'English nationalism' behind the four-nation-state, is a moot point to which I will return below. Less controversial examples of the 'civic' nation-state are to be found in the American and French republics after their respective revolutions of 1776 and 1789. It must be remembered, however, that even here citizenship was still largely confined, for many decades, to the enfranchised elite of white, propertied males and did not always include women, slaves or aboriginal peoples.[3]

A second common understanding of nation is as *territory*. This definition need not always involve a state as such, but it does, minimally, lay claim to a specific place or land which constitutes the so-called *national territory*. To fully exist the nation thus geographically defined must cover the entire national territory – 'the land which the nationalists believe to be the nation's by right and [which] embraces all the members of the putative nation therein domiciled'.[4] In the case of Ireland, geography has been one of the most commonly invoked criteria for justifying the aspiration to unity within the island and separation from the neighbouring island of Britain. The fact that Ireland is an integral island, 'surrounded by water', has been a mainstay of separatist nationalism.[5] The problem here is that *both* the Irish Republic and Great Britain have considered Northern Ireland to be part of their respective 'national territories'. Many nations have, of course, existed *without* a land – e.g. the Jews for centuries, the Kurds, the Palestinians – but there are few, if any, examples of nations with *no* sense of territorial identification.

A third common sense of nation is that of *ethnicity*. Here the definition of belonging is one of blood rather than law. The nation is defined, accordingly, in terms of a racially homogeneous 'people' which seeks out a state appropriate to its unique identity. In contrast to most Western nation-states, which today define their nationhood in terms of common citizenship (by birth, residence or allegiance), Germany is an example of a nation which still defines itself ethnically.[6] For the ethnic nation, a person's deepest identity is inherited rather than chosen; what unifies a society is common *roots* rather than laws. 'Regardless of the real nature of the state-society, the nation-state treats it as a mass of ethnically uniform individuals who exist to serve its welfare and convenience. It *is*, after all, the nation'.[7] In such a scenario, it is the national community – the *Volk* – which defines the individual citizens rather than the other way around; the People before persons. We thus find several German romantics of the nineteenth century repudiating the Enlightenment idea that the state created the nation, and mobilizing German patriotic resistance to Napoleon's invasion of the German principalities around a specifically German – as opposed to French revolutionary – understanding of the nation-state. The extraordinary appeal of this ethnic model of nationalism for emergent nations in the nineteenth century is described by Michael Ignatieff as follows: 'What gave unity to the nation, what made it a home, a place of passionate attachment, was not the cold contrivance of shared rights but the people's preexisting ethnic characteristics: their language, religion, customs and traditions. The nation as Volk had begun its long and troubling career in European thought. All the peoples of nineteenth-century Europe under imperial subjection – the Poles and Baltic peoples under the Russian yoke, the Serbs under Turkish rule, the Croats under the Habsburgs – looked to the German ideal of ethnic nationalism when articulating their right to self-determination'.[8] When Germany was finally unified under Bismarck in 1871 and assumed world-power status, it served as an examplar of ethnic nationalism for the 'captive nations' of imperial Europe – and beyond.

Certain instances of Irish nationalism also display an ethnic feature, based on alleged differences between Gaelic and non-Gaelic. This is, admittedly, uncharacteristic from an historic point of view. Ideological geneticism or Darwinian biology were rarely invoked in the Irish separatist cause. Probably the closest one gets to some kind of racialist inference was Douglas Hyde's odd, and largely innocuous, theory about natural selection and language. 'As President of the linguistic revivalist Gaelic League, [Hyde] actually argued in the mid-1890s that Irish people had been speaking Gaelic for so long that their mouths were unfitted physically for English'.[9] Even the most zealous nationalists of the time took little heed. Less impervious, alas, were certain members of the Irish Ministry of Justice in the 1940s who refused to shelter Jews fleeing from Nazi persecution on the grounds that 'they do not assimilate with our own people but remain a sort of colony of a worldwide Jewish community. This makes them a potential irritant in the body politic and has led to disastrous results from time to time in other countries'.[10] Racialism may have been rare in Ireland; it was not nonexistent.

A fourth, more generous, understanding of the nation comes under the rubric of the *'migrant* nation' – or the nation as 'extended family'. Here the definition of the nation remains partially ethnic, but is enlarged to embrace all those emigrants and exiles who live beyond the territory of the nation-state *per se*.[11] The most celebrated example of this is no doubt that of the Jewish diaspora. But it also pertains to that of many other emigrant nationalities, not least the Irish. If over seventy million people in the world today claim to be of Irish descent, it is evident that this definition of nationality, or at least of national genealogy, extends far beyond the borders of a state or territory.[12] Irish-Americans, Irish-Australians or Irish-Britons, for example, can affirm a strong sense of national allegiance to their 'land of origin' even though they may be three or four generations from that land and frequently of mixed ethnicity. With the formulation of a 'new nationalism' in the Forum for a New Ireland (1983–84), the then Foreign Minister, Peter Barry, included the Irish emigrant population in his definition of the nation. (He appealed, for example, to 'Irish nationalists North and South and everywhere else in the world'.) As did President Mary Robinson when she came to office in 1992–93. And similar appeals are heard whenever the international community is solicited to support peace in Northern Ireland (the International Ireland Funds etc.), or when it is a question of debating emigrant voting rights in national elections and selecting national football teams.

In short, while the 'migrant nation' still retains an ethnic base, it is far more inclusive than the ethnic nation-state in that it embraces the exiled along with the indigenous. By implication, this means accepting that the Irish diaspora comprises not only different Irish peoples ('Ulster Scots' as well as 'Gaels') but, through intermarriage in the melting pots of overseas continents, different racial confections as well. One wonders how many of the Irish Irelanders – who sought to confine the nation to those of 'pure' extraction or adoption – would have believed that by the 1994 World Cup the Irish team would be over half British-born with a centre forward called Cascarino.

A fifth, and final, variable which merits attention here is what might broadly be called the 'nation as *culture*'. This is not unrelated to the two preceding definitions but differs in this crucial respect: the cultural paradigm of national identity is not reducible to race. National culture can include many things besides ethnicity. For example, religion, language, art, sport, dance, music, cuisine, clothes, literature, philosophy, even (some believe) economics. As such, it is by nature far more pluralist than any strictly racial understanding of nationhood. For its part, the Irish nation includes several different religions – as Wolfe Tone's reference to 'Catholic, Protestant and Dissenter' recognized – two different languages (Irish and English) and a rich variety of philosophical traditions (see Chapters 9–11 below). Indeed, even when cultural nationalism does refer to ethnicity, it is obliged – if it is to be consistent – to invoke several different ethnic legacies. In the case of the Irish cultural nation this requires acknowledgement of the Viking, Norman, Scots and Anglo-Saxon contributions alongside those of the 'ancient Celtic race'. Thus we might say that the exclusivist equation of 'Irish Irish' with Gaelic and Catholic by D.P. Moran and other fundamentalists in the first decades of this century, was in fact a betrayal of the full complexity of Irish culture.

While the Irish language is the official 'first language' of the Republic, and an invaluable resource to the nation, it is not the first tongue spoken by the majority of the population. Nor is it the tongue responsible for making Irish writing one of the world's great modern literatures. Joyce, Yeats, Wilde, Kavanagh, Heaney may well be haunted by the Gaelic ghost as their souls 'fret in the shadow of the [English] language' – but it is the English language that they speak and write, albeit in a singularly Irish way. The language question is even more vexed when it comes to politics. Elements in the Gaelic League did, for a time, pursue the quasi-Herderian thesis that the collective 'genius of the race' found its true expression in the Irish tongue – hence the view that Gaelic equalled rurality, purity and authenticity while English equalled urbanity, decadence and vice. The implication here was that because Ireland had a unique and ancient language it had a natural right to separate political status.

Several recent commentators challenge this assumption. Political theorist, Tom Garvin, notes the fact that the more the Irish embraced *English* the more nationalist they became. 'English has always been the language of Irish political separatism, in an extraordinary succession from Swift and Molyneux in the early eighteenth century, through Theobald Wolfe Tone and William Drennan in the 1790s, to John Mitchel, Arthur Griffith, James Connolly and Patrick Pearse in the nineteenth and twentieth centuries. Political sentiment in the Irish Gaelic language tended to be rather pre-political, rarely getting further than a sentimental and rather rhetorical Jacobitism'.[13] Whatever the validity of the last claim, it seems the case that it was through English that the republican principles of the French and American revolutions spread through Ireland in the 1790s, leading eventually to the United Irishmen rebellion in 1798. Thus, it has been remarked that the acquisition of English, 'far from making the Irish assimilate to English attitudes and loyalites, rather gave the weapons of European Enlightenment to a previously impotent tradition . . .'.[14] By such accounts, the historical relationship between language and Irish nationality is, to say the least, far from evident.

The same could be said about religion and Irish nationalism. While the Catholic religion is the majority creed of Ireland, it is by no means the only one, and besides carries an 'internationalist' ingredient which contrasts with the notion of a closed insular *Volk* – e.g. the missionary tradition of diaspora throughout Europe, Africa, Asia and the Americas. That said, one should not underestimate the powerful role religion has played in Irish nationalism. The fact that nationalism, particularly in its modern republican guises, is an offspring of Enlightenment secularism, has not prevented its more popular manifestations from being fuelled by the collectivist energies of traditional religion. Though this connection has been greatly underrated in much academic literature, recent research by Marianne Elliott shows a strong symbiosis between Irish nationalism and Catholicism in our own century and argues that this dominates Ulster Protestanism's rejection of nationalism.[15] Tom Garvin makes a similar point when, conceding that the founding fathers of the separatist Irish tradition were Protestant rather than Catholic (largely due to the Protestants' near-monopoly of higher education in Ireland up to the twentieth century), he observes that the nationalist rank and file have been overwhelmingly Catholic since the 1790s and the nationalist leadership so since the 1900s. 'Irish nationalism', he concludes, 'has always been rhetorically anti-sectarian, but is tempted into sectarianism because of its anthropological rooting in the Catholic majority and in the ideology of dispossession and repossession'.[16] The fact that Protestantism was the religion of the dominant Ascendancy class, which disenfranchised the Catholic majority, was an additional factor in the equation.

Here once again, history is complex. One of the main reasons the Catholic hierarchy was not officially allied to Irish nationalism, during the eighteenth and nineteenth centuries, was because it feared the nationalist-republican ideas being imported into Ireland from the French Revoution were anti-Catholic. The fact that these ideas were also anti-British meant, logically, that a tacit alliance of interests bound Maynooth and Westminster together: the Catholic hierarchy actually approved the abolition of the Irish parliament and union with Britain in 1800, while the English government financed the establishment of the Catholic seminary at Maynooth in 1795. After the fall of Parnell and 1916, however, it became clear to the Church that the soul of the Irish nation was up for grabs and that the need for a unifying collective identity for the newly emerging state could best be provided by a form of Catholic nationalism which allowed (in Joyce's words) 'Christ and Caesar go hand in hand'. Indeed, the 1937 Constitution of Dáil Eireann came close, at times, to ratifying the equation of Catholic, Gael and Irishman. While this was modified by subsequent amendments, the strong influence of the Catholic Church on matters of state was witnessed as late as the knife-edge 1995 referendum on divorce.

The Irish republic was not, of course, unique in its early tendency to accommodate religion as a badge of national identity. North of the border, one found a Protestant Parliament for a Protestant People being rapidly established, while on the neighbouring island the Church of England was still a primary means of asserting English national identity. And those who consider the link between nation and religion to be now no more than an anachronism need only look to the continuing sectarianism in Ulster, or to the more global fate of former Yugoslavia and the ex-Soviet Union.

Finally, while some cultural nationalists of the Sinn Féin school argued for an 'economic nationalism' in the 1930s and 1940s, this ultimately came to grief. Independent Ireland's original policy of national capitalism – economic self-sufficiency – foundered because Ireland (a) lacked a sufficiently large internal market and a sufficient number of industrial entrepreneurs, (b) inherited a bureaucratic and centralized state apparatus from the British and (c) continued to look to Britain for ultimate solutions. As Desmond Fennell remarks in his analysis of economic nationalism, 'The state was changed only to make it more what it was – more centralized, interventionist, uncoordinated, and uncontrolled by citizen's decisions'.[17] Economic nationalism also failed because the world economy was becoming such that nation-states were no longer the determining units in the regulation of wealth but were increasingly subject to a transnational network of global banks, markets and industries.[18] The notion of a quintessentially 'Gaelic-Catholic-Nationalist' economy was never more than an ideological illusion.

In short, Irish cultural nationalism, whether it was predicated upon religious, linguistic or economic grounds, has proved extremely variegated, displaying an unusual capacity, *pace* the stereotypes, to change its mind about itself. Whence the old quip: whenever the English thought they'd found the answer, the Irish changed the question.[19]

All five definitions of 'nation' share an equation of 'people' with 'nationality', although the precise criteria of belonging varies from nation to nation. Thus while nationalism, Irish or otherwise, displays a certain Protean, multiform and elusive character, it observes a common organizing principle – namely, the structural function of *unifying* a variety of elements (territory, language, statehood, tradition, history, race, religion, ideology) into a certain *identity*, thereby imparting to them a special function of inclusion and exclusion. 'National identity in its distinctive sense is', as Liah Greenfeld observes, 'an identity which derives from membership in a "people", the fundamental characteristic of which is that it is defined as a "nation". Every member of the "people" thus interpreted partakes in its superior, elite quality, and it is in consequence that a stratified national population is perceived as essentially homogeneous, and the lines of status and class as superficial. This principle lies at the basis of all nationalisms and justifies viewing them as expressions of the same general phenomenon'.[20]

BEYOND IRISH AND BRITISH NATIONALISM

Each of the chapters below attempts, as stated at the outset, a *separation of identities*. Such an endeavour is not inspired by motives of disavowal or dismissal. It is intended, rather, to properly acknowledge, by means of vigilant decipherment and discernment, the distinct singularities that make up the nation or state.

My critique of Irish nationalism is, however also a critique of its mirror-image, British nationalism.[21] Any analysis of the 'national question', cognizant of the full ideological implications of the British–Irish conflict, demands no less. One cannot adequately identify the parts if one does not also have a grasp of the original whole. The dismantling of nationalism can only be effective, in the Anglo-Irish context, if it is a dismantling of *nationalisms*. Critical surgery cuts both ways. Far too often, the sins of nationalism have been laid exclusively on the Irish side, with the result that Britain's implication in the nationalist quarrel is conveniently occluded. This, I would argue, has been one of the most ingenious ploys of British (or more particularly English) nationalism: to pretend that it *doesn't exist*, that the irrational and unreasonable claimants to sovereignty, territory, power and nationhood are always *others* – Palestinians, Indians, Africans, Irish. By thus externalizing the crisis of national legitimation onto its neighbours or adversaries, British–English nationalism conveniently forgot that it was in fact the first of its kind in the world: 'At a certain point in history – to be precise, in early sixteenth-century England – the word "nation" in its conciliar meaning of "an elite" was applied to the population of the country and made synonymous with the word "people". *This semantic transformation signalled the emergence of the first nation in the world, in the sense in which the word is understood today, and launched the era of nationalism*'.[22]

Irish and British nationalism are Siamese twins. Britain has always been obsessed by Ireland, and oblivious of it, at one and the same time. Ireland, and in particular Irish nationalism, is its alter ego, its ally and enemy, familiar and foreign. The other which defines, and undermines, its very identity.[23] The double which haunts and fascinates. Its phantom limb.

What the crisis of Irish nationalism brings home to Britain is the realization that it too is founded upon a nationalist principle of sovereignty; and that this principle is in fact more *absolutist* than the former's. Indeed, political theorists like Neal Ascherson and Tom Nairn have gone so far as to claim that Britain is the *most* absolutist nation-state in Europe. 'There is nothing else like it in the developed world', writes Ascherson. 'What happened in the seventeenth century was that the English parliament just took absolutism away from the King, from the divine right of Kings, and gave it to parliament, where it still is. So there is no concept of *popular* sovereignty. Instead, you have an elected parliament, but it is completely sovereign in itself – it is not subject to the people as a concept or to a constitution'.[24] The British national parliament cannot give away power in any sense – federate or regionalize – without ceasing to exist. This all-or-nothing nationalism stands in contradiction, of course, to the fact that the British state is ostensibly a 'multinational state' made up of England, Northern Ireland, Scotland and Wales. But to acknowledge this seminal fact would entail exposing and challenging 'the almost total sovereignty of an English-dominated parliament over these parts'.[25] This explains why Irish (or, for example, Scots) nationalism, and the increasing demand for greater regional democracy, has put the very basis of British nationalism in question. 'In order to approach regionalism of some kind, which would fit into the currently growing concept of a Europe of the regions, the way forward has to be a change in the basic constitutional doctrine of the British state. They have got to admit, first of all, that this is a multi-national state; secondly, that power which is devolved or federated to the component nations of this state cannot simply be taken back; and thirdly, they have got to break the age-old tradition of centralising authority'.[26]

In short, behind the British ideology of 'parliamentary sovereignty' lurks what Nairn has termed 'an intense neo-tribal nationalism' predicated upon a 'fossilized Constitution and an outdated national identity'. The real question of nationalism was never resolved in Britain, for the simple reason that it was never raised.[27] And the reason it was never raised was that its longevity as a modern nation – dating back to the founding of the English–Welsh nation in the sixteenth century (two hundred years before the French) – together with its imperial designs on neighbouring nations and its suppression of its own hybridity (the

Anglo-Saxons were themselves hyphenated before they commingled with the 'foreign' Welsh) gave it a false sense of self-righteousness. It has always been difficult for British nationalism to respect the fundamentally pluralist and multi-ethnic character of its own civic nationalism, encompassing other peoples on equal terms. The deep Tory suspicion of Europe is an obvious case in point.[28]

The spectre of Irish nationalism might be said to represent Britain's return of the repressed. It compels it to look in the mirror and see its own cracked image. How British nationalism survives the break-out of peace in Ulster and the increasing momentum of European politics towards a postnationalist paradigm remains to be seen.

The shibboleths of both Irish and British nationalism begin to come undone when exposed to the razor of contemporary change. Britain and Ireland are, in Benedict Anderson's resonant phrase, 'imagined communities'.[29] As such, they are capable of reimagining their ideological legacies in the light of present crises and future possibilities. Rethinking Ireland and Britain means thinking *otherwise*. The 'break-up' of the United Kingdom is no more unimaginable at this historical juncture than the surrender of the dream of a United Ireland. Why? Because the break-down of Northern Ireland, as commonly claimed territory of both nation-states, has, through the violence of the last quarter-century, exposed the ultimate infeasibility of 'unitary nationalism' predicated upon absolutist sovereignty claims. The tragic war in Ulster was the direct result of the ineluctable clash between two such rival claims – one to preserve a United Kingdom, the other to forge a United Ireland. The beginnings of a solution may reside, I would suggest, in, first, a mutual acceptance of this historical misfortune and, second, a mutual commitment to rethink the 'totality of relations' between these islands.

Such rethinking requires us to think beyond our inherited models of sovereignty, nation-state and nationalism, in order to create new paradigms of political and cultural accommodation between all the citizens on these islands.[30] It requires our seeing the situation since 1921 as an interim one. With this in mind, I return, again and again, throughout these chapters to the idea of a Council of the Islands of Britain and Ireland, eventually evolving towards a federal British–Irish archipelago in the larger context of a Europe of Regions. That, at least, is my wager. But whatever the outcome, the important thing at this decisive historical juncture is that we begin to rethink who and what we are, not just on both sides of the Irish border, but on both sides of the Irish sea.[31]

* * *

In summary, our eleven chapters will broadly adhere to the following lines of inquiry:

1 Is nationalism a hangover of tribal primitivism or a secular modern movement inspired by the Enlightenment and the French Revolutionary principle of *le droit du peuple?*

2 Does nationalism necessarily lay claim to a nation-state or can it remain a regulative principle of regional self-rule and local participatory democracy?

3 Is the nationalist claim to self-determination and unitary identity compatible with the republican claim to universal rights and cosmopolitan pluralism?

4 Is nationalism an imagined construct based largely on narratives, myths and symbols (Anderson) or a natural, organically based given of communal identity (Herder, Fichte and the Romantics)?

5 Finally, is nationalism: (a) a regression to atavistic irrationalism (Minogue/Kerdourie); (b) a necessity of humane and rational modernity (Gellner/Anderson); or (c) an ambivalent mix of both (Hobsbawm/Greenfeld/Breuilly)?[32]

If the last conjecture is correct, and nationalism is to be treated as ideologically agnostic and ambiguous, the decisive question for us then becomes: how might what is best in the nationalist legacy be sublated and transformed into a postnationalist paradigm?[33] This is one of the key challenges the present work seeks to address.

Part I
Politics

1 Beyond sovereignty

> In modern republics the origin of sovereignty is in the people, but
> now we recognize that we have many peoples. And many peoples
> means many centres of sovereignty – we have to deal with that.
>
> (Paul Ricoeur)[1]

'What ish my nation?' asks Captain Macmorris in *Henry V* in what
must surely be one of the first expressions of Ireland's identity crisis.
Ever since, the same question has found multiple forms of response,
each contriving to make sense of complex, and often conflicting, allegiances – Gael and planter, Catholic and Protestant, Republican and
Loyalist, tribal and cosmopolitan.

A change seems to be occurring in recent times, however, as Irish
people, North and South, move gradually beyond the orthodox equations of political and cultural identity. For unionists and nationalists
alike, this means rethinking traditional fidelities to unitary ideals of
nation-statehood: a United Kingdom for the former, a 32-county
Republic for the latter. The 25-year war in Ulster epitomized the clash
of irreconcilable territorial claims. Hence the need for a movement
beyond sovereignty – at least understood as an absolute principle of
'one and indivisible' power. And the attendant need to think further
than the conflict between British and Irish nation-states towards a new
configuration of identities.[2]

The central wager of this opening chapter may be stated accordingly:
contemporary Ireland is in historic transition and calls for new modes
of self-definition in keeping with an overall move towards a more federal
and regional Europe. In the new European dispensation, nation-states
will, arguably, become increasingly anachronistic. Power will be disseminated *upwards* from the state to transnational government and
downwards to subnational government. In this context, future identities
may, conceivably, be less nation-statist and more local and cosmopolitan.

A EUROPEAN SOLUTION TO THE IRISH–BRITISH PROBLEM?

Ulster is an Irish problem and a British problem. But it is also a European problem. Ireland's historical divisions are, in significant measure, European in origin. We often forget that the Viking invasion was plotted in Norse; the twelfth-century conquest in French; the Battle of the Boyne in Dutch; the Great Armada in Spanish; the 1798 landing in French; the 1941 blitz of Belfast (where five hundred died in one raid alone) in German. Ireland is also a European problem requiring a European solution.

In the New Ireland Forum in 1983, Bernard Cullen and I proposed a form of joint-sovereignty for Northern Ireland (a model retained as one of the three options in the final Forum Report, 1985). But it became clear over the years that many unionists resisted the principle of dividing or diluting sovereignty in an Anglo-Irish context. The only parameters within which they seemed prepared to share sovereignty were, tellingly, those of the European Community. With the signing of the Single European Act in 1988, both the United Kingdom and the Republic agreed to a significant sharing of sovereignty with the other ten members of the EU – and, by implication, with *each other*. The unionists raised no objection. (Unlike the Anglo-Irish Agreement of 1989 which they vehemently opposed.) Moreover, unionist representatives, disinclined to cooperate with their nationalist counterparts in Westminister or Dublin, had little difficulty voting and campaigning with them in Brussels or Strasbourg. Why? Because, once removed from the disabling conflict of Anglo-Irish sovereignty claims, the urgent social and economic needs of their common Ulster region became paramount. Thus, Paisley and Hume, while implacably at odds on the issue of national sovereignty were almost invariably at one on regional issues of agricultural policy, fishing quotas, social cohesion funding, etc. The lesson? That unionists and nationalists can agree at *regional* and *European* level, but not at *national* level. Once again, the vexed issue of nation-state sovereignty remained the bone in the craw of Ulster.

It was precisely the manifest failure to divide or share sovereignty within the British–Irish context that prompted me to try to think beyond the 'joint-sovereignty' option of 1984 in favour of more 'European' options (see below the joint submissions with Robin Wilson to the Opsahl Commission in Belfast, 1994, and the Forum for Peace and Reconciliation in Dublin, 1995). The basic line of thinking here was: Could a European model not supplement and ultimately subsume the existing Anglo-Irish initiative? Was there not a compelling logic to the notion of Ulster as a quasi-autonomous region relating, inter-dependently, to other regions on (a) the *island* of Ireland, (b) the *archipelago* of Britain and (c) the *continent* of Europe? Might such a tri-lateral allegiance to the concentric circles of Ireland–Britain–Europe not enable both nationalist and unionist communities to put their sovereignty-quarrel behind them and work for the common good of their region under a broad European roof? Indeed, was the model of a federal Europe of regional participatory democracies not what Voltaire, the Enlightenment visionary, originally had in mind when he dreamt of 'one great Europe made up of parts each corresponding equally to the other'?

The wager, simply put, was that the reconciling of divided com-munities – in Ulster, no less than in Gibraltar, Germany, Belgium or the Basque country – could no longer be confined to isolated nation-states. The claims of absolute national independence, predicated upon exclu-sivist notions of state sovereignty, were no longer feasible, nor desirable, in the emerging European configuration.[3] Approaching a new mil-lennium – in the wake of the paramilitary ceasefires of 1994 and ongoing Peace Process – it seemed that Northern Ireland might well, ironically, be in a position to take the lead in the European resolution of national conflicts.

CONCEPTS OF SOVEREIGNTY

One of the most pressing tasks in this attempt to rethink Ireland is the separation of 'nation' and 'state'. Is it possible to break the equation of national self-determination and state sovereignty? Is it possible to re-think the question of sovereignty *culturally* as well as *politically*? In terms of identity rather than territory? Or, given Hannah Arendt's ar-gument in *Crises of the Republic* that 'as long as national independence and the sovereignty of the state are equated ... not even a theoretical solution of the problem of war is conceivable' – where do we begin looking for an alternative theoretical model?

I have already alluded to the practical, and I believe practicable, pos-sibilties contained within the European Union charters. But we cannot think forward without at the same time thinking back. How, after all, are we to supersede the limits of sovereignty if we do not first under-stand something of its genesis in Western political thought? By sum-marily retracing the genealogy of this key concept I hope to free up some conceptual space to *think again* about some of its more immediate implications today.

Originally, the concept of sovereignty meant 'supreme power'. As derived from the Latin *superanus* through the French *souveraineté*, the term connoted the ultimate authority or overseer of order. Initially attributed to a divine ruler, the mantle was gradually passed onto divinely elected 'representatives' in history – kings, pontiffs, emperors, monarchs – before being finally delegated to the 'people' themselves in many post-revolutionary republics and nation-states. Today, sovereignty is one of the most controversial concepts in political theory and international law, intimately related to concepts of state government and/or national independence.

The term 'sovereignty' first came to prominence, as a modern theoretical principle, in the sixteenth century when Jean Bodin invoked it to consolidate the power of the French King over the insurgent feudal lords. The historic transition from traditional feudalism to modern nationalism was thus facilitated – albeit within a monarchical system. In 1576 Bodin promoted a concept of *absolutist sovereignty*, defining the sovereign as one who makes the laws but is not himself bound by the laws he makes (*Majestas est summa in cives ac subditos legibusque soluta potestas*). With the publication of *Leviathan* in 1651, Thomas Hobbes confirmed the identification of the sovereign with might rather than law. Sovereign power is as absolute as men can make it, he argued, and since law is what the sovereign commands it cannot itself command or limit the sovereign.[4]

With the contractual theories of John Locke at the end of the seventeenth century and of Jean-Jacques Rousseau in the eighteenth, we witness a shift towards a concept of *popular sovereignty*. The state is now considered to be founded upon a compact or contract between citizens through which they entrust such powers to a government as is deemed necessary for common protection. This doctrine of popular sovereignty found clear expression in the US Declaration of Independence in 1776. But it underwent yet another shift with the French revolutionary constitution of 1791 where it assumed the guise of *national sovereignty*. Citing key phrases from Rousseau's *The Social Contract*, this constitution states that 'sovereignty is one, indivisible, unalienable and imprescriptible; it belongs to the Nation; no group can attribute sovereignty to itself nor can an individual arrogate it to himself'. The sovereign people now becomes identified with a sovereign nation embodied in an organized, centralized state.

This standard modern equation of sovereignty and nation-state underwent certain subsequent readjustments. In the nineteenth century, the English jurist John Austin and others argued that sovereignty was ultimately vested in a nation's parliament, thus promoting the concept of *parliamentary sovereignty*. Parliament was now envisaged as the supreme body that enacted laws binding upon everyone but itself – since it, and it alone, had the right to change these laws at will. This notion of legislative sovereignty – still conceived in absolute and indivisible terms – was, however, somewhat revised when applied to the American situation where the US Constitution did not endow the national state legislature with supreme power but imposed important limits upon it – the famous principle of 'checks and balances'. Hence the principle of *constitutional sovereignty* where ultimate power is invested in the fundamental document of the Constitution itself.

The principle of nation-state sovereignty thus evolved through a number of genealogical mutations – *popular, national, legislative, constitutional.* But with each shift, a basic consciousness was emerging: sovereignty cannot finally be considered as synonymous with absolute and unrestricted power. This deconstruction of the principle of absolute sovereignty came from two directions at once – from within and from without. Sovereignty became challenged *internally* by (a) the recognition that power may well reside in several centres at once, e.g. in different political, economic, social or religious groups that govern a state (the notion of *pluralist sovereignty* developed by Guguit, Krabbe and Laski in the twentieth century); or (b) the partition of sovereignty between the union and its constituent units in the federal structure of the USA (a *de facto* form of *dual sovereignty* as required by the 10th Amendment of the Constitution whereby separate states retain powers not delegated to the US state Congress). Besides the USA, other countries found it increasingly difficult to attribute all power to a *single* repository of sovereignty as competing criteria were invoked in different legal cases – the laws of nature, reason, God, region, community (*ius gentium*) in addition to the nation-state itself.

But sovereignty was also challenged *externally* by the development of international law in the twentieth century. With the Hague Conferences of 1899 and 1907, followed by the Covenant of the League of Nations and the Charter of the United Nations (art. 2), significant restrictions on the action of states were laid down. A system of international checks and balances was now being introduced limiting the rights of sovereign states to act as they please in all matters. Moreover, the increasing *interdependence* of states – accompanied by a sharing of sovereignties in the interests of greater peace, social justice and economic exchange – qualified the principle of absolute independence for the nation-state. 'The peoples of the world have recognized that there can be no peace without law, and that there can be no law without some limitations on sovereignty. They have started, therefore, to pool their sovereignties to the extent needed to maintain peace; and sovereignty is being increasingly exercised on behalf of the peoples of the world not only by national governments but also by organs of the world community'.[5]

If this pertains to the 'peoples of the world' generally, and to the peoples of Europe particularly, how much more does it pertain to the peoples of the islands of Britain and Ireland? This is why I argue, in my three opening chapters, for a surpassing of the modern nation-state model in the direction of a federal Europe of regions – postmodern, postnationalist and postsovereign. The nation-state has, I believe, become too large *and* too small as a model of contemporary Irish identity. Too large for the growing need of regional, participatory democracy; and too small for the increasing drift towards transnational exchange and power-sharing, at both British–Irish and European levels. Hence the relevance, in my opinion, of the the Nordic Council analogy as a model for resolving the historical sovereignty dispute over Ulster, declaring it a demilitarized zone, along with the Spitsbergen and Aland islands.[6]

NATIONAL–POPULAR SOVEREIGNTY AND IRISH NATIONALISM

Before leaving our summary genealogy of sovereignty I would like, however, to take a closer look at the specific development of national–popular sovereignty in the eighteenth century, which exerted a formative influence on Irish nationalism.

A famous 1791 document of the United Irish Society hailed the French Revolution's transfer of absolute sovereignty from the King to the people as follows: 'on the 14th of July, the day which shall ever commemorate the French Revolution, let this Society pour out its first libation to European Liberty . . . '.[7] While Bodin had argued in *Les Six Livres de la République* that sovereignty could only be effectively maintained in a true monarchy, the French Revolution replied that the proper place for sovereignty – still understood as the 'unitary will' of 'absolute and perpetual power' – was in the nation itself.[8] With the reign of Louis XIV, sovereign power had begun to distinguish itself from the juridical order which it was in theory supposed to preserve. The 'state' (understood as the active agency of power) began to separate itself from 'society'. Kings were no longer conceived as servants of God; they became identified with gods themselves who 'in some fashion partake of divine independence'.[9] The monarch was sovereign therefore precisely because the law, the state and the divine will were deemed to express themselves through his individual person. He alone was the truly public will; or as Bossuet put it: 'the whole state is in him, the will of all the people is encompassed in his'.[10] The establishment of absolutist sovereignty thus witnessed the imposition of centralized command on local practices of participation and consent, with judicial government being replaced more and more by administration government. For the *ancien régime* in the seventeenth and eighteenth centuries, 'sovereign power – the power of the state in the active modern sense – no longer simply upheld the social order from within; it acted upon society from without'.[11]

From the mid-eighteenth century on, a noticeable shift occurred where the locus (if not the character) of sovereignty transferred from the body of the king to the body of the *nation*. As noted above, Rousseau was a key theorist of this transfer. Rousseau agreed with Hobbes and other advocates of absolutist sovereignty, that the transmutation of multiplicity into unity could only be effected by the 'irrevocable submission of every individual to a single, unitary person'.[12] But according to Rousseau's *The Social Contract*, this person could no longer be identified with the actual person of a king but with the collective personification of citizens as a whole. While inheriting the monarchical doctrine that sovereignty is inalienable and indivisible (it cannot be delegated or represented without subverting the unity of the body in which it inheres), he reintegrated sovereign power back into the social order by situating sovereignty in the body of the people understood as a collective abstraction: the famous 'general will'. Rousseau thus provided the theoretical basis for the French Revolution's transfer of power from Crown to nation.

The most influential doctrine of national sovereignty to emerge from the revolutionary debates was, however, Sieyès pamphlet, *Qu'est-ce que le Tiers Etat?* Revising the notion of the historical nation, Sieyès empowered it with the immediate active sovereignty of the people (understood in Rousseau's sense). The nation assumed the status of both the popular and the natural order, deriving its authority from no source other than itself. And with this radical formulation of national sovereignty, we encounter one of the most formative models of the modern nation-state. As Keith Baker explains: 'By a dramatic inversion, the nation, created in the course of centuries by the persistent efforts of the monarchical state, now became metaphysically prior to it. The logic of *Qu'est-ce que le Tiers Etat?* threatened the entire standing order of international relations no less radically than it subverted the institutional order of the French monarchy. Once it was adopted, the history of humanity could be nothing but the story of national self-determination inflicted everywhere upon it in the two centuries since the

French Revolution'.[13] The national will becomes its own origin and end, with nothing before or after it. The common will of the nation is a justification in itself: it is legitimate by virtue of the fact that it *is*. It is absolutely representative precisely because it represents – quite literally – itself. When it comes to the nation, there is no dualism of body and soul. This is why, for Sieyès, 'the national will needs only to exist in order to be legal at all times; it is the source of all legality'.[14] And it is also why, in Sieyès's cryptic formula, a 'nation cannot decide that it will *not* be the nation'. The nation is self-founding, self-representative, self-evident.

It was a short step from the arguments of Rousseau on popular sovereignty, and Sieyès on national sovereignty, to the creation of the National Assembly and the Revolutionary Constitution's claim that 'sovereignty is one, indivisible, inalienable, and imprescriptible. It belongs to the nation'.

The story does not end there, however. Several difficulties ensued from this equation of absolute sovereignty with the nation. First of all, there was the vexed problem of *representation* inherent in the very concept of national/popular sovereignty – a problem by no means confined to French nationalism. The problem runs something as follows: If the people of the nation are everywhere – since sovereignty is inalienable – does that mean that everyone is the people? In other words, if the people are the totality, how are they to be 'represented' at the level of bodies such as the National Assembly where they (the totality of the people) are not immediately or directly present? If the 'people is always there', as the conventionnels proclaimed, why is there a need for them to be 'represented' at all? And how are individual wills to be identified with the general will?

And so the rub: if representative government is said to emanate directly from the unitary body of the people/nation, it must embody the same inalienable unity as the people/nation – that is, admit of no difference or dissension. The seeds of the Terror, and more generally of absolutist nationalism, were already sown. By this logic, as Baker argues, 'unity was the condition of sovereignty; the nation was unanimous or it was nothing. Hence the constant aversion, throughout the revolutionary period, to any form of political activity that threatened the unity of the sovereign will by the apparent articulation of particular wills or partial interests. Hence the constant impetus to achieve unity by way of exclusion'. Baker concludes accordingly that this logic of a unitary sovereign will, aggravated by war and internal division, 'required constant elimination of difference through restriction of the category of "nation" or "people"'.[15]

The endeavour to locate sovereignty in the unitary body of the nation fed the logic of the Terror, transmuting a 'theory of collective liberty into the practice of despotism'.[16] Whence the critique of sovereignty – understood in the absolutist sense running from Hobbes and Bodin to Rousseau and Sieyès – as the claim to legislate for all society by the exercise of a sovereign will. Critics as different as Benjamin Constant, Hannah Arendt, Claude Lefort and Charles Taylor share the view that the transfer of absolute sovereignty from God and God-King to Nation and State is not an escape from absolutism but a continuation of it by other means. Without some critical line of demarcation between civil society and the state, between the nation and the communities and individuals it purports to 'represent', the question of pluralism seems irresolvable.[17]

Liah Greenfeld introduces a useful distinction here in her book, *Nationalism – Five Ways to Modernity* (1992), between an individualistic-libertarian and a collectivistic-authoritarian type of national sovereignty. The former she identifies with the initial emergence of popular sovereignty as national *democracy.* 'Originally, nationalism developed *as* democracy . . . but as the emphasis in the idea of the nation moved from the sovereign character to the uniqueness of the people, the original equivalence between it and democratic principles was lost'.[18] This initiatory form of democratic popular sovereignty meant that some individuals, who were *of* the people, members of the nation, exercised sovereignty. But once popular sovereignty became a question of a particular nation's exclusive 'uniqueness', the national principle became collectivistic and authoritarian. 'The national principle was collectivisitic; it reflected the collective being. Collectivistic ideologies are inherently authoritarian, for, when the collectivity is seen in unitary terms, it tends to assume the character of a collective individual possessed of a single will, and someone is bound to be its *interpreter.* The reification of a community introduces (or preserves) fundamental inequality between those of its few members who are qualified to interpret the collective will and the many who have no such qualifications; the select few dictate to the masses who must obey'.[19]

The crisis of absolutist or 'authoritarian' sovereignty was not confined to the French Revolution and its influence on national independence movements in the nineteenth and twentieth centuries. Britain also experienced deep crises of *representation–interpretation* at the level of both nation-state and empire. In the 1860s Disraeli contrived to introduce the notion of 'one nation Toryism' by way of embracing the diverse classes and nations that made up modern Britain. In this scheme of things, Queen Victoria served as emblematic veneer of sovereignty, seeking to represent consensus and unity where it was needed (that is, didn't already exist). Victorian Britain thus sought to overcome the 'break-up of Britain' by extending the image of a unitary national body over an increasingly fragmented Kingdom. Triumphalist statues of the grey regal matron began to pop up in major cities of the Empire, from Edinburgh, Dublin and Belfast to Calcutta, Adelaide and Toronto. But the triple crisis which 'one nation Toryism' sought to address – of identity, of legitimation and of representative democracy – did not go away. Talk of the break-up of Britain is once again on the agenda, particularly in the context of European integration, regional government for Scotland, and, most importantly of all, the vexed sovereignty clash in Northern Ireland.[20]

IMPLICATIONS FOR NORTHERN IRELAND

The most obvious implication of the above analyses for the question of Northern Ireland is this: the dual claims of absolute sovereignty exercised over the same territory by two sovereign governments are inevitably condemned to conflict. Unless, that is, the understanding of sovereignty is radically revised and superseded. By extension, the claim of either national government to 'represent' both Ulster communities (British and Irish) as 'one and indivisible' is doomed to failure. No matter how it is viewed – as part of a United Kingdom or of an eventual United Ireland – the pluralist character of Northern Ireland defies the equation of absolute sovereignty with a unitary body. Hence the need (i) to separate the notion of nation from that of state; (ii) to acknowledge the co-existence of different identities in the same society; and (iii) to extend the models of identification *beyond unitary sovereignty* to include more inclusive and pluralist forms of association – such as a British–Irish Council or European Federation of Regions.[21]

In the chapters which follow I attempt to explore certain ways of rethinking Ireland – politically, culturally and philosophically – in the hope that alternative models of identity may point, in time, towards alternative ways of living on these islands.

2 Ideas of a republic

Almost four million people in Ireland live in what is called a 'republic'. The majority of Irish citizens vote for parties which lay claim to a 'republican' heritage. In fact, on the island as a whole, only the unionist parties reject the idea of a republic – this being largely due to the fact that a republic is not a Kingdom, and so precludes the basic unionist principle of loyalty to the Protestant British Crown.

But even the unionist position admits of exceptions. Certain proponents of a liberal unionist tradition proudly, if selectively, invoke the original project of pro-Enlightenment Irish Protestants for a society based on 'civil and religious liberties'. Thus, paradoxically, a reason sometimes cited for Northern Protestant opposition to unity with the South is the view that the existing republic has *betrayed* the original goal of the United Irishmen to reconcile 'Protestant, Catholic and Dissenter'. It was after all the episcopalian Tone, a leader of the 1798 rebellion, who denounced the Catholic clergy as 'tyrants of the people and slaves of Government'. Here was a secular enlightened view of a non-denominational republic. 'When it comes to religion', Tone explained, 'my belief is that we should work for the overthrow of the official church, without erecting another in its place'. A far cry from the common equation of Irish republicanism with Catholic nationalism!

Mainstream unionism resists the idea of a republic because it sees it (rightly or wrongly) as representing a threefold threat: (1) to the continuation of Ulster within the United Kingdom; (2) to the religious tradition of Protestantism; (3) to the distinct integrity of the Ulster British as a people. This threefold threat was focused, for several decades, on the use of the term 'republican' by the IRA. Since the inception of the Provisional IRA campaign in 1971, to be 'anti-republican' increasingly came to mean, on both sides of the border, to be against bombing a million Protestants into a republic (Cardinal Conway's phrase). Little wonder then that the very term 'republican' fell into disrepute in the 1970s and 1980s, putting pressure on constitutional Irish parties to replace it with the term 'nationalist'. Thus the Forum for a New Ireland, set up in 1983, frequently presented itself as a meeting of 'constitutional nationalists', in contrast to non-constitutional republicans (Sinn Féin and the IRA). Nationalism became the covering term for some 80 per cent of the electorate on the island of Ireland; while republicanism came to designate a non-democratic violent movement, often dubbed as 'terrorism' by the media.

This semantic switching between nationalism and republicanism led to much confusion, not just in Ireland but abroad. In continental Europe, for instance, the term 'republican' generally carried positive and progressive connotations, 'nationalist' the contrary: memories of Hitler's Germany, Mussolini's Italy, or Franco's Spain being still very much alive. Indeed, the further one travelled from Ireland the more one found the cause of the Irish Republican Army being identified with that of democratic liberation and self-determination, especially in Third World countries. The 'republican' hunger-striker, Bobby Sands, had streets called after him in Paris, Tripoli and Islamabad, while a prominent Noraid figure led the St Patrick's Day Parade in New York in 1988. Nor was it insignificant that a sizeable proportion of the seventy million people claiming Irish descent around the world were sufficiently confused about the meaning of 'republicanism' to believe that giving money to the IRA was emancipating the land of their Fathers.

So what do we mean when we talk of Irish republicanism today? Do we mean *sectarian nationalism*, as exemplified by the legacy of paramilitary violence? Do we mean *romantic nationalism* as expressed by the Fenian visionaries of the nineteenth century and most of the leaders of 1916 and the first independent Irish state? Do we mean *separatist nationalism*, espoused by many of the founders of the United Irishmen in the 1790s, as a means of breaking the subservient link to the English Crown (thereby entering a 'Republican Alliance' with France and other post-monarchical states of Europe)? Do we mean a *conservative nationalism*, closer to the American model of republicanism which, in practice, had little time for the radical theories of the European Enlightenment, seeing rebellion in the more practical terms of a colony taking redress against the British government in the name of the basic constitutional principle: 'No taxes without Representation'? Or do we mean, finally, a *new republicanism* – postnationalist and postunionist – which would allow the inhabitants of Ireland to reaffirm their local identities while embracing a new internationalism?

Such a new republicanism might learn much, I suggest, from the project for a federal European community as originally inspired by

Monet, Schumann and Spinelli – a project determined to overcome the 'national rivalries' that devastated Europe in two World Wars this century. But it might look still further back to the libertarian vision of Tom Paine (theorist of the American and French Revolutions befriended by Tone in Paris) and the enlightenment vision of Kant and Voltaire, who dreamt of Europe as a multi-state cosmopolitan republic.

The United Irishmen, and Tone as one of its founding figures, were closely attuned to the international spirit of republicanism. One document of the United Irish Society, published in 1792, hailed the American Revolution as a 'sudden light from America shining through our prison'. While the movement's original manifesto of 1791 appealed to the cosmopolitan spirit of the French Republic thus: ' "Dieu et *mon* Droit" is the motto of Kings. "Dieu et la Liberté", exclaimed Voltaire, when he first beheld Franklin his Fellow-Citizen of the World. "Dieu et *nos* Droits" – let Irishmen cry aloud to each other. The cry of Mercy and Justice . . . '.

What I am suggesting is that if we wish to rethink republicanism for the future we first need to think back to the philosophical source of Irish republicanism, inspired as it was by the American and French Revolutions. Such a debate on the origins and ends of Irish republicanism is above all a battle of ideas.

THE REPUBLICAN PARADOX: UNIVERSALISM VERSUS NATIONALISM

There is a fundamental paradox coiled at the heart of modern republicanism – in France, America and Ireland. On the one hand, republicanism promoted an *enlightened universalism* of world citizens. On the other, it permitted a *separatist nationalism* which subordinates the universal rights of the citizen to the rights of the nation-state.

It is this latter – nationalist – legacy of republicanism which critics like Conor Cruise O'Brien and J.L. Talmon deplore, identifying it ultimately with the heritage of the French Revolutionary Terror. O'Brien, for example, pushes his Burkean suspicion of the French Revolution to the point of denouncing it as a cradle of modern totalitarian nationalisms.[1] He argues that the 'bloodiest of all new terrestrial creeds' – the Cult of the Nation – was 'already present, fully formed, in 1789 in France'. The removal of God and the delegitimizing of monarchy left an unholy vacuum which the revolutionaries contrived to fill by deifying the nation. Universal rights and individual liberties were thus subordinated to the nationalist Right of the People (*le Droit du Peuple*). Henceforth, 'it would be in the name of the nation that men would be most likely to feel it legitimate to hate and kill other men and women and children'. Indeed, O'Brien does not refrain from asserting a direct link between this brand of French republicanism and the Nazi extermination of six million Jews.

If O'Brien is selective in his choice of nationalisms – he says much of the French and German but nothing of the British for example – he is equally selective in his reading of French republicanism. He ignores the universalist principles of the Declaration of the Rights of Man in 1789, choosing to focus instead on Abbé Sieyès' claim that the 'nation is the law itself', and a petition to the French Assembly in 1792 declaring the '*patrie*' as 'sole divinity'. What O'Brien has to say about the evils of German nationalism is acute, but his attempt to tar the French Revolutionary heritage with the Nazi brush is less than credible. What distinguished the French Declaration of Rights from both the English Bill of Rights of 1689 and the American Bill of Rights of 1789 was its *universalism*. For the first time the rights of individuals and nations were being applied to the universal community of mankind as a whole. Here we had a document proposing to legislate for all citizens of the world, not just the citizens of a single nation, France. And this particular Declaration was not, as its advocates made clear, some timeless abstraction but a dynamic legacy inviting ongoing interpretation and action. It was less a *point d'aboutissement* than a *point de départ*.[2] This was one of the reasons, of course, why the republicanism of 1789 proved to be so exportable – as the United Irishmen realized.

A signal feature of the French *République* was the conviction that the Rights of Man and the Rights of the People were mutually inclusive. Although the original Declaration of the Rights of Man and of the Citizen in 1789 made no explicit reference to the Rights of the People, the French Constitution of 3 September 1791 made up for this. We read: 'The French nation renounces any war undertaken with a view to conquest and will never use her powers against the liberty of any other people'. This principle was further ratified and reformulated in the Jacobin Constitution of 24 June 1793. Article 118 reads: 'The French people are the friend and natural ally of all free peoples'. And the same text goes on to proclaim the equal and inseparable legitimacy of the Rights of Man and the Rights of the People (or what soon became known as the 'principle of nationalities').

Napoleon's campaigns did, admittedly, inject a dose of pernicious ambiguity into this principle – in so far as his conquests of other nations were frequently carried out in the name of liberation. But this did not prevent later revolutions from positively invoking the French Declaration of the 'rights of peoples'. This was particularly true of the

1848 revolts which swept through Europe, taking the form of intense popular agitation for national independence. So widespread was this movement for national self-determination that 1848 was christened '*le printemps des peuples*'. The legacy of this double declaration – of the rights of nations and of man – was not confined to Europe. It extended to the continents of Latin America, Africa and Asia where, well into our own century, peoples have been rebelling against imperial regimes in the name of democratic liberation. And it is these same Siamese twins of individual and national rights which were confirmed in their universal dimension on 10 December 1948, by the Universal Declaration of Human Rights in the General Assembly of the UN.

It is undeniable that some of those republics which have been most voluble in support of human rights – France and America for example – have also been guilty of conducting imperial campaigns against smaller nations over the last two centuries. But it would be disingenuous to dismiss the extraordinary appeal of the Rights of Man (as collective humanity or individual citizen) and the Rights of the People for nations struggling against despotism. In this respect, it is surely telling that the first action taken by Alfred Rosenberg, principal ideologue of the Nazis, after Hitler's invasion of Paris in 1943, was to declare war on the ideas of 1789. Rosenberg fully recognized the 'universalist' appeal of the French Declaration of human rights.

But what impact did this legacy of rights have on Ireland? How did the French republican principles of 1789–93 influence the United Irishmen rebellion of 1798, and later the Easter Rebellion of 1916? Was Irish Republicanism historically capable of sustaining the delicate but indispensable balance between the Rights of Man and the Rights of the Nation? Have the rights of the Irish nation served to safeguard the corollary rights of individual citizens and minorities (in keeping with the the original pluralist agenda of republicanism)? Or have they served instead to subordinate them? In short, if we speak of Irish republicanism today are we speaking of the Rights of the People *against* the Rights of Man or *in accordance with* the Rights of Man?

CATHOLIC, PROTESTANT AND DISSENTER

In the manifesto of the Dublin Society of the United Irishmen – one of the first republican clubs founded in the 1790s – both legacies of the *République* were in evidence: the universalist and the nationalist. The document addresses its readers as 'citizens of the world', bidding them to 'swear to maintain the rights and prerogatives of their nature as men and the right and prerogative of Ireland as an Independent People'. The universalist and cosmopolitan tendency seems to prevail as the document proceeds to speak of overcoming the 'brazen walls of separation' erected by 'religious persuasion', and acknowledges that the inhabitants of Ireland are 'separate nations met and settled together, not mingled but convened'. In other words, the original founders of Irish republicanism sought to overcome the opposed nations and religions which existed in their country, establishing in their stead a non-ethnic secular society, based on Enlightenment values of tolerance. Wolfe Tone could hardly have been clearer on this point when he stated his ambition to 'abolish the memory of all past dissensions, and to substitute the common name of Irishman in place of the denominations of Protestant, Catholic and Dissenter'. The French Revolutionary principle of fraternity was to become paramount here, superseding the separate ethnic nations of Anglican Planters (who saw themselves as colonial representatives of England in Ireland), Scots Presbyterians (who saw themselves as a people of exodus and election) and Irish Catholics (who saw themselves as true inheritors of the ancient motherland). These constituent groups were now to enter a relationship of 'equality' – a new republic where conquered and conqueror would take equal part in the body politic.

This early idea of the Irish republic was largely universalist, therefore, in the sense that it operated on the assumption that once the antagonisms of embattled religions, languages and races disappeared a new culture of world citizenship would take its place. The challenge would be how to reconcile the Right of the People (under the common name of a single Irish Nation) with the respective rights of the three constituent peoples that made up this aspirational Nation – Protestant, Catholic and Dissenter? Let us take each in turn.

Protestants

Protestants were susceptible to republican ideas to the extent that they were bitterly disappointed by the outcome for Ireland of the Glorious Revolution in England in 1688. The latter had given rise to the Protestant 'patriot' campaign against England led by the Ascendancy MP William Molyneux, demanding legislative independence for Ireland (1782–83). But the radical implications of a Protestant political movement really only emerged when it developed a sense of pride in its own 'Irishness' between 1770 and 1790 – or what has been described by Marianne Elliott as the 'Golden Age of confident Protestant liberalism' in Ireland. The settlers were now turning patriots, promoting a kind of secular state in line with Enlightenment principles. But the main aim behind the Protestants' attempt to forge a collective sense of Irishness, uniting them with the indigenous majority, was autonomy from England. In other words, there were more material reasons for the Ascendancy Protestants' disposal towards a new Republic than revolutionary universalism. The colonial settlers were now feeling oppressed by England along with the colonized natives, as is plain from this 1792 extract from the *Proceedings of the Society of United Irishmen of Dublin*: 'It was not 'till very lately that the part of the nation which is truly colonial, reflected that though their ancestors had been victorious, they themselves were now included in the general subjection; subduing only to be subdued, and trampled upon by Britain as a servile dependency. When therefore the Protestants began to suffer what the Catholics had suffered; when from serving as the instruments they were made themselves the objects of foreign domination, then they became conscious they had a country – Ireland. They resisted British dominion, renounced colonial subserviency and . . . asserted the exclusive jurisdiction of this island'.

Fully aware of this line of thinking, Edmund Burke, perhaps the most trenchant critic of revolutionary republicanism of his time, warned that the chief source of sedition in Ireland was the Protestant community. 'The crimes of Jacobinism', as he complained in a letter of 1797, are 'unfortunately not disagreeable to the principles and inclinations of the majority of what we call the Protestants of Ireland'. And he added, lest there be any doubt as to his meaning: 'The Protestant part of the kingdom is represented by the British Government itself to be, by whole counties, in nothing less than open rebellion. I am sure that it is everywhere teeming with dangerous conspiracy'.[3]

Dissenters

It was, however, with the *Dissenters* – largely middle-class Ulster Presbyterians – that the revolutionary project of a new republic took firmest hold. Here, as with the colonial Protestants, it was a minority group of rebellious minds. The Irish Presbyterian tradition as a whole was strongly loyalist – even to the point of outspoken protest by the Ulster Presbytery against the execution of King Charles I! But this did not prevent a significant minority of Ulster Presbyterians from banding together in the early 1790s and appealing to the revolutionary principles of the French Republic. Many of these principles, it is arguable, were quite compatible with certain Enlightenment sentiments contained within the more radical strains of Presbyterianism itself. Amongst such radical sentiments might be counted: (i) the rejection of the tradition of

absolute authority; (ii) the priority given to a direct communion between man and the Divine, irrespective of institutions and traditions;
(iii) the belief in the primacy of the individual and of the liberty of
conscience – principles still reflected in the democratic structure of the
Presbyterian Church; and (iv) the conviction that Christ had delivered
humanity from the slavish fear of dogma and tradition.

These radical sentiments conspired happily with the French
Revolutionary abhorrence of obedience to absolute authority. Tom
Paine, observer of both French and American Revolutions, regarded
the Presbyterian movement of Ulster Volunteers (which evolved into
the United Irishmen) as the only true revolutionary body in Ireland.
And, as Marianne Elliott remarks, it is surely a reflection 'of the *loyalist*
and *nationalist* misrepresentation of Irish history that the United
Irishmen are traditonally regarded as part of catholic nationalist heritage. In reality they were a further manifestation of presbyterian
libertarianism'.[4]

Non-Presbyterian United Irishmen also acknowledged their debt to
this tradition (as in the case of Thomas Emmet who described the
Ulster Presbyterians as 'Lovers of Liberty, and almost republicans from
religion, from education and from early habits'). Nor should it be forgotten that certain Presbyterian church bells rang out in Ulster to celebrate news of the French Revolution. The fact that the Ulster
Presbyterian middle classes were those who stood to lose most from
English trade restrictions was, arguably, a decisive factor in their espousal of the republican project.

Catholics

The third and largest denomination included under the 'common name
of Irishman' was the *Catholic*. Surprisingly, it was difficult to find
members of the Roman Catholic hierarchy of the era who were also
true republicans. That, at least, is the contention of historian Liam de
Paor in 'The Rebel Mind: Republican and Loyalist'.[5] The main reason
for this was that the great enemy of Tridentine Catholicism taking hold
in Ireland at the end of the eighteenth century was the Enlightenment.
Prudence, patience and continuity were the Tridentine precepts: hardly
grist to the mill of a republican revolution.

The now commonplace identification of Catholicism with republican
nationalism is a relatively recent phenomenon. And the same can be
said of the image of Ireland as a devoutly Catholic country. There was
little regard, up to the nineteenth century, for the dogmas of the
Catholic hierarchy among a population which was only nominally

Catholic. The stereotypical equation of Irish Catholic and violent republican has, in fact, little historical basis. To quote Marianne Elliott:
'Whatever conclusion futher commentators will draw from current IRA
activities in Ireland, the Irish catholic populace has never been naturally
rebellious and the entire experience of modern Irish rebellion, from
1798, 1848, 1867 through to 1916, has shown the error of identifying
the physical force tradition of Irish nationalism with Catholicism in
general'.[6] It was, ironically, the *anti-revolutionary* influence of Catholic
members of the United Irish executive after 1797 which – in addition to
the violence of the Wexford Rebels – reanimated the tacit suspicion of
the Ulster Protestants for Catholics (and 'southerners' generally) provoking an irremediable break between Ulster and Dublin leaders.

The material condition of most Irish Catholics in the late eighteenth
century was, of course, dire. This, more than any theological doctrine of
liberation or Roman conspiracy, was to mobilize certain Catholics to
revolt. In rural areas, rebellion was prompted by massive increases in
rents and tithes, enclosure and overcrowding. Destitution saw secret
societies and gangs springing up, including the influential Defenders
movement. The new gospel of republicanism could thus be proclaimed
to the rural Catholic masses in the guise of a simplified millennialism
whose basic message was: the New Age begins with the End of Rent!
Many of the flock rallied to the cause, despite official ecclesiastical
hostility to the spread of secular republican ideas infiltrating the country from abroad. The misery of the Catholic population as a whole
meant that the winds blowing from France would stir this class to insur-
rection. Their support was finally given, therefore, not for doctrinal, but
for socio-economic reasons. In the moment of decision, class needs
proved stronger than confessional restraint.

While encouraged by the Protestant leaders of the United Irishmen,
the Catholics were rarely treated as complete equals. The Protestant
community, which initially articulated the republican ideology, was
marked by an insecure and basically ambiguous mentality of colonizer-
and-colonized, settler-and-native. Most Anglicans and Presbyterians of
the time had contempt for the Catholics whom they considered 'unfit
for liberty'. And when a sufficient number of United Irishmen over-
came such inherited prejudice to campaign for the emancipation of
Catholics, they frequently did so on the pretext that it was they, the
settlers, who had 'educated the indigenous populace to liberty'.

This 'condescending elitism' of some United Irishmen hardly fits the
common image of that movement as a military wing of Irish Catholic
nationalism. Indeed, it is often conveniently forgotten that Tone himself, who appealed for Catholic emancipation in the 'common name of

Irishman', did so not as an end, but as a means towards the separation of Ireland from England. Beneath such strategic motivation, Tone despised the Catholic religion. He considered priests as bigoted and illiterate – 'low bred rustics of vulgar sentiment' – and rejoiced in the French Directory's defeat of the Pope which left him 'nothing but his keys'. In his Journal, Tone went so far as to record his delight at the retribution inflicted at last on this 'Old Priest' from Rome, whose 'predecessors had for so many centuries sucked dry the marrow of Europe'. Wolfe Tone's hope was that once liberated from colonial oppression into a free republic, the Irish 'papists' would renounce their superstitions and be transformed into 'emancipated Irishmen'. At the very least, Tone anticipated a secular alliance between the common material interests of middle-class Catholics and Presbyterians – 'those catholics who had contributed successfully to commerce in Ireland', and those Presbyterians who had enriched themselves 'from trade and manufacture particularly in textiles'.

It has even been suggested that some Irish republicans' insistence on military assistance from France was prompted, not just by their obvious concern to strike an alliance with a common enemy of England, but also by their distrust of how the Catholic lower classes would behave in a revolutionary situation. The *Gaeil* could not be trusted. Populist movements like Defenderism were enlisted for support largely as part of a 'numbers game' (they did after all represent the majority population in what purported to be a 'democratic' uprising). The Protestant leadership of the United Irishmen never fully abandoned their distrust of Catholics, persuaded that one of their main goals was 'to knock the protestants on the head and take their place'.[7] But that did not stop Protestant republicans from *needing* them. For many of the Planter communities, the great appeal of the 'common name of Irishman' lay in its power to galvanize and exploit the support of the colonized Catholic majority against the imperial nation of England which was now oppressing the Protestant colonizers themselves. A Catholic means towards a Protestant end! Indeed, when one recalls such attitudes towards Catholics, one can perhaps concede Marianne Elliott's argument that the 'transformation of Ulster from the heartland of early Irish republicanism in the 1790s to the later centre of bitterly anti-catholic loyalism was not such a dramatic reversal as it may appear'.[8]

When it came to confessional differences, then, the ideology of the United Irishmen was marked, almost from the outset, by a curious confection of radicalism and reaction. The republican attempt to overcome religious tribalism was soon to be vitiated by its own brand of sectarianism – and opportunism. The rhetoric of a non-ethnic and non-confessional republic did not, alas, always match the reality.

THE REPUBLICAN LEGACY: IDEALS AND REALITIES

Protestant loyalism and Catholic nationalism were not, however, the only offspring of the failed project of early republicanism. Another important movement to emerge in the wake of '98 was *romantic nationalism*. While respecting the original republican vision of a united non-sectarian community, this ideology looked less to a future Enlightenment dream of world citizenry than to a memory of an ancient 'Celtic Race' which pre-existed colonial divisions and differences. Here the 'common name of Irishman' appealed to a long-lost heritage of shared 'Celticism' rather than a yet-to-be realized universalism. Davis and Ferguson were passionate advocates of such a 'romantic nationalism' in the nineteenth century; as were Pearse, Hyde and Yeats in the twentieth (see 'Myths of Motherland' below). In fact, Yeats's repudiation of Enlightenment thinkers – who, like Locke, had, he insisted, 'taken away the world and given us excrement instead' – and his celebration of a separate and sacrosanct 'Celtic nation' based on ancestral Unity of Culture, exemplified the *revivalist* spirit of romantic nationalism.

The legacy of the United Irishmen, in this context, was to prove less *republican* (in the Enlightenment sense) than *separatist* (in the romantic sense). That is, it had ultimately less to do with the overcoming of monarchy and religious rule in the name of a secular pluralist republic than with breaking the connection with the English – politically and culturally. The 'deanglicization' of the island became the overriding goal. The promotion of a non-confessional cosmopolitan ideology, in tune with the French *république*, was sidelined. In the long run, Irish republicanism was to become a synonym for Irish nationalism. Or to put it another way, the idea of a republic become less an end in itself than a means towards a nationalist end.

The reasons for this were, however, perhaps more complex than we have suggested. There were external as well as internal factors which prompted the abandonment of the original 'republican alliance' with revolutionary France and its allies. The deep confusions on the French side were also responsible for the catastrophic outcome of the 1798 uprising, which witnessed the collapse of the United Irish Society into a 'pitiful rump of exiles' by 1800. The delays of the French Directory, the dispersal of Hoche's fleet, the diversion of Napoleon from the English and Irish campaigns to the Mediterranean, the dispatch of General

Clarke to Italy, the muddle within the Republican Alliance in Europe generally: these were *external* contingencies effecting the failure of the original project of Irish republicanism.

But whatever the exact reasons, the betrayal of the original republican vision was incontrovertible. The carnage of 1798 was almost immediately followed by the Act of Union of 1800 (copperfastening the 'connection' with England) and the exacerbation of sectarian tensions between Protestant, Catholic and Dissenter. Robert Emmet's failed rebellion in the early nineteenth century merely exacerbated this eclipse of the republican ideal. And if Daniel O'Connell's campaign briefly revived its energies, it did not restore its ideology. Moreover, when some republican ideas did begin to make a come-back in the 1840s, in the transposed guise of Davis's romantic cultural nationalism, one was dealing with a very confused ideology indeed. Davis preached the rehabilitation of a timeless Celtic nation – to which Norman, Saxon, Gael and Dane could belong; and though he did not invoke Voltaire or Jefferson as ideological models, some of his contemporaries did subscribe to vaguely republican principles in their arguments for separation from the English Crown.

The 'second phase' of Irish republicanism, emerging after the Famine, was basically a version of separatist nationalism. Proclaiming a broad democratic ideal of 'government of the people by the people', it was most decisively fuelled by everyday practical struggles against the local tyranny of bailiffs, landlords and battering-rams. This was a matter of practical reaction to tyranny rather than a visonary project for a new world. More colonial rebellion than radical revolution: it knew what it was *against* rather than what it was *for*. As such, it could be said to approximate more to the American than the French idea of a republic – more, in short, to Lincoln's campaign for a democratic national union, than to Voltaire's philosophy of an international enlightened republic of equal parts. 'America rather than France', as de Paor puts it, 'inspired the Irish republicans of the later 19th century'.[9]

How, finally, did events in the twentieth century affect the legacy of Irish republicanism? The 1916 proclamation? The Anglo-Irish and Civil wars? The rise to power of self-proclaimed 'republican' parties like Sinn Féin and Fianna Fail? The ratification of Ireland as a Republic by Dail Eireann in 1949? The emergence of the Civil Rights campaign in Ulster in the 1960s? The 25-year campaign of violence conducted by the Irish Republican Army north of the border? The signing of the Single European Act and the Anglo-Irish Agreement by both British and Irish governments in the 1980s? In the light of these and other decisive changes in the political climate, what does Irish republicanism actually mean today?

It is surely in rethinking, and redebating, the various strands of the republican heritage that a new political paradigm might emerge: one capable of transmuting the old ideologies into new visions, denouncing aberrations in order to save the honour of the name, reconciling the particular rights of the people(s) on this island with the universal rights of man. In this respect, there is, I believe, a great need for a novel appreciation of the *universalist* dimension of republicanism, as we move toward greater integration with the common house of Europe and the wider world. And there is a corresponding need for a reappreciation of its *localist* dimension, if we are ever to realize the possibilities of participatory democracy which the project for a decentralized Europe of regions will, if achieved, open up. In his formative essay, 'Europe of the Regions', published in 1988, John Hume had this to say about such a project: 'This is the real new republicanism, the development of processes which will allow people to preserve their culture, rights and dignity; to promote their well-being and have a means of controlling the forces which will affect their lives . . . this will allow us better to fulfil our potential as a people; to contribute to our world; to rediscover the cultural interaction between Ireland and Europe; to reinvolve ourselves in political relationships with those on the Continental mainland and to enjoy properly the inchoate European outlook and vision which was lost in our oppressive and obsessive relationship with Britain. It maintains the necessary synchrony between the scope of democracy and economic and technological circumstances. . . . On this basis we can provide a social, regional and Irish dimension to our Europe'.[10]

There is a battle to be fought over the meaning of the term 'republicanism' for Irish citizens in the emerging Europe. Waging this debate means confronting the following questions: Is the term so tainted by the campaign of IRA violence in Ulster as to stand unredeemed and unredeemable? Has it degenerated irreversibly into the adversarial extremes of sectarian nationalism and loyalism? Or is there still something to be retrieved from the United Irishmen's initial vision of a non-sectarian, cosmopolitan and enlightened republic of liberty and tolerance?

The debate on the authentic legacy of Irish republicanism is, above all, a contest of ideas. The ideas of a republic discussed above (and in Chapter 3 below) derive from both Anglo-American and French–Continental ideologies and, as such, need to be constantly checked against the changing needs of the communities that make up Irish society, north and south of the border – and, if one is to grant the rights of

Irish emigrants, beyond the border. A new republic would surely only be 'representative' in a genuine sense if it acknowledged that the common name of Irishman includes diverse groups both within the frontiers of the island (subnational communities) and in the wider world (international communities). If the idea of a republic is to have any positive meaning for Ireland in the year 2000 it will not, I am persuaded, be one reducible to the boundaries of an insular nation-state. But that is another story: one that we take up in the chapters which follow.

3 Genealogy of the republic

In Chapter 2 we explored what the notion of 'Republic' has come to mean in the contemporary Anglo-Irish context and sought to compare this with certain aspects of revolutionary republicanism. In what follows I propose to trace the genealogy of republicanism from its origin in classical and Renaissance thought through English, French and American versions of the term. I take as guiding motto Cicero's statement: 'When we inquire what a Republic means, we should first of all understand the nature of the thing itself about which we inquire' (*The Republic of Cicero*, Book 1, pp. 24–25).

The term 'republic' may be defined according to the following eight characteristics:

1 primary power invested in the people;
2 a mixed balance of separate powers – executive, legislative, judicial;
3 primacy of a 'political life' of civic participation based on the Aristotelian model of the citizen as a *zoon politikon*;
4 the virtue of autonomy and self-government in contradistinction to the absolute sovereignty of monarch or despot;
5 the appeal to a certain universality of value tailored to the historical needs of particular communities in particular times and places;
6 a commitment to a plurality of views on justice, transcending inherited dogma and cultivating open debates about the nature of civic *virtue* – i.e. a democratic conflict of interpretations;
7 a government by law rather than by persons – with crucial emphasis on the original moment of law-giving, on the founding constitution of first principles;
8 a society of equal rights of access, in accordance with the old Athenian principle of *isonomia* – a society in which office was to be widely accessible on an equal footing.

CLASSICAL REPUBLICANISM

I begin our genealogy with what is arguably the most 'originary' text on republicanism, Cicero's *De Republica*. It was here that the term 'republic' first achieved systematic articulation. Many of the principles of republicanism had already been adumbrated by Greek authors such as Plato, Aristotle and Polybius, or in Greek constitutions such as Sparta, Athens or Carthage. But it was Cicero who synthesized these diverse formulations into a single *summa*. Almost all subsequent versions of 'classical' republicanism refer to Cicero's seminal text, right down to Renaissance thinkers like Machiavelli and Guicciardini or later English theorists such as Harrington, Sydney and Neville.

Acknowledging that there are differing opinions on the exact nature of a republic, Cicero (in the persona of Scipio Africanus) seeks to clarify the debate at the outset by offering this basic definition: 'The Republic is the property of the people' *(res publica [est] res populi)* (I, 24–25). He immediately goes on to add, however, the all-important proviso that 'the people does not mean every association of men however congregated but an association of many under the sanction of the law, and associated for a common object of public service (*utilitatis communione sociatus*)'. Cicero observes that the reason for people associating for the sake of common purpose and law is not merely preventative, i.e. to compensate for or curb weakness (*imbellicitas*); it also serves the positive purpose of fufilling our being as political citizens. That Cicero is here confirming Aristotle's famous definition of man as *zoon politikon* in *The Politics* would appear evident from his claim that 'man's nature is neither singular nor solitary, but so constituted that . . . it is his natural disposition to congregate together' (I, 24–25).

Cicero entertains a number of different accounts of the origin of human society – or, as he puts it, of how a 'scattered and wandering multitude formed a state by general accord (*concordium civitas*). Quite apart from the obvious reasons of utility, necessity and convenience, Cicero also suggests that it is in the 'nature of men to associate together and, fleeing from solitude, to seek intercourse and form societies' (I, 26). This Aristotelian–Ciceronian doctrine of our intrinsically political nature was to have a profound impact on the development of republican theory from Florentine thinkers like Machiavelli and Giacciardini to John Adams, a founding father of the American Constitution, who declared that the most essential character of all peoples is that of public emulation and recognition – 'the desire to be seen, heard, talked of, approved and respected by people'.[1]

If these are the 'seeds' (*semina*) of motivation founding human society, Cicero claims that every civic body which is a constitution of people
requires to be governed by some kind of council (*consilium*).[2] This
council is needed 'in order to be lasting' (*diuturna*). And, interestingly,
this enduringness is only ensured when the council called upon to
govern the republic is that which has already founded it in the first
place: 'that council which organised the community is the fundamental
purpose (*prima causa*) to which its constitution must ever be referred'
(I, 26 *et seq.*). Thus, from the outset, we are confronted by two recurring features of classical republicanism: (i) the desired *longevity* of the
republic; and (ii) the circular nature of the *foundational* argument.

Cicero proceeds to mention a third important feature: the model of
mixed government. The power of council, and by implication constitution, can be given to one person (monarchy), to a select few (aristocracy), or to all (democracy as *civitas popularis*). A government can
only attain stability, however, if the original bond (*vinculum*) 'which first
induced [citizens] to associate together for public purposes holds
good'.[3] In other words, all forms of government are bound by the original moment of constitution. But this introduces a certain precarious-
ness since the founding bond is not some timeless essence but an event
of history exposed to the vicissitudes of time and place. Cicero is cognizant of this, as his frequent allusions to the previous rise and fall of
republics – Carthage, Athens, Sparta – makes plain. Cicero thus recommends an intermixture of each of the three forms of government
by way of counteracting the extreme of any one left to itself. Rule by the
one can lead to *tyranny*, rule by the few to *oligarchy*, rule by the many to
anarchy. Or as Cicero puts it, 'a despot springs from a king, a faction
from the nobles, a mob from the people' (I, 45). Against the danger of
these three extremes, Cicero recommends a fourth kind of government
– one compounded of all three.[4]

What is particularly 'republican' about Cicero's position here is his
insistence that rule by the people be included as an indispensable part
of this new mix. Criticizing the reign of King Cyrus for ignoring the
interests of the people, Cicero pens this argument for popular participation in government: 'Liberty hath its home in no other form of government except where the power of the people is supreme; and where that is
so, certainly nothing can be sweeter; and where there is no equality,
there can indeed be no liberty'. A list of instances of democractic equality follows: 'states in which all are free of speech, for they possess the
suffrage, confer military commands, create magistrates, go about can-
vassing and soliciting appointments'. Citing the historic examples of
Athens and Rhodes, Cicero claims that in a genuinely united people 'all

references are to its safety and freedom' (I, 30–32). A republic of the people is, he repeats, a republic for the people: *res publica est res populi*.

And so we come to the next stage of the argument: a republic of the people is a republic governed by *law*. 'When the law is the bond of civil society', writes Cicero, 'and there is an equal right to the law, in what way is it possible for an association of citizens to be held together when the talents of all are not equal? For if fortunes cannot be made equal – if genius cannot be given equally to all – still rights ought to be equal amongst those who are citizens of the same republic. For what is a state (*civitas*), but an association of right regulated by law (*juris societas*)' (I, 33–34).

At this point Cicero defends the notion of a republic against hereditary power. Neither monarchy nor aristocracy should be called republics. A free people, he insists, is one which selects its own form of government and its leader, repudiating the election of kings by blood lineage (I, 33–34). One who rules by oppressing the people is a tyrant, reducing citizens to the condition of servants. Whenever monarchy opts for tyranny rather than a balance of powers (as in the case of Tarquinius Superbus in Rome), a wise and courageous republican (such as Lucius Brutus) must arise to readjust the balance and restore a sufficient element of popular participation.[5] Aristocracy does not merit the title of republic either, for here one simply replaces the tyrannical rule of the one with the tyrannical rule of the many. Elitist 'factions' are no more deserving of power than individual despots. Cicero's *apologia pro re popula* protests the prejudice that those with wealth or noble blood are best suited to rule. A republic should be governed by virtue rather than by royal race or vulgar wealth (I, 34).[6] Here we encounter a powerful prefiguration of the Florentine Renaissance argument for widespread civic participation.

It is true that Cicero qualifies this argument subsequently in favour of a benign equilibrium (*aequabilitas*) between all three forms of government (I, 35–36). It is also true that he invokes a Platonic critique of the many excesses of popular rule – chaos and confusion, neglect of the laws, refusal of authority, licentiousness, etc. All too easily, a *polis* ruled by the many can degenerate into a 'house without a master, a family without a father' (I, 43–44). In other words, populist extremism, unchecked by government, can betray republican virtue and provoke a return to the opposite extreme of tryanny from above. 'A tyrant springs up from the excess of liberty . . . tyrannizing over the very persons by whom he has been raised to power' (I, 45). Hence the argument that if the republican demand for a relatively stable and lasting constitution is to be met, the best solution is a 'moderately mixed' government (*moder-*

ateque permixta conformatione rei publicae – I, 45). But this preference
for a balance between the three forms of government does not diminish
the fact that Cicero's text offers one of the most cogent classical por-
traits of a participatory republic.

RENAISSANCE REPUBLICANISM

Cicero's text was to have an enduring impact on the entire tradition of
classical republicanism extending down through the centuries to such
Renaissance thinkers as Plutarch, Machiavelli and Guiccardini. What
these thinkers took from Cicero was the realization that republics are
founded in historical time and, as history demonstrates, undergo numerous mutations, appearing and disappearing at various different
times and places – Athens, Carthage, Sparta, Rome, and later again,
Venice and Florence. The theorists of Renaissance republicanism inherited from Cicero the puzzling paradox that a republic sought to be at
once universal and particular, permanent yet responsive to a specific set
of temporal circumstances. The leading question now became: how do
republics arise and remain stable over time, given the vicissitudes of
historical change?

In his remarkable study, *The Machiavellian Moment: Florentine
Political Thought and the Atlantic Republican Tradition*, J.G.A. Pocock
extrapolates some of the salient consequences of this question. The
revival of the classical republican ideal in sixteenth-century Florence
and Venice amounted to an attempt by civic humanists to resolve the
problem of a society 'in which the political nature of man as described
by Aristotle was to receive its fulfillment, seeking to exist in the framework of a Christian time-scheme which denied the possibility of any
secular fulfillment'.[7] To put it another way, how is one to institute a
meaningful mode of civic being – a republican *polis* – in a secular time
independent of transcendent meaning? The task of Renaissance republicans, from Bruni and Machiavelli to Guicciardini and Contrarini, was
to reconcile the claim of a republic to actualize universal values with
the circumstantial contingency of its historical existence. This was to
prove a central feature of civic humanists committed to the basic neo-
Aristotelian ideal of active citizenship in a republic: what the
Florentine republicans named the *vivere civile*.[8] The main obstacle here
was the Platonic doctrine that true ideals are universal essences existing
beyond time, space and circumstance. And this was not aided by the
Judaeo-Christian view of history as meaningful at both its beginning
(creation) and its end (redemption) but not during the historical period
in between. In its most extreme form, this meant that history was a time

of fallenness which could only be redeemed from the outside, eschato-
logically, by grace.

The problem was crystallized for Renaissance republicans around the
question (already touched on by Cicero and the Roman republicans) of
the foundation of a law which, in each republic, would incorporate both
the rational principles of universal citizenship and the circumstantial
conditions and customs attached to each specific community. It was,
after all, one thing to deduce the statutes of a *polis* from the principles
of natural justice and reason; quite another to render them compatible
with the specific practices of particular peoples.

It was in response to this dilemma that the republicans of Venice and
Florence proposed the notion of good 'usage' to justify the suitability
of law for peculiar conditions. A political custom becomes good because it lasts over time, and it lasts because it works. A culturally and
socially conditioned second-nature – called wise custom or prudence
(based on Aristotle's *phronesis*) thus comes to supplement our first or
rational nature. Though the longevity of the republic was a myth, it
was a necessary one for its own self-legitimation. By declaring that
custom, predicated on long-lasting experience and reason, was the
mainspring of political legitimacy, the Renaissance humanists were basically saying that a single sovereign has no more privileged access to
these than any other citizen. Republican government could now be
recognized as an art rather than some divinely ordained dogma: an art
guided by prudence and usage and mobilized by a secular concern to
combine the universal and the particular. The republic sought to found
its authority on *lex* rather than *rex*, on *prudentia* rather than *providen-
tia*. It called for a theory investing humans with the ability to inaugurate
new orders in the realm of secular history. This ability became identified
with the Latin term, *virtus*, a reworking of the Greek term, *arete,* meaning the power by which persons act effectively in a civic context. It is a
form of civic action, largely influenced by the Aristotelian conviction
that political and social association are natural to human beings and
their ability to perceive particular things in terms of their true essences
or ends (the universal). As such, this model of republican thinking
poses a direct challenge to the medieval and Augustinian dichotomy
between history and eschatology, the world of action and of
contemplation.[9]

The Florentine experiments in republican thinking and practice in
the fifteenth and sixteenth century were undoubtedly the most formative attempts of the early modern period to emancipate citizens from
the heavy baggage of imposed authority, inviting them to take their
civic life, *vivere civile*, into their own hands. Not surprisingly, Brutus

was revived as the exemplar of the republican citizen who defended the *res publica* against Caesar and the Empire. Florentines like Bruni made the radical step of renouncing imperial tradition in favour of the republican principles of active participation and civic partnership. Hence the basic option of 'civic humanism' for a republican *polis* over a hierarchical *civitas dei*. For Renaissance humanists, the intellect was not just there to contemplate eternal verities but to participate in a 'conversation between men in time'.[10] It was, Pocock suggests, from this Renaissance culture of civic humanism that a primary emphasis on rights of speech, pluralist debate and public decision became an indispensable feature of modern republicanism. In short, any genuine republic requires the possibility of open conversation between its citizens.

The challenge for this republican ideal of democratic communication is, once again, to explain how particular citizens at particular times can lay claim to reliable, universally valid meanings. To save the republican system of values from mere relativism, it would be necessary to establish a body of constitutional theory, replacing the old appeal to divine election or cosmic order. In pursuit of this theory, the Italian republicans revived not only Cicero but Aristotle's insistence that the *demos* – the citizen body as a whole – should have a key role to play in the determination of values lest the good of any one group, or individual, become identical with the good of the whole. A revised version of Aristotle's model of balanced government or *politeia* was thus invoked as a constitution or functionally differentiated structure of participation permitting a wide diversity of citizens to associate in pursuit of a *res publica*. This represented the politicization of virtue. In short, virtue is acknowledged as a moral and political relation of citizenship, a relation in which each citizen agrees to rule and be ruled in such a way that one's own civic virtue is intimately bound up with that of one's fellow citizens. The pursuit of one's own particular goods must be perpetually balanced with one's pursuit of a common universal good which is shared with the other citizens of the *polis*. The civic humanists of the Renaissance recognized – as Cicero and Aristotle before them – that if *politeia* represented the most widespread participation of citizens in power, it also ran the risk, unless held in check, of degenerating into a formless democracy. The feared result was: rule by a numerical mass of undifferentiated and depersonalized men, a tyranny of numbers, or what de Tocqueville would later refer to as the 'tyranny of equality' – majoritarian democracy.

A balanced polity, by contrast, reconciling the interests of the particular and the universal, is one where the good of citizenship becomes a relation of interdependency between each citizen's virtue and that of the others. And so for the Italian republicans of the sixteenth century in search of a constitutional theory, virtue was to be based, not as with the medievals on the operation of divine grace, nor with the monarchists on the powers of a single rule, but on the political interaction between fellow citizens actively participating in a *vivere civile*. The universality of the republic, henceforth, was to be predicated upon the stable harmonization of its particular values. But here again there are attendant dangers. The move from a divine to a distributive model of justice, from power as salvific to power as social, carries the risk of reducing human beings to an extreme form of collective dependency. If the mystical body of Christ, in which all parts interact, is replaced by the mystical body of the republic, the degree of public responsibility for each citizen becomes almost intolerable. In other words, if virtue becomes completely public, subsuming one's private interior life completely to the *vivere civile*, there would appear to be no escape from the all-seeing eye of society's Law. The identification of *virtus* with the civic life of the republican *polis* could no longer be taken for granted. Indeed, the horrific activities of the Committees for Public Safety during the French Revolutionary Terror would show just how destructive certain extremes of republicanism can be.

In a certain sense, Machiavelli already anticipates this swing from republicanism to despotism, from the rule of the many to rule by the one, when he writes: 'To found a new republic, or to reform entirely the old institutions of an existing one, must be the work of one man only'.[11] Machiavelli's astute insight into the thin line between democracy and autocracy is evident in his appeal to the authority of a single founder in the *Discourses* and to the strategy of the single-rule of dictatorship in *The Prince*. Because republics are historically founded and humanly instituted, they must have resort to dictatorship in times of transition or crisis – albeit a dictatorship that is constitutionally provided.

But if conservative republicanism sought the solution to the crisis of legitimation in returning to first principles (*recursi principi*) or constitutional dictatorship, monarchists would dismiss all forms of republic outright. The key theorist of the anti-republicans of this period turned out to be Jean Bodin who responded to the threat of republicanism with a single recipe – absolutist *sovereignty*. In his *Six Livres de la République*, published in 1576, Bodin argued that since sovereignty was by its very nature indivisible, it could only reside in one place, not two or three or more. The very idea of mixed government or a balance of separate powers – executive, legislative and judicial – is therefore a nonsense. Bodin's book was, in the view of Zera Fink, 'one of the most widely read works of the sixteenth and seventeenth centuries', and was, moreover, to supply 'in the doctrine of sovereignty a concept which . . . was made by succeeding absolutists in France and England into an argument against attempts to limit the royal power'.[12] It became clear to royalists throughout Europe that the theory of mixed government supported the cause of republicans in their opposition to monarchy. Monarchy was fundamentally incompatible with the republican principle of mixed power because it was government by the *one*!

ENGLISH REPUBLICANISM

The republican tradition, in both its classical and Renaissance forms, was to be revived in the modern revolutions of America and France. But it also exerted a considerable influence on theories of a commonwealth in civil war England. Despite the fact that England was only a republic for a short spell between 1646 and 1660, the influence of its republican theorists – in particular Harrington, Milton and Smith – was considerable, especially in North America. While English republicanism was ostensibly revolutionary, it was, as Pocock notes, in reality deeply conservative in its nationalist, evangelical and ultimately imperialist aims.[13] Not surprisingly, the model of an expansionist republic advanced by Machiavelli was to appeal to the imperial interests of seventeenth-century England.

James Harrington's *Oceana*, published in 1656, was undoubtedly the most influential tract of English republicanism. It argued for a retrieval of the ancient 'prudence' of republics by way of challenging the tyranny of modern despots. Harrington's genealogy of the commonwealth ran something like this: while prudence had been granted by God directly to the Israelites, and indirectly through nature to the Greeks and Romans, it had been abruptly dispensed with by the 'execrable reign of the roman emperors', followed by the subsequent tyrannies of Huns, Vandals and Lombards. The great heritage of classical republicanism – which Harrington identified with Sparta, Rome and the Hebrew commonwealth – was most powerfully revived by Machiavelli and challenged by Hobbes's anti-republican *Leviathan*. To Hobbes's doctrine of single-headed state power (or monarchy), Harrington opposed the Machiavellian model of active citizenship.

The Italian city-republics – and especially Florence and Venice – were the chosen prototypes for Harrington's utopian commonwealth. While Florence proffered a blueprint for an ever-exanding commonwealth ('the growth of Oceana givith law unto the sea'), Venice was favoured as the 'most democratic and popular of all'.[14] Harrington insists, moreover, on the myth of Venetian longevity, first promoted by Contrarini, in order to support his argument that mixed government – of which Venice was a supreme example with its balance of democratic equality and aristocratic administration – could be as stable and hereditary as monarchical rule by the one. He thus predicts the imminent collapse of the 'Gothic' monarchies of seventeenth-century Europe and the modern revival of classical and Renaissance republicanism.

The curious feature of Harrington's English republicanism is that it was attracted to 'mixed government' not just because it was more *egalitarian*, but because it was more *powerful* than all other forms. Invoking the classical thesis of Aristotle, Polybius and Cicero that any *single* form of government led to corruption (monarchy to tyranny, aristocracy to oligarchy, democracy to anarchy), Harrington believed that the emerging English Empire would be best served by a republican balance of powers. This included the active participation of citizens in popular power. Every citizen, after all, had a right to robustly contribute to the expanding empire! No one was excluded from the colonizing campaign of the English nation!

But quite apart from this ideological consideration, Harrington was committed to a genuine form of power by the people. Law made in the interest of the few (albeit the most wise and noble) was not to 'the profit of a commonwealth'. Hence his support for a bicameral system of government – i.e. a balance of lords *and* commons. While the First Council (Senate) would propose, it would be the people's representatives in the Second Council (popular assembly) who reserved the right of decision. No single Council could, on its own, be equal or just.[15] Anticipating here certain aspects of the revolutionary republicanism of France and America, Harrington argued for a government of 'equal mixed polity' that would be 'free', 'popular' and 'democratic', with sovereignty residing in the people. He advocated the equal rotation of all offices, including the magistracy (or third branch of government), such rotation to be decided upon by the 'free election or suffrage of the people'.[16] To keep power fixed in one person or party was, he believed, to destroy the very life of the commonwealth. Harrington's *Oceana* thus represented a radical challenge to the 'Gothic' formula of power confined to the one or few, together with the old feudal system of land tenure.

Harrington is republican, therefore, to the extent that he promotes a state where the major portion of power lies in the people. This he describes as a 'democracy' where the 'people have the election of the senate and the result which is the sovereign power', in addition to 'safety of the common-wealth'.[17] He opposes all forms of hereditary monarchy and, naturally, approves the deposition of Charles I by the Puritan Revolution. In the dispute between royalists and parliamentarians as to where the sovereign power to make laws resides, Harrington is clear: 'power should be in the people'.[18]

Harrington interprets this appeal to popular sovereignty in terms of the old republican maxim that government should be 'of laws not of men'. In other words, it is not good or bad men that made good or bad republics, but good or bad *constitutions*. Harrington adheres thus to the basic principle, shared by both classical and modern republicanism, that republics are founded on legal constitutions rather than on the will, whim or fiat of a single ruler. The problem here is, of course, the perennial question of who *founds* the constitution? And this problem becomes almost a paradox, if not a contradiction, when Harrington invites Cromwell, in the preliminary essay of *Oceana*, to imitate the action of Lycurgus in Sparta by deploying supreme authority, not to set himself up as an absolute, but to initiate a perfect mixed state on behalf of the people. As Zera Fink observes: 'In view of Harrington's great indebtedness to Machiavelli, it is significant that the role he would have Cromwell play had a close parallel in that which the Italian theorist proposed to the Medicis in his tract on the reform of the government of Florence'.[19]

That said, Harrington recognized that the republic set up in England in 1649 was not a *real* republic but a single-council oligarchy of inspired zealots doomed to early dissolution. The *real* republic would be the realization of the utopian *ideal*, as outlined in *Oceana*, established on the ballot and agrarian legislation, with rotating national government and senate, based on the best principles of Venice and Rome. Not surprisingly, Cromwell was not unduly impressed with *Oceana,* declaring he would not change his ways for a 'little paper shot'.[20] But this did not prevent the utopian text causing a profound stir in the political community at large, in Britain and later in America. The major achievement of Harrington, in his more Machiavellian moments, was to make certain basic republican principles – in particular popular democracy at national level – compatible with the prospect of a lasting world empire of ever-expanding frontiers. Here he reconnects with the radical Puritan nationalism of Milton who believed that England was an 'elect nation' with a vocation to lead the world. England's ideal republic, Oceana, was not to be made for 'herself only', insisted Harrington, but for all mankind – 'for the vindication of Common Right, and the Law of Nature'.[21] Indeed, it is highly ironic, but not surprising, to recall that republicanism was first introduced into Ireland by Cromwell in the guise of English imperialism.

If imperialism lurks behind the mask of English republicanism, nationalism lurks behind the mask of English imperialism. Harrington himself was undoubtedly both a nationalist and an imperialist – and the influence of his thinking on the modern emergence of nation-state republicanism is important in this respect. While nation-state republics had the virtue of transferring sovereignty from king (the one) to people (the many), they did so largely within the nationalist framework of sovereignty. Hence Harrington's critique of the Swiss and Dutch republics for their lack of central authority and defence. The ideal republic outlined in *Oceana* was one predicated upon the centralized rule of national sovereignty. This crucial point has often been ignored by the English, who throughout their imperial history have generally considered nationalism a defect of the nations they colonized. Thus if Ireland, and many another colony, did indeed mix their republicanism with nationalism, it was in many respects a mirror-image response to their English overlords.

The fragile marriage between British nationalism and classical republicanism dissolved into open conflict on the sovereignty issue. The indivisibility of sovereignty, advanced by theorists like Bodin and Hobbes, appeared to be in direct contradiction with the republican model of mixed government. Sovereignty had found its original model in the divine power of an absolute God, then in the delegation of that power to the Patriarch of family or tribe, and finally to the king, monarchy or centralized nation-state. In all such cases, sovereignty was considered absolute, inalienable and indivisible. In the *Leviathan* (II, XIX), Hobbes was to deliver a blistering attack on the republican support of rebellion against monarchy, along lines similar to Bodin's critique of *la partage de la puissance souveraine*. Simply put, because sovereign power is indivisible it cannot be divided. Because it is one, it cannot be mixed. The republican government of the Puritan Revolution in England epitomized this contradiction as it attempted to pay dual allegiance to a mixed state and an absolute sovereignty. This was particularly acute in the attempt by republicans like Cromwell, Milton or Sydney to combine the interests of nationalism (based on absolute, albeit popular, sovereignty) and republicanism (based on the *partage* of powers).[22]

Another major problem arising from this republican transfer of absolute sovereignty from monarch to people, was that there could be no acceptance of differences between different groups or parties representing the people. Now the people, not the monarch, must be one and indivisible. There could be no way of accounting for 'good' and 'bad' forms of republican parliament given the notion of undivided popular sovereignty (members of parliament working with the 'full suffrage of the people'). If the people is now sovereign, it must be a single whole – or 'one holy nation' as the Puritan rebels put it. Any individuals, or parts, of the nation-state not conforming to the will of the sovereign 'people' were thus dismissed as unworthy of parliamentary representation. To dissent from the absolute oneness of the English nation, even as a colony, was simply not to exist. Indeed, it is surely no accident that the aligning of English republicanism with this absolutist form of nationalism in the 1650s coincided with Cromwell's campaign in Ireland.

AMERICAN REPUBLICANISM

The transatlantic connection between English and American republicanism has been somewhat eclipsed historically by the more conspicuous influence of the constitutionalist tradition of Locke and Burke. The extensive research of scholars like Pocock and Fink on the English-speaking legacy of classical and Renaissance republicanism has, however, done much to redress the balance. Even before the official republicanism of the American Revolution, republican theory had left its mark on the founding charters of New World colonies. Both the Carolina government plan of 1669 and the New Jersey charter of 1676 included a free ballot, and an accountable Grand Council of the Harringtonian–Venetian variety.[23] (Wolfe Tone expressed particular interest in the latter.) The charter of Pennsylvania, devised by William Penn in the 1680s, comprised these and other such republican features as rotating committees, a popular Assembly and secret ballot. Admittedly, the republican model of mixed government migrated to America largely through a Lockean reading together with Montesquieu's notion of the separation and balance of powers. At any rate, when the founding fathers met at Philadelphia to draft a constitution, predicated on the superiority of mixed government – what John Adams called 'a constitution of balanced powers' – the legacy of English and Classical republicanism was not far from their minds.

American republicanism also included, as de Tocqueville later recognized, a dose of the Enlightenment ideology of equality and liberty inherited via Montesquieu and Locke. But recent theorists such as Boorstin and Arendt tend to downplay this ideological legacy, stressing the more Burkean reading of the American Revolution as a form of conservative rebellion.[24] According to this reading, the greatness of the American republic was to dispense with ideology and ideas in favour of experience and pragmatism. And this pragmatism dictated that the American rebels of the Boston Assembly of 1770 declared themselves even more faithful to British constitutional principles – 'No Taxes without Representation' – than the British themselves! Whence the quip that the English revolution succeeded twice, once in England (1688) and once in America (1776). The founders of the American Republic, from Adams and Jefferson to Madison and Lincoln, were practical, common-sense lawyers rather than radical theorists, determined to conflate ideological differences between political factions in favour of a basic consensus about the American way of life – supported by legal guarantees. For the Americans, in their more Burkean mood, a republic was good if it *worked*: that is, if it subordinated abstract aspirations to home-grown efficiency and experiential wisdom. The federal consitution was ultimately more about compromise on practical details than agreement on theory. Indeed it is no accident that the first republican tract issued in America arguing for independence, was published not *before* the revolution of 1776 but in the same year.

Daniel Boorstin has argued that the recurrence of organic images of landscape and geography in the tracts of the founding fathers was a way of reassuring American citizens that, in spite of differences of colour and creed, there was a basic experience of *givenness* which bound them all together. This Boorstin calls the 'pre-formation' principle of the American Republic. According to it, the American way of life is a common fact of law and land, with no need of ideology to legitimate it. The genius of American republicanism, in this view, was to cultivate institutions suited to a particular time and place, in historical continuity with the past. So that when Lincoln invokes the republican principle of liberty in his Gettysburg Address of 1863, he invokes the same British parliamentary principles which the fathers of the Revolution of 1776 believed the British themselves had betrayed. Similarly, the Declaration of Independence itself, with its inalienable rights to 'life, liberty and the pursuit of happiness', was not intended to initiate a new order in rupture with the past but rather to respect the basic consitutionalist principles of the Puritan pioneers of the seventeenth century. Boorstin's conclusion is, accordingly, that the more continuous and orthodox the American model of a republican constitution, the more capable it was of absorbing the mixed character of its emigrant populations. Everything from Civil War divisions to the rights to free speech and life are continually referred back to legal interpretations of US constitutional amendments, irrespective of ideology. This is why, Boorstin argues, the Americans experience their republic in terms of common continuity (two hundred years of internal unity) in contrast, for example, to the French revolutionary experience of ideological discontinuity and rupture. The fact that the American Republic has more to do with a conservative colonial rebellion than a radical revolution means that 'Americans are reared with an unprecedented belief in the normality of [their] kind of life to [their] place on earth'.[25] Native Americans and Afro-Americans notwithstanding.

American republicanism also exerted its influence on the development of Irish republicanism. The United Irishmen invoked the American Declaration of Independence as a 'light shining through our prison'. And it was no accident that Wolfe Tone made his way to Paris in the 1790s via America with an alias provided by the Foreign Ministry in Philadelphia, 'James Smith, American Citizen'. While Tone approved the American model of national-colonial rebellion against Britain, he was also partial to the more openly revolutionary ideas of Tom Paine, whom he befriended in Paris and described thus: 'Paine . . . has done wonders for the cause of liberty, both in America and Europe'. The Patriot campaign against English rule in the 1790s was deeply influenced by the colonial rebellion of the Americans in 1776. And the United Irishmen's newspaper, the *Northern Star*, championed Paine's arguments against hereditary monarchy, denouncing kingship as mere 'delegated power' in 1792. Indeed, this initial link between Irish and American republicanism could be said to have continued, in later centuries, through the Fenian campaigns, De Valera's famous visit to the USA in the 1940s, and the recent support of the Northern Irish peace policy by the influential 'American-Irish' lobby in Washington. In summary, it might be said that Irish republicanism took certain guidelines from the American model of colonial rebellion – in particular its leaning towards a pragmatic nationalism. But if Irish republicanism was frequently American in practice it was, as noted in Chapter 2 above, largely French in theory.

FRENCH REPUBLICANISM

The anti-sectarian philosophy of the French Republic, which initially inspired Wolfe Tone and the United Irishmen, was encapsulated in the Declaration of the Rights of Man and of the Citizen (1789–93). As I have already discussed this Declaration in Chapter 2, suffice it to offer the following summary. The rights in question were threefold: those of the individual citizen; those of the people or nation; and those of mankind as a whole. It was in this last respect – *universalism* – that French republicanism was original, going beyond both the English Bill of Rights of 1689 and the American Bill of Rights of 1789, and prefiguring the UN Charter of Human Rights of 1948. The French Republic espoused, for the first time in history, the project of a universal civilization transcending racial, social and national boundaries by advancing the inviolable rights of all peoples of the world to freedom and equality. And in spite of compromising this revolutionary ideal – especially with the Terror of 1793–95 and later with Napoleon's imperialism – a number of radical reforms were achieved: the abolition of slavery, the granting of full civic rights to Protestants and Jews, the democractic separation of Church and State, the restoration of sovereignty to the people, family law provision including equal rights to inheritance, divorce and the according of legal status to illegitimate children. The argument against the French *République*, levelled by critics like Burke, Carlyle and Talleyrand, was that it was essentially a revolution of abstract ideas, an invention of fanatical *philosophes* with no real grasp of reality. The fact that thinkers like Diderot, Rousseau and Voltaire were revered by the new republic confirmed this suspicion that the revolution was little more than an 'idolatry of ideas'. In Britain the attack on the revolutionary ideology was spearheaded by Burke who condemned the founders of *La République* as 'banditti assuming the tone of an academy of philosophers'. Burke's main fear was that it elevated ideological principles to the exclusion of inherited wisdom and traditional experience. And he believed, moreover, that the 'crimes of French Jacobinism' would soon spill over into Ireland.

The French Republic differed fundamentally from English democracy in its refutation of monarchy – as evidenced in Condorcet's influential address of 12 July 1791, 'On the Republic or, Is a King Necessary to the Preservation of Liberty?' And it differed from the American model in that it was, as noted above, more universalist than 'colonial' or 'conservative'. But it shared in common with all forms of previous republicanism the ancient notion of the *res publica* as a community bound together by civic virtue and participation. There were naturally competing views on how large or how small such a republic should be. Was it to be confined to regional units like the city states of the ancient world, the Italian Renaissance, Geneva or a modest political unit like the Netherlands? Could it work in a large country of over twenty million people like France aspiring to the condition of a nation-state? Or could it extend to the size of America with its federation of independent states? Might a new republic serve as a direct democracy in the guise of 'representative government' in which the members were invested with the sovereignty of the people? And was it possible to destroy the old absolutism of hereditary monarchy without replacing it with a new absolutism of the people conceived as 'one will' and represented by one (unicameral) assembly? If the executive was no more than a means of implementing the indivisible and sovereign will of the legislature in the form of an Assembly whose jurisdiction was unlimited, how was one to cater for democratic dissent and pluralism? It was surely no accident that Article 1, title 2, of the revolutionary Constitution of 1791 declared that the phrase 'Kingdom one and indivisible' be simply replaced by the formula 'French Republic one and indivisible'.

The three great principles intended to characterize the republican order were (1) the separation of powers, especially the legislative and the executive; (2) respect for law based on a constitution; and (3) the exercise of national sovereignty through elected representatives.[26] Each of these was betrayed by the Terror, when the Republic patently failed to respect the rule of law and constitutional principles. Republicanism degenerated into insular nationalism when the Montagnard republic mobilized a mass defence of the French fatherland. This patriotism – linked to Robespierre's appeal to ancient 'public virtue' as the 'unique foundation of civil society' – led to a moralistic scapegoating of the 'enemies of the people'. Once again, the French Republic was to witness a ruinously absolutist invocation of the 'people' as a unified general will – dissent being branded as betrayal or crime. As Pierre Nora notes: 'Even in the twentieth century, with the Popular Front, the Resistance, the National Front, and the Common Program, the idea of the "people" has remained the heart and soul of republican ideology. The Republic needs enemies in order to define itself and steel itself for combat, and it has always lived off its adversaries. The storming of the Bastille remains one of its central symbols not only because it commemorates an inaugural act but because it is the key theme in a recurrent program'.[27] In fact, the extension of this equation between French republicanism and military violence against the enemies of the nation eventually led to Bonaparte, 'at first the hero of the Republic but ultimately its executioner'.[28]

IRISH REPUBLICANISM

What Irish republicanism took from its French prototype – in theory at least – was less its imperial nationalism, than its universalist principle of liberty. There can be little doubt that the event which most directly influenced the original ideology of the United Irishmen was the French Revolution (see Chapter 2). Through the energetic mediations of Tone, the French Directory agreed to four revolutionary expeditions to Ireland – in 1796 and 1798, respectively. And the fact that all resulted in failure probably accounts for the delay in establishing an independent Irish Republic for almost one and a half centuries.

Ireland in the 1790s was, as we saw above, ripe for republican revolution, particularly with the growth of the United Irish Society issuing in the 1798 revolution. As one English spokesman remarked at the time: 'If the Irish are in some respects a century behind us in point of civilisation, they are at least two centuries before us in their revolutionary principles: and if we are to be agitated hereafter by those doctrines which now shake Europe to her centre, we are as likely to have them imported from Ireland as from France'. Tone himself was partly responsible for the republicanization of the United Irishmen in the mid-1790s. He saw himself as a '*cosmopolite*', transcending sectarian divisions in support of the Enlightenment principle of religious and civil liberties. He saw the revolutionary situation in Ireland – fuelled by severe economic and political disability – as part of a broad 'Republican Alliance' on a European scale. Tone's preference was for a Republicanism of universal principles over one of Terror. But his Enlightenment appeal to the 'common name of Irishmen' was ultimately to slip into sectarian nationalism as the rebellion of 1798 failed and another kind of 'terror' took its toll. Yet, in spite of these setbacks, the Irish republican project for a more just and fraternal society, based on universal rights, never faded completely, and eventually saw itself at least partially realized in 1949. Clearly the Irish republican heritage is a complex one, requiring to be rethought in terms of its origins and ends. Just as it is necessary to discriminate between the French *République*'s postive legacy of rights and negative legacy of terror, contemporary Irish citizens also have an intellectual duty to ask what exactly 'republicanism' means today, and seek to distinguish between the enabling and disabling legacies of its evolution in Ireland from the 1790s to the 1990s.[29]

It may well be the case, at this historical juncture of Irish–British *rapprochement*, that what is required is a combination of the best aspects of the British–American and Irish–French democratic traditions, which would transcend both.[30]

4 Postnationalism and postmodernity

L'Europe des patries souveraines, laminées par une interdépendence économique et une harmonisation croissante des législations, est en train de s'effacer. La nation n'existe plus; l'Europe politique, n'existe pas encore; nous sommes dans le malaise de cet entre-deux.

(Pascal Bruckner, *La Mélancolie démocratique*, 1990)

BEYOND NATIONALISM

To critique the nation-state is not to repudiate all forms of nationalism. It is unwise, in particular, to ignore how certain forms of nationalism have served, historically, as legitimate ideologies of resistance and emancipation. In the last half-century, one could cite examples such as the nationalist opposition of local peoples to US involvement in Latin America or Soviet imperialism in Eastern Europe and Afghanistan. Not to mention the struggle of European nations themselves against Nazi occupation in the Second World War or the campaigns waged by African nations against supremacist colonial policies. One might also note here that the history of Irish nationalism was itself a relatively noble one – with the exception of the IRA campaign after the 1960s.

A consideration of such cases exposes, I believe, a need to discriminate between different kinds of nationalism – civic and ethnocentric, resistant and hegemonic, those that emancipate and those that incarcerate, those that affirm a community's genuine right to self-identification and those that degenerate into ideological closure, xenophobia and bigotry.[1]

Take the first of these distinctions: *civic* and *ethnocentric*. Civic nationalism conceives of the nation as including all of its citizens – regardless of blood, creed or colour. Ethnocentric nationalism believes, by contrast, that what holds a community together is not common rights of citizenship (or humanity) but common ethnicity (or race). The former derives largely from the modern legacy of the French and American Revolutions, while the latter finds its roots in the German romantic conviction (Fichte, Herder, Schlegel) that it is the native *Volk* that founds the state – an ideology which underlay the drive to unify Germany as a nation-state in 1871.[2] Fascism is one of the most extreme forms of ethnic nationalism, predicated as it is on the supremacy of one 'people' over all others. Nationalism of this kind is not pride in one's national identity or character (a perfectly legitimate sentiment). It is, as Isaiah Berlin remarks, 'the belief in the unique mission of a nation, as being intrinsically superior to the goals or attributes of whatever is outside it; so that if there is a conflict between my nation and other men, I am obliged to fight for my nation no matter what the cost to other men. . . . My gods are in conflict with those of others, my values with those of strangers, and there exists no higher authority – certainly no universal tribunal – by which the claims of the rival divinities can be adjudicated. That is why war must be the only solution'.[3] Ethnic nationalism repudiates the existence of universal laws above the nation or subnational identities (e.g. minorities) within it. The nation is conceived as a 'natural' given, with a pre-existing fixed essence and a divine right to realize itself – organically and ineluctably – as a nation-state. This ignores the fact that 'national identities' are also historical constructs or 'imagined communities' in Benedict Anderson's apt formula. And to acknowledge this last fact, as civic nationalism does, is to realize that nationality may actually be strengthened by its decoupling from ethnicity and permitted to find more appropriate forms of expression than a centralist nation-state.[4]

In endeavouring to go beyond negative nationalism one must be wary, therefore, not to succumb to the opposite extreme of anti-nationalism. Those who identify all forms of nationalism with irredentist fanaticism habitually do so in the name of some neutral standpoint that masks their own ideological bias. To roundly condemn Irish nationalism, for instance, refusing to distinguish between its constitutional and non-constitutional expressions and omitting reference to the historical injustices of British colonialism and unionism, amounts to a tacit *apologia* of the latter. It also fails to appreciate the fundamental role of nationalist ideology in the formation of the *British* nation-state at the end of the eighteenth century. (Nationalism is not the prerogative of the Irish.) Indeed, the critical strains in Britain's vexed relationship to European Union in the 1990s reveals how the very economic processes which helped form the nation-state are now undermining it. The growing discrepancy between economic growth and national sovereignty is exposing, as well as testing, the very basis of British nationalism.[5]

Republican nationalism played a legitimate part in the shaping of modern Ireland, just as monarchical nationalism did in the shaping of the United Kingdom. But it is now time to move beyond the competing nationalisms of these islands. Surely what is required as we approach the millennium is a transition from traditional nationalism to a post-nationalism which preserves what is valuable in the respective cultural memories of nationalism (Irish and British) while superseding them. Postnationalism is not Pol-Potism. It does not solicit a liquidation of the past but its reinterpretation or *Aufhebung*. As such, it recommends a series of discriminations: (a) between various forms of nationalism (civic, ethnic and so on, as mentioned above); (b) between nationalism and nationality (i.e. national identity as cultural memory, tradition, belonging); (c) between nation and state; and (d) between nation/state and other models of community (federal, international, regional, local, conciliar). It is this latter kind of discrimination, already touched on in our introduction, which Agnes Heller has in mind when she advocates a 'postmodern' version of cosmopolitan identity in opposition to modern versions of narrow nationalism. Speaking of Europe, she writes, 'one feels that this tiny Continent now has both the need and the opportunity for becoming more cosmopolitan. . . . The nationalism of race harbours the single greatest danger for our world, and also for Europe. One can only hope that Europe will fall victim no more to such a temptation. The external limits of Europe as a cosmo-polis can once again be transformed into internal limits. This time, the internal *limes* can assume the form of practical humanism as the spontaneous and active toleration of otherness. . . . After the great century of nations, of national literature, national music, national painting and national philosophy, the postmodern art and taste gives the finishing touch to the accomplishment of high modernism: it leaps over national borders . . . '.[6]

But the federal-cosmopolitan Europe, envisaged by people like Heller, Arendt and Berlin, is not to be confused with a move to a 'European national state', analogous to the United States of America, for that would be merely to replace one model of nation-state with a super-nation-state still dominated by nationalist ideology. 'European-ism' and 'Americanism' are nationalisms amplified to the upper case of geo-political power; they still operate according to the old absolutist principles of inclusion and exclusion. By contrast, the cosmopolitan Europe promoted by Heller is one based on a common right to 'fellow-citizenship', and a corresponding right to one or more identities of nationality and regionality. In this scenario, one may be Irish and British (in Ulster), Spanish and British (in Gibraltar), Spanish and

Catalan (in Catalonia), Basque and French (in *Le Pays Basque*), Arab and French (in Marseilles), Flemish and Belgian (in Northern Belgium), Swiss and Italian (in Tyrol) – while being *European* in all.

Beyond the 'modern' alternatives of national independence and multinational dependence lies another possibility – a postnational model of interdependence. But what might this third model actually look like? Here I return to the suggestion, discussed in our previous chapters, of a new federalism counterbalanced by a new regionalism. 'The question of identity', writes Erhard Eppler, a leader of Germany's SDP, 'no longer necessarily connects to nation-states. . . . And it may even be that the European nation-states are being overcome from both sides at once: by the European Community, and from below, by regional cultures'.[7] Several EU countries have already made significant moves towards greater regional democracy (notably Italy, Denmark, Spain and Germany). And it is not insignificant that former EU President, Jacques Delors, explicitly endorsed a European triad of region–nation–federation as preferred model for an integrated Europe of Regions.[8] Moreover, the formative EC Reports on Regional Policy by Martin (1986) and Hume (1987), together with art. 23 of the SEA (1988) and the proposed Committee of Regions in the Maastricht Treaty (1993), confirm the need to provide for a Europe of equal regions. The proposals are still largely unrealized – due to resistance by respective nation-states – but are no less urgent for that. The European project is still a wager, not a *fait accompli.*

Let us take Germany, one of the EU's most influential member states, as a test case here. Germany has, to date, been enthusiastic about the ideal of a federal Europe, in large part, one supposes, because of its successful experience of federal government within its frontiers since the Second World War. Germany has led the push away from central administration toward increased regional and local goverment (since unification the Federal Republic includes 16 *Länder*). The case of Germany is also telling in that it has suffered – and made others suffer – more than any other country from excesses of national sovereignty. Two World Wars this century and over fifty million dead speaks for itself. This point is made forcefully by the poet Hans-Magnus Enzensberger in his book *Europe, Europe* (1989). Nation-state sovereignty, he reminds us, is an invention of recent centuries. In the case of Germany, it lasted less than a hundred years – 'and what did it do for the Germans between Bismarck and Hitler? One crash landing after another'. Enzensberger observes that the history of almost every European nation is a 'millennium of patchwork'. Diversity, not homogeneity, is the best recipe for a new Europe. 'Particularism is the true home of all

Germans', he concludes, 'and that's not just true of Germany, it's really a European phenomenon . . .'.[9] Another influential German intellectual to endorse the decentralizing of power in a federal Europe is Peter Glotz. He promotes the thesis that 'at the end of the twentieth century the nation-state is economically, ecologically, militarily and culturally out of date.' And he argues, accordingly, for a two-pronged movement 'down to regional autonomy and up to trans-national structures'. For democracy to succeed in the new postmodern scenario, what is required is 'a pan-European federation – with maximal guarantees for ethnic groups and minority rights'.[10]

Such a pan-European Federation of regions is becoming less and less utopian. Even in the two most centralized states of the EU – Britain and Ireland – pioneering voices have made themselves heard. Foremost among these is Neal Ascherson who foresees a larger Community, including the EFTA countries plus much of the former Eastern Europe. The marginal nation-states would still be represented, but most of their existing powers would be exercised either from Brussels or through a diversity of smaller units, coordinated through a Council of Regions. As far as the British archipelago was concerned, suggests Ascherson, these units might be England (or possibly several English regions), Scotland, Wales, Ulster and either the Republic of Ireland as a whole or its provinces acting as autonomous regions. 'The cultural and economic links between Ulster, Southern Ireland and England would remain strong, but they would no longer carry connotations of *sovereignty*'.[11] What Ascherson has to say here is in line with much of the 'new regionalist' thinking in the Irish/British context;[12] it also supports my critique of nation-state sovereignty in Chapter 1 – a subject which I propose to explore further in what follows.

TOWARDS A POLITICAL THEORY OF THE POSTMODERN

It has been suggested by Heller and others that postmodern theory can have radical implications for politics.[13] One frequently encounters the claim, for instance, that the postmodern critiques of the centre – as logos, arché, origin, presence, identity, unity or sovereignty – challenges the categories of established power. The most often cited examples here relate to the critique of totalitarianism, colonialism and nationalism. The postmodern theory of power puts the 'modern' concept of the nation-state into question. It points towards a decentralizing and disseminating of sovereignty which, in the European context at least, signals the possibility of new configurations of federal–regional government.

A formative contribution to the postmodern critique of centralized power has come from Derrida's reading of Western 'logocentrism'. After deconstruction, we are told, the centre cannot hold. The accredited notion of a single origin or end is replaced – or displaced – by a play of multiple meaning. 'It was necessary', says Derrida, 'to begin to think that there was no centre, that the centre could not be thought in the form of a being-present, that the centre had no natural locus, that it was not a fixed locus but a function, a sort of non-locus in which an infinite number of sign-substitutions came into play. This moment was that in which . . . the original or transcendental signified, is never absolutely present outside a system of differences'.[14] The translation of this deconstructive moment into political terms has subversive consequences for inherited ideologies. Totalizing notions of identity (imperial, colonial, national) are submitted to scrutiny, the theory goes, in the name of an irreducible play of differences.

Several of these consequences are explored by Michel Foucault in *Governmentality* (1978) and by Jean-François Lyotard in *The Postmodern Condition* (1979). Foucault argues that the modern 'problematic of government' first emerges in the sixteenth century with the phenomenon of 'state centralization' – or what he calls the establishment of the 'great territorial, administrative and colonial states'.[15] Machiavelli's *The Prince* was to play a pivotal role in these deliberations, nowhere more so than in nineteenth-century Europe where the Napoleonic heritage of the French Revolution, and the German and Italian claims for territorial unity, were confronting the question of how and under what conditions a ruler's sovereignty over the state could be maintained. Gradually we find the transcendent singularity of Machiavelli's Prince being replaced by an immanent 'economy' of state power. With this introduction of economy into political practice, sovereignty is no longer merely defined in terms of power exercised on a territory and its subjects but of power exercised on all relations between 'men and things'. A new and more pervasive paternalism replaces the old paternity of the feudal kingdom. The task of government now becomes a question of how to introduce the father's economic management of the family into the management of the state. 'To govern a state will therefore mean to apply economy, to set up an economy at the level of the entire state, which means exercising towards its inhabitants, and the wealth and behaviour of each and all, a form of surveillance and control as attentive as that of the head of a family over his household and his goods'.[16] Over time, this economic model of family management is replaced, in turn, by the political-economic model of population management.

One of the consequences of this paradigm shift is that the old goal of sovereignty – which was the exercise of sovereignty itself – now takes the modern form of a 'state rationality' governed by four sciences: (i) *statistics* (the science of the state directed upon the administration of the 'population'); (ii) the *Cameralist science of police* (which ensured law served the state rather than the contrary); (iii) *Mercantilism* (the first rationalization of the exercise of power as a practice of government – wealth accumulation); and (iv) *political economy* (the intervention of government in the relations between population, territory and wealth). With the birth of the so-called 'governmental state', sovereignty becomes inseparable from practices of centralization and discipline. In reality, concludes Foucault, 'one has a triangle , sovereignty–discipline–government, which has as its primary target the population and as its essential mechanism the apparatuses of security'.[17] Against this triangular state, Foucault suggests we experiment with 'local struggles' aimed at de-governmentalizing the practice of politics.

For his part, Lyotard defines the postmodern turn as a dismantling of Grand Narratives – which seek to totalize meaning around a single foundation – in favour of 'little narratives' (*petits récits*). The ultimate reference of postmodern narrative is not some totalizing centre of meaning – Party, King, Nation-State – but other narratives. In other words, postmodern narratives are multiple, diverse, non-subsumable into some final solution. As Lyotard says: 'Let us wage war on totality. Let us activate the differences . . .'.[18]

On this reading, the postmodern critique of power implies the replacement of absolute sovereignty – theocracy, monarchy, bureaucracy – with 'republican principles' of freedom.[19] 'As the common inheritance is more and more measured in terms of the law of freedom, the uncertainty about previously held beliefs increases, and the social network becomes more fragile, insubstantial', writes Lyotard. 'In the political field, a sign of [this] can be found in the extension in people's mind of Republican principles'.[20] To the extent that we can speak here of a political or ethical community, it is one which 'always remains *in statu nascendi* or *moriendi*, always keeping open the issue of whether or not it actually exists'.[21] It is, in short, a community where identity is part of a permanent process of narrative retelling, where each citizen is in a 'state of dependency on others'.[22] In such a postmodern republic, the principle of interdependency is seen as a virtue rather than a vice; it serves, in fact, as reminder that every citizen's story is related to every other's.

Postmodern politics favours the dissenting stories of the detainee in opposition to the Official Story of the Commissar – the latter masquerading as a meta-narrative which merely conceals its narrative status.

The postmodern turn seeks to deconstruct the Official Story (which presents itself as Official History) into the open plurality of stories that make it up. Modern imperialism and modern nationalism are two sides of the Official Story. Genuine internationalism (working at a global level) and critical regionalism (working at a local level) represent the two sides of a postmodern alternative.

But, before examining some of the practical implications of these positions, there are two further contributors to the debate who merit specific acknowledgment: Kenneth Frampton and Charles Jencks, both, as it happens, theorists of architecture, the discipline which first launched the term postmodernism in the 1970s and 1980s. In a seminal essay in *Postmodern Culture* (1985), Frampton advances a model of 'critical regionalism' as the most appropriate response to our contemporary predicament. He defines it as 'an attempt to mediate the impact of universal civilization with elements derived from the peculiarities of a particular place'.[23] Whereas modernism, in architecture at least, tended to represent the 'victory of universal culture over locally inflected culture',[24] the postmodern paradigm of critical regionalism opposes 'the cultural domination of hegemonic power'[25] – a domination which seeks to sacrifice local concerns to abstract ones. Advocating a postmodern resistance to the modernist avant-garde, Frampton argues that 'architecture can only be sustained today as a critical practice if it assumes an *arrière-garde* position, that is to say, one which distances itself equally from the Enlightenment myth of progress and from a reactionary, unrealistic impulse to return to the architectonic forms of the preindustrial past. A critical *arrière-garde* has to remove itself from both the optimization of advanced technology and the ever-present tendency to regress into nostalgic historicism or the glibly decorative. It is my contention that only an *arrière-garde* has the capacity to cultivate a resistant . . . culture while at the same time having discreet recourse to universal technique'.[26] Such a programme, Frampton believes, offers the best prospect of a postmodern regionalism of emancipation.

Charles Jencks adds a further inflection to this position when he advances a poetics of 'radical eclecticism' in *The Language of Postmodern Architecture*.[27] All tendencies toward cultural uniformity are to be resisted. As applied to architecture, this entails the liberty to mix together stylistic 'quotations' drawn from a variety of periods and styles (Egyptian, Graeco-Roman, Celtic, medieval, Renaissance, Baroque, late-modernist, high-tech, functionalist). As applied to literature, it might be said to correspond to Roland Barthes's notion of 'multiple writing' where the cultural text is recognized as a pluridimensional space of open reinvention. One of the goals of 'radical eclecticism', Jencks reminds us, is to rid us of the illusion of englobing ideologies which erode cultural differences. But it is important to distinguish this radical eclecticism from the 'weak' or 'conservative' kind which tolerates multiplicity by default, by simply discarding commitment or purpose, by succumbing uncritically to the dispersive trends of consumer society. The challenge is to turn 'weak eclectism' into 'radical eclecticism' – to transform the existing jumble of cultural fragments into carnivalesque collage.

Taking the example of *Finnegans Wake* – a prototypical postmodern text – we witness a blending of indigenous myth with a 'polygutteral' assortment of foreign narratives (Judaic, Greek, Babylonian, Chinese). Joyce portrays culture as a 'circumbendibus' of multiple aspects, a transmigration of perspectives which – like the Vico Road – goes round and round to end where terms begin. To be true to ourselves, as Joyce put it, is to be 'othered': to exit from our own time frame in order to return to it, enlarged and enriched by the detour. This signals a new attitude not only to culture but to history. The very notion of evolving historical periods (tradition, modernity, etc.) following each other in causal order is put into question. Rather than construing history as a continuity leading inexorably back to a lost paradise or forward to a guaranteed future, postmodernism views it as collage. It resists the belief in history as inevitable progress or regress, recommending instead that we draw from old and new in 'recreative', non-dogmatic ways. The 'post' in postmodern refers then not just to what comes *after* modernity. It signals rather another way of seeing things, which transmutes linear history into a multiplicity of time-spans. Thus the modern idea of a millenarian state in which cultural and political differences might be subsumed into consensus, is challenged by the postmodern preference for *dissensus* - diversity without synthesis.

When Lyotard, finally, opposes 'dissensus' to totalizing models of identity, he is careful to distinguish it from mere relativism (or lazy pluralism). There is, he concludes, a significant distinction between a relativist refusal to judge, on the one hand, and a postmodern hermeneutic of indeterminate judgment, on the other. The latter crucially involves the recognition that there exist certain *differends* (conflicts of incompatible but equally valid interests) which cannot be resolved. This does not mean that *any* judgment is as good as any other. It means, rather, that history will never end because we will never be done with doing justice. 'The just judgment leaves the question of what justice might be open to discussion: it does not allow justice to become a determinate concept. The multiplicity of justices evoked by the heterogeneity of language games is thus not a mere relativism, since it is regulated by a justice of multiplicity. This judgment is not an undifferentiated pluralism, rather it is based in the most rigorous respect for difference'.[28] In short, a postmodern hermeneutic would be one guided not by sceptical solipsism but by an idea of justice always to be determined. Not 'any kind' of justice, therefore, but the right kind of justice – one which necessitates that we keep open the discussion about the nature of justice.

DEMOCRACY – REPRESENTATIVE AND PARTICIPATORY

How does all this relate to the critique of nationalism? Apart from the obvious challenge to exclusivist notions of race, centralized notions of power and absolute notions of sovereignty, postmodern theory also provides us with a useful insight into the contemporary crisis of 'representative' government. Representative democracies are those where the people supposedly empower certain elected individuals to represent them in parliament, to act in their name and on their behalf. When we hear talk of the loss of confidence in a governing power, as we do more and more, this signifies that the people are withdrawing their consent from their representatives. (Less than half of US citizens vote in Presidential elections; less than 40 per cent of the British electorate voted in the May 1995 local elections.) The nation-state is falling into crisis. Realizing this, and fearful that the people will also realize it, those in power often begin to react as sovereign rulers or monarchs. They substitute communications propaganda for the assent of the people (*demos*). They try to fill the 'credibility gap' no longer by police or military force – as in former times – but by media seduction or simulation.

Another more predictable strategy for resolving the crisis of consent is scapegoating: one fabricates an inner sense of national solidarity by focusing on a common external enemy. Hence the use of the Falklands factor in Thatcherite Britain; the reds-under-the-beds syndrome in McCarthyite America; the witch-hunt of 'foreign-backed' counter-revolutionaries in communist China. But scapegoating does not work in the long run – for the scapegoaters know, though they seek to hide it from themselves, that those scapegoated are not really what they are denounced as being. As Sartre points out in *Portrait of an Anti-Semite*, liars can fool others but not themselves. A sense of national unity predicated upon the projection of inner hostilities onto some outer adversary is ultimately condemned to fail. The ploy of demonizing others returns to plague the inventor.

Rather than face the consequences of inner disunity and diversity, nation-states will sometimes push the scapegoating stratagem to the point of war. The irresolvable conflict now becomes one *between* nation-states rather than *within* them. As Hannah Arendt observes in *Crises of the Republic*: 'So long as *national independence*, namely freedom from foreign rule, and the *sovereignty of the state*, namely the claim to unchecked and unlimited power in foreign affairs are *equated* . . . not even a theoretical solution of the problem of war is conceivable, and a guaranteed peace on earth is as utopian as the squaring of the circle'.[29]

Since Arendt believes that war is no longer acceptable as a last resort for the resolution of conflicts between sovereign states, she opts for a federal alternative where power would operate horizontally rather than vertically, the federated units – regional governments, councils or cantons – mutually checking and controlling each other's powers. But a genuinely transnational federation of this kind must be distinguished from a supernational administration which lends itself to monopolization by the strongest nation or by a single global security state. An equitable and just internationalism is one which draws its authority from below (not above), from the participatory democracy of local councils.

The most practicable alternative to the state or superstate system of centralized authority is, by this argument, a federated council of councils. (See, for example, our 1995 Proposal, in Chapter 5, to the Forum for Peace and Reconciliation in Dublin Castle.) Every time it has emerged in history, the council model has been destroyed by party or state bureaucracy. This is true of the French Revolution, the American Revolution (as pioneered by Jefferson's original vision of a federation of 'elementary republics'), the Paris Commune, the original Russian soviets of 1905 and 1917, the German and Austrian revolutions at the end of the First World War, and the Hungarian councils of 1956. In each of these, the council system emerged spontaneously as a direct response to the requirements of democratic political action. It grew from the actual experience of local participatory democracy. A council network of this kind, to which the principles of absolute sovereignty and nationalist hegemony would be alien, is arguably best suited to the possibility of an international federation.[30]

William Dewey recognized as much and in response to the traumas of the Second World War, which he experienced at first hand, he spoke of a 'Great Community' consisting of a confederation of local communities. 'Unless local communal life can be restored', he argued, 'the public cannot adequately resolve its most urgent problem: to find and identify itself'. And, in parallel fashion, such local forms of self-identification and participation need to avoid isolationism by establishing networks of mutual association and coordination with other local councils in the wider community. This would ensure the direct participation of each citizen in the public affairs of society. The council model thus represents, for Arendt as for Dewey, nothing less than 'a direct regeneration of democracy', valorizing 'the average citizen's capacity to act and to form his own opinion'. In contrast to the regime of unitary national sovereignty, the council system acknowledges multiple layers of political membership, from the local to the confederal. It fosters a pluralism of identities – and cultural specificities – in defiance of the them-and-us polarity of ideological nationalism. And, finally, it demonstrates that 'centralized nation-states are not hospitable agencies of . . . democratic political empowerment, and that any challenge to the principle of nation-state sovereignty must envision a new world order'.[31]

Such a confederation of councils represents a robust challenge to the modern equation of political authority with the sovereignty of unitary states, proposing as it does to bi-locate authority in both a universalism of rights (at odds with the national exclusivism of territorially based sovereignty) and a particularism of responsibilities. This renunciation of sovereignty in favour of federated political communities requires the renunciation 'not of one's own tradition and national past, but of the binding authority which tradition and past have always claimed'.[32] In short, it calls not for the surrender of our particular attachments but a preparedness to incorporate into them the standpoints of the particular attachments of others. Such a process of reciprocal incorporation entails the idea of a universality-in-diversity operating within a framework of 'mutual agreements'.[33] It calls, in short, for a reconciliation between Kant's cosmopolitan vision and Burke's fidelity to locally rooted relations.[34]

CONCLUSION

The fact that such a process *has* not yet been realized does not mean that it *will* never be. Indeed, our own proposals for a federal Europe of regions, outlined in Chapter 5 below, are largely motivated by a conviction that the time is ripe to explore such a council-of-councils in response to the British–Irish sovereignty crisis.

Without such a dissemination of sovereignty *beyond* the frontiers of the nation-state and *within* it, Ireland will continue to find itself at odds with neighbouring Britain and at sea in an EU market where existing economies of scale benefit the larger complexes over peripheral regions.

More than any other region in Europe, Northern Ireland needs to escape from the stranglehold of nation-state conflict. To do so means confronting a double crisis of *representation*. First, the crisis of representative democracy outlined above; and, second, the correlative crisis of imaginative representation. This last requires us to invent, or re-invent, new images of communal identity – replacing (for example) the Four-Green-Fields with the Fifth Province. Or, on the British side, replacing the triumphalist emblems of Empire (Britannia, Sceptre and Crown, King and Country) with alternative images of accommodation: Britain as 'archipelago', as 'North-West Islands' and so on.

It is not enough to be 'represented' by elected members of parliament. The crisis of representation, which afflicts the history of British–Irish sovereignty, is one with roots deep in the socio-political imaginary of these communities. Citizens identify with their community by internalizing the 'imaginary significations' which in each society organize the human and non-human worlds and give them meaning. Political institutions and constitutions are creations of the social imagination and cannot function, or retain legitimacy, without the latter (as manifest in languages, images, myths, memories, ideas). A community of whatever kind – nation, state or otherwise – can only exist as *instituted*: 'Its institutions are always its own creation, but usually, once created, they appear to the collectivity as given (by ancestors, gods, God, nature, reason, the laws of history, the workings of competition, etc.); they become fixed, rigid and worshipped'.[35] The answer to this reification of institutions is to remind ourselves that nations and states are of our own making and can be *remade* according to other images.

In this respect, a liberated postmodern community would be one which not only acknowledges that it has created its own laws, but is prepared to reconstitute itself 'so as to free its radical imaginary and enable itself to alter its institutions through a collective, self-reflexive and deliberate activity'.[36] The critiques of national myths conducted in the second part of this volume are attempts to reopen the 'radical imaginary' of Irish society.

5   Rethinking Ireland

A proposal for a joint sovereignty solution

Richard Kearney and Bernard Cullen (Submission to the New Ireland Forum, Dublin Castle, 8 December 1983)

The problem of Northern Ireland has proved to be so intractable because two groups of people with significantly conflicting senses of their own national and cultural identity inhabit the same territory. This has resulted in the perceived illegitimacy of the Northern Ireland state by a large minority of its inhabitants, which underlies the fundamental and continuing instability of that jurisdiction. Any serious proposal for lasting peace and stability in Northern Ireland must take account of these twin concepts of *identity* and *legitimacy*.

In Northern Ireland, there are two communities with quite distinct identities. Each of these communities has a set of traditional ideals, with an ultimate aspiration. On the one hand, there is a substantial minority of the population of Northern Ireland who identify themselves as Catholics. The great majority of these are Irish nationalists, since their ultimate aspiration is for a united Ireland, in some form or other, separate and independent.

It is important to emphasize that there is a wide spectrum of commitment to this ideal: from those who don't really care too much, but who think it would be 'nice' to have a united Ireland for sentimental reasons (as long as it doesn't cost them anything); through those who are prepared to dedicate themselves to the peaceful pursuit of a united Ireland; to those few who are prepared to kill for it, both inflicting and undergoing much suffering.

More specifically, the degree and quality of support within the Catholic community for the IRA is continually shifting, often as a direct response to external factors (such as a decision of the government or a particular action of the security forces). Furthermore, votes for Sinn Féin must not be construed unthinkingly as support for the IRA. Although this is something which unionists, understandably, find difficult to accept, people do vote for Sinn Féin for a variety of reasons: and this point will be particularly important when we come to discuss the legitimacy of government institutions in Northern Ireland.

On the other hand, the majority of the inhabitants of Northern Ireland identify themselves as Protestants and as unionists. (The fact that many members of either community do not practise their religion is quite irrelevant to their self-identification in religious terms.) The ultimate aspiration of the unionists is for complete constitutional separation from the Republic of Ireland, which is perceived as alien and threatening; and dependence on Great Britain as the guarantor of that separation. Unionists are much more homogeneous than nationalists in their commitment to the union with Britain: so that the most moderate of unionists could recently describe the idea of a united Ireland as 'a destructive fantasy'.

The two Northern Irish communities, therefore, have opposing national and cultural identities, with deep roots in history, together with conflicting aspirations. We are convinced that any lasting solution to the problem of devising stable governmental institutions for Northern Ireland must give meaningful expression to both identities: Irish/Catholic and British/Protestant. Unfortunately, far too much of the discussion of a 'New Ireland' has been in terms of a united Irish republic separate from Britain, whether of a unitary, federal or canton structure.

We suggest that the Forum acknowledge the force of the unionists' refusal to countenance integration into what they perceive (rightly or wrongly) to be an essentially Roman Catholic state. The least that could be said is that such a republic would be considered illegitimate for the foreseeable future by a significant enough proportion of the unionists to render it every bit as unstable as the Northern state currently is.

On the other hand, any future arrangement in Northern Ireland must enshrine the deeply held Irish identity of the nationalists there, which is not the case at present. The long and powerful historical memories of the nationalist community – closely bound up with the persecution of Catholics in Ireland, and present even in those who would vehemently deny that they are 'anti-British' – make any arrangement which excludes the Republic from a say in the affairs of the North ultimately unworkable. They can too easily be tapped by those seeking to perpetuate the destabilization of Northern Ireland.

Political discourse in Ireland has, until now, been in terms of the hegemony of one community over the other; and proposed solutions to the problem of governing Northern Ireland have been couched in terms of the denial of its national identity to one or other of the communities. We hope we have shown that if the two communities are to live together in peace (and we rule out as unacceptable massive shifts of population), then significant concessions have to be made on both sides.

A key feature of our proposal is that it eschews all holier-than-thou claims that the 'primary responsibility' for the present impasse lies with one side or the other and that one side must change before the deadlock can be broken. The present violent impasse is the result of a dynamic of mutually reinforced hostility, fear and distrust which has a long and dialectical genesis. If the two communities must share responsibility for arriving at that impasse, then both communities must share responsibility for extricating themselves from it. Joint governance would involve an equal degree of generosity and an equal degree of concession on both sides. For any solution to be successful, the other side must not be seen to 'win'.

Northern Ireland, administered under joint sovereignty, would have a bi-national cultural identity. It would be equally legitimate to hold a British or an Irish passport. There would be two national anthems and two national flags, each set of national symbols having equal prominence in all official circumstances. The Irish language would be recognized as a perfectly legitimate cultural expression, and lack of proficiency in Irish would not handicap any citizen in employment. While Gaelic games could increasingly be seen as an enjoyable and healthful option in state schools (which are predominantly Protestant), the GAA would have to delete its rules banning members of the police or security forces.

The society would have to be legislatively pluralist, to the extent that the religious views of one particular denomination could not be enshrined in law, in matters as diverse as family or sexual ethics, or attitudes to Sabbath observance. This would not involve any dilution of the religious convictions of individuals or groups: but those convictions would not now be translated into legislation. The 'historical memories' of the two communities would not be impaired. Instead of being affirmed as weapons in the struggle for ideological/symbolical/cultural hegemony of one community over the other, they would become co-equals.

Once the principle of joint sovereignty is accepted, we believe that the details of the appropriate political, legal and economic institutions could be worked out in negotiations among all the interested parties – namely, the Irish and British communities within Northern Ireland and the Irish and British governments – and then enshrined in a treaty between the two states.

We mention here only some general guidelines. Northern Ireland would ideally have a devolved parliament and government, structured so as to guarantee the adequate representation of all interests. While we believe such a devolved administration should enjoy as much autonomy as possible within the new state, it could be subject to an intergovernmental commission, perhaps interministerial, perhaps interparliamentary. Northern Ireland could send elected representatives to Westminster and the Dail.

There would be areas, such as foreign affairs and defence policy, on which the two sovereign powers could be expected to have differing views. There are historical precedents for permitting Northern Ireland to opt out of such divisive issues (for example, the exemption from conscription and national service): and it would be reasonable to insist that the Republic's neutrality remain intact. (Perhaps Northern Ireland could be formally declared a demilitarized zone?) Resolution of such issues, however, would emerge from the comprehensive re-examination of the totality of relations within these islands which our proposal implies. Much closer cooperation between Ireland and Great Britain – which we would welcome – need not jeopardize the two states' independence in matters of foreign policy.

Although the new government could have considerable power over its own economic affairs, its income would have to be supplemented. We consider it entirely reasonable to expect the British and Irish governments to contribute on a proportional basis; and the frequently promised development aid from the EEC and the USA could also be called up at this point.

Trans-communal legal arrangements and law enforcement agencies could be so structured that they be acceptable to locally elected police committees (perhaps sub-committees of local councils) and to a joint police authority, with firmly entrenched impartial complaints procedures. The whole could be monitored and overseen by the European Court of Human Rights at Strasbourg (or a permanent sub-committee of that body), which would be the ultimate guarantee of fairness and justice in the administration of law. Alternatively, the European Convention on Human Rights (to which both governments are signatories) could be enshrined in Northern Ireland law.

Our proposals do not represent a panacea to end all paramilitary violence. We expect that some sort of militant republicanism will be with us for some time. There will always be some unionists prepared to kill at the prospect of the tricolour flying over Belfast City Hall. But this brings us back to our insistence on the importance of the concept of legitimacy. Paramilitary violence thrives on a widespread sense of *illegitimacy*. If we could develop a constitutional arrangement in Northern Ireland such that almost all the citizens would regard policemen and judges as 'ours' and not 'theirs', and such that all Catholics were not seen by most unionists as crypto-subversives, then the paramilitaries on both sides could be so marginalized as not to survive on anything like the same scale.

Will anyone buy it? We believe they will, provided certain necessary conditions are fulfilled. First, joint sovereignty must emphatically not be seen as transitional, but as a durable solution. Specifically, the Irishness of the nationalists must be unequivocally affirmed, while the Britishness of the unionists must be similarly guaranteed, for once and for all. The British will accept any arrangement that we Irish – nationalist Irish and unionist Irish – can live with.

We Irish must accept, each one of us, that none of us can get what we might ideally want. However, we believe the nationalists can be persuaded to accept an arrangement which enshrines throughout Ireland the legitimacy of their Irish nationality and cultural identity. The unionists can be persuaded to accept an arrangement which guarantees that their constitutional link with Britain (which they see as underwriting their cultural identity) will remain; but they will do so only if it is unequivocally declared by the Irish government that joint sovereignty is not a stepping-stone to a united Ireland.

The carrot for the unionists would be the prospect of the trans-communal acceptance of the legitimacy of the Northern Ireland state, which it has never enjoyed since its inception.

Finally, joint sovereignty must not be imposed. Once it is agreed upon by the two sovereign governments, it must be presented to the people of Northern Ireland and some means must be devised of providing evidence that it receives significant support in both communities. Ideally, it would be presented to the people of the North with the all-party support of Westminster and the Dail.

We are proposing joint sovereignty because we are convinced that it holds out the only hope of devising an arrangement in which sectarianism would lose its political stranglehold, and the less murderous left/right politics typical of other European states would be allowed to develop. It offers the best option, we believe, for reconciling the two distinct cultural and national identities which must be reconciled if Northern Ireland is to have lasting peace and stability, and a tolerable quality of life for all its citizens.

Northern Ireland's future as a European region

Richard Kearney and Robin Wilson (Submission to the Opsahl Commission, Belfast, 2 February 1993)

The European dimension

In his review of the literature on the Ulster 'troubles', *Interpreting Northern Ireland*, John Whyte charted the trajectory of intellectual debate in the 1970s and 1980s, demonstrating how there had been a convergence around an 'internal conflict' explanation of the conflict. Whyte wrote: 'Both the traditional nationalist and traditional unionist intepretations have lost their popularity ... [in favour of] ... the internal-conflict interpretation. According to this interpretation, the crucial conflict is between the communities in Northern Ireland. Though this conflict is influenced by the relations which Northern Ireland has with Britain on the one hand and the Republic on the other, those relations are not the heart of it. There would still be tensions between the two communities no matter what wider framework was adopted for the region'.[1] But Whyte argued that even though the internal-conflict interpretation had come to prevail intellectually, a new paradigm was necessary to address its weaknesses. One of these is the tendency to represent the poles of the conflict as two monolithic blocs, whereas Whyte argued that the local diversity of Northern Ireland could usefully be explored. The growth of local studies in the region is part of a growing emphasis on cultural diversity which, as we indicate below, is a paradigmatic shift we strongly endorse.

We believe, however, that the dramatic changes in Europe since Whyte's text was written signal a more all-encompassing shift – to re-focus Northern Ireland's internal conflict within the rapidly evolving European context. A crucial weakness of the internal-conflict interpretation is that it is vulnerable to the superficial reading that the conflict is unique – a hangover of seventeenth-century religious quarrels which the rest of Europe has long left behind.

The fall of the Berlin Wall has demolished that rather trite assessment.

Raymond Pearson captured the significance of the 1989 revolutions for Comparative Approaches to Community Relations: 'Northern Ireland has so often been represented in the past as a thankfully *sui generis*, untypical and even anachronistic phenomenon within western European society. 1989 may well change all that: a likely by-product of the transformation of eastern Europe will be a fundamental refocus in international, particularly European, perceptions of the "Ulster Question" over the 1990s. In future, the "troubles" of Northern Ireland will be perceived as less anomalous than has been conventionally represented. Though conceded indisputably unique characteristics, Northern Ireland will be viewed in a more comparative, possibly a more charitable light: as the most north-westerly manifestation of a continent-wide phenomenon of social and political community conflict mounting in intensity and range through the Greater Europe of the 1990s'.[2]

Which Europe?

It is important to stress initially that there are three different senses of 'Europe', as *The Financial Times*'s foreign editor, Edward Mortimer, makes clear in his paper 'European Security after the Cold War'.[3] First of all, there is 'Europe' in the simple sense of the institutions of the European Community. Like 1989 in the east, 1991 in the west marked a key moment. Despite the compromises entailed in the Maastricht Treaty and its subsequent travails, we agree with the European editor of *The Guardian*, John Palmer, that the logic of further moves from intergovernmentalism to supranationalism is unanswerable (which is not to say there will not be reverses and fluctuations of pace). We want to place the elaboration of new democratic structures for Northern Ireland institutionally within this context.

Secondly, there is 'Europe' as the continent. This is necessary not only to avoid the common elision between 'Europe' and the EC, but also because on a continent-wide basis, as indicated above, questions of nationalism, ethnicity and minority rights are raging everywhere. This perspective is essential to place the politics of conflict-resolution and human rights in Northern Ireland in their right comparative place.

Thirdly, there is 'Europe' in a much more general sense: Joseph Lee's sense of a way of ordering and administering society, or Mortimer's of a common cultural patrimony. If this is a vague idea, it acquires some sharpness, nevertheless, in the negative counterposition of the British (and hence, often, Irish) way of doing things to that which may prevail elsewhere. And it is our view that the modernization of Northern

Ireland may entail leapfrogging the two states which currently preside over it into the mainstream of European practice.

Our overall vision is of a federal 'Europe of regions' in which European integration and enlargement is marked by a progressive transfer of power down to regions from the 'nation-state' as much as by a transfer of power upwards through economic and monetary, and political union. This new European 'architecture' would be buttressed by a filling of the 'democratic deficit' at the heart of the EC and a new concept of European citizenship underpinned by human rights guarantees overseen by pan-European institutions.

We would stress, however, that a resolution of the conflict in Northern Ireland need not await such a full-scale construction. Indeed, the former could in some significant ways prefigure elements of the latter.

Everyone a minority

It is in the most intense, and intractable, conflicts in the 'new Europe' where the parallels with Northern Ireland are most evident. In both the former Yugoslavia and in Nagorno-Karabakh, as in Northern Ireland, it is the clash of competing nationalist groups which has caused the explosion of polarization and violence. It is the 'double minority' structure of all three conflicts that makes the clash so bitter. As Misha Glenny has written: 'The central conflict which destabilised Yugoslavia was between the desire to create or consolidate (in the case of Serbia) a state in which one national group was dominant; and the perceived or demonstrable vulnerability of minority populations in these projected states'.[4] It would be easier by far if in each of these situations, one side was clearly 'right', the other 'wrong'. But, just as it was reasonable for the Armenian majority in Nagorno-Karabakh to resist domination by the much larger Azeribaijan, so also it was reasonable for the Azeri minority in Nagorno-Karabakh to fear a hand-over to Armenian sovereignty. Similarly, it was, and remains, entirely reasonable for Northern Ireland Catholics to feel fearful for their fate under a unionist régime. And unionists, conscious of their minority position on the island, can reasonably fear that accommodation of Irish nationalism, given its ultimate goal, will be to their constitutional disadvantage.

Such double-minority problems throw into question the applicability of the Westminster convention of majority rule, on which unionists rely, and, indeed, the international convention of the right of nations to self-determination, rehearsed by nationalists. As to the former, it is striking that no emerging east European democracy has sought to emulate the

British first-past-the-post electoral system. As for the latter, as Nora Beloff has put it in the context of ex-Yugoslavia, what does 'self-determination' mean when there are many different 'selves'?

From nation-state to region

The metamorphosis of Europe raises fundamental questions about the very nature of sovereignty, about the meaning of words like 'nationalism' and 'unionism'. Each is premised on the 'winner take all' concept of sovereignty, residing in a centralized state, which dictates a zero-sum game over its seizure or abandonment.

These conventional notions of 'national sovereignty' in Ireland have historically entailed either colonial dependence or nationalist independence. The idea of European interdependence, combined with the application of the principle of subsidiarity, can, however, for Northern Ireland transcend both. The emerging Europe has a unique opportunity to be truly democratic by fostering notions of sovereignty that are inclusive rather than absolute, shared rather than insular, disseminated rather than closed in upon some bureaucratic centre. Northern Ireland could be a testing ground.

The multi-coloured map we gazed upon at school no longer tells the full story. Traditional borders have become too large and too small: too large to cater for the growing sense of regional differences in Europe, and too small to respond to the movement towards European integration. As Neal Ascherson has argued: 'European integration means that the nation-state is leaking power both upwards and downwards to the regional level. Within the new outer shell of the integrated community, the tough skin of the old nation-states will swiftly grow permeable and porous'.[5]

Ascherson's map of 'The New Europe' demonstrates this strikingly. Dividing up as it does European countries into constituent regions to which power has been devolved, the sheer geographical size of the Republic and England immediately stand out in their centralized power – only comparable, indeed, to the former dictatorships of the east. However artificial its foundation, Northern Ireland, by contrast, is approximately the size of the Italian autonomous regions (of which there are 22), or Wallonia and Flanders in Belgium, or the smaller German *Länder* (18) and French regions (22).[6]

The manifesto of the European Regionalist Network (ERN of which we are respectively representatives in Northern Ireland and the Republic) envisages for Europe 'a decentralised, federal structure which would bring substantial power closer to its peoples'. Within such a context, it says, while border changes might take place between the relatively equal, interdependent communities involved, these could only be achieved non-violently, preferably by negotiation. In turn, any of the constituent regions would have to respect the human rights of any minorities they contained.

This dual approach – respecting existing borders while addressing minority rights – reflects a wider, evolving practice on the part of pan-European institutions, notably the Conference on Security and Cooperation in Europe, faced as the CSCE has been since 1989 with many conflicts, especially in the east, where 'ethnic' and state boundaries do not coincide. It captures both aspects of the 'double-minority' dilemma by reducing tensions and grievances affecting both parties. The alternative – as is now all too clear – is, on the one hand, irredentist campaigning for borders to be moved to reincorporate the people caught on the 'wrong' side, and, on the other, 'ethnic cleansing' to expel them. The ERN manifesto says: 'We believe that this type of federation based around small nations and regions, by fostering allegiances both more universal and more particular than the traditional nation-states, would greatly help to resolve national and ethnic conflicts within and between existing European states – for example, in Northern Ireland, the Basque Country, Corsica, South Tyrol, Gibraltar and [ex-] Yugoslavia'.

We have seen the future

Some positive signposts can already be detected. As Hugh Miall argues in *New Conflicts in Europe: Prevention and Resolution*: 'On the whole the European integration process has had beneficial effects on regional conflicts. For example, tensions between Spain and Gibraltar have eased with the admission of Spain to the Community. Spain's own internal conflicts between the Castilian Spanish majority and the Basques and Catalans have improved considerably, partly in the context of democratic government, but also because the Basques and Catalans see a future for themselves as regions within the EC. It has been easier for the German minority in South Tyrol to accept its autonomy in Italy given the free flow of people and goods between states'.[7]

Ferdinand Willeit, deputy president of the German-speakers' Sudtiroler Volkspartei, spelt out his Euro-regionalist vision thus: 'Personally, I want a greater degree of autonomy within the current borders, just like a *Land* in Germany. I view Europe as a confederation of states within which each region, each of the *Länder*, will have a specific role'.[8]

Another instance which points to ways forward from conflict is the

Istrian peninsula (mainly in Croatia), which has so far been insulated from the ex-Yugoslav maelstrom, despite its combination of Croats, Slovenes and Italians. The Istrian Democratic League has prevailed over the nationalist Croatian Democratic Community party and the IDL leader hopes that 'Istria could be a laboratory for Europe, socio-politically'.

According to Mark Thompson, a writer on ex-Yugoslavia, 'What matters is that no community tries to claim ownership of the territory. A scholastic distinction? By no means. The basis of Istrian identity is cultural, not given by genealogy; artificial, if you like, but also pragmatic. It will always lack the gut appeal of the national identities which surround it. Conversely, it has a clearer democratic potential: an Istrian is simply someone who lives and works here'.[9] Asking himself what should be the characteristics of the new European regions, Ascherson replied: 'One is the cluster of a sense of home and place, a sense of common purpose and of common tradition – which may mean more than one tradition, in a community which is confident enough about itself to accept cultural pluralism as something less than a threat to identity. A second characteristic should be a sceptical but pragmatic sense of democracy, of a smaller and more manageable arena which requires less of a leap of imagination, or of an act of faith, to believe that one's collective identity is shared by others whom one will never meet . . . . Third, I would hope that such a region would show a degree of openness to the outside world which the nation-state found hard to afford. The region would require to understand itself less by exclusivity – by which "we define ourselves against the ways in which you are not like us". This sort of openness is also about a new way of seeing minorities – not as a threat, but as an enrichment'.

A European rights regime

In the year after the fall of the Wall, a CSCE meeting in Copenhagen on the 'human dimension' endorsed this concept of cultural diversity: 'The persons belonging to a national minority have the rights to fully and effectively exercise the rights of man and the fundamental freedoms without any kind of discrimination and with full equality before the law . . . . The persons belonging to national minorities have the rights to freely express, preserve and develop their own ethnic, cultural, linguistic and religious identity and to maintain and develop their own culture in all its aspects, protected from all attempts of assimilation against their will'.

Since such minorities may feel affinity with an external group – as applicable to many Northern Ireland Catholics as to Hungarians in Romania or Slovakia – the Copenhagen meeting itemized, among others, the right 'to establish and maintain free contacts between their own country as well as across borders with citizens of other States with which they have a common national or ethnic origin, a cultural network or religious convictions'. The 1991 CSCE expert meeting on national minorities not only emphasized for minorities the centrality of human rights, the rule of law and judicial independence, but also affirmed that: 'appropriate democratic participation of persons belonging to national minorities or their representatives in decision-making or consultative bodies constitutes an important element of effective participation in public affairs'.

These three affirmations, it should be noted, re-position the traditional questions of power-sharing, civil rights and an Irish dimension for Northern Ireland in the context of accepted European conventions, defusing without loss of principle the charged character they have acquired in purely domestic negotiations.

Civil and political liberties represent a key concern for Catholics in Northern Ireland. The British government has, as is well known, been brought before the European Commission and Court of Human Rights more than any other member of the Council of Europe, many arising from Northern Ireland cases. It has been a frustrating experience for the plaintiffs. In this context, an important breach was made in the principle of 'national sovereignty' at the Moscow CSCE conference on the 'human dimension' in 1991: 'Participating states emphasise that issues relating to human rights, fundamental freedoms, democracy and the rule of law are of international concern, as respect for these rights and freedoms constitutes one of the foundations of the international order. They categorically and irrevocably declare that the commitments undertaken in the field of the human dimension of the CSCE are matters of direct and legitimate concern to all participating states and do not belong exclusively to the internal affairs of the state concerned'.

At the 1992 follow-up meeting in Helsinki, the CSCE, against the backdrop of the Nagorno-Karabakh and ex-Yugoslav conflicts, agreed a Dutch proposal for a High Commissoner for Minorities, 'an outstanding international personality with considerable political experience' who would, in emerging conflicts, collect information from a range of sources, including from non-state parties. S/he could draw on expert assistance from other CSCE and Council of Europe sources. This proposal was agreed, despite Turkish, US and British objections. Miall reports: 'The strongest objection was from the UK, fearful that in a far advanced conflict such as Northern Ireland the introduction of an outsider might not be helpful'. It is of note in this context that in its 1992 policy statement, 'Towards a Lasting Peace in Ireland', Sinn Féin said: 'While we travel the road to peace, continued abuse[s] of human rights seem inevitably to continue. The Conference on Security and Cooperation in Europe is empowered to check abuses of human rights in any European country. Britain should not be allowed to hide behind the argument that human rights are the exclusive preserve of each government'.

A role for civil society

The CSCE recognized importantly in Helsinki that it should be more than an intergovernmental forum, involving civil society as well: 'The CSCE is a process whose activities go far beyond formal relations among governments to involve citizens and societies of the participating states . . . . Successful efforts to build a lasting and democratic order and to manage the process of change require more structure and substantive input from groups, individuals, states and organisations outside the CSCE process'. Miall concludes – and his comments are as applicable to Northern Ireland as to eastern Europe – 'One of the major sources of conflict in the new Europe is the disjuncture between peoples and states. States are seen to be the legitimate international actors, and the source of rule-making authority and power. Peoples, on the other hand, have no international standing, unless they have their own state. For those who do not, such as minorities, or peoples spread in compact or dispersed patterns across several states, obtaining recognition and equal rights can be difficult. There is an understandable wish to create new states, which existing states then resist. This problem is especially acute in eastern Europe, where ethnic heterogeneity is high and states are poorly aligned with peoples. If Europe is to retain as a key principle the maintenance of existing borders, until they are changed by agreement, it is essential to give peoples a bigger say in the international system. This applies both within states (where democracy and accountability are crucial aspects of conflict prevention) and in international organisations'.

The next logical step for the CSCE is to pursue the proposal by Antonio Papisca of the University of Padua Human Rights Centre. Papisca has called for 'a pan-European charter of human rights and the rights of peoples', which would include all human rights and address questions of self-determination and minority rights. There would also be 'pan-European machinery' for enforcement of these rights, with individuals, minorities and non-governmental organizations all able to appeal for redress. Papisca urges the CSCE to initiate this project, with involvement of institutions drawn from civil society, with a view to such a convention being ratified by the European Parliament and national parliaments elsewhere in Europe.

There is another reason why peoples, why civil society, must be involved in the resolution of conflict. Writing of another chronic conflict situation – Cyprus – in *Comparative Approaches to Community Relations*, Stephen Ryan identified the destructive processes perpetuating conflict, and perpetuated by it: militarization, physical separation of communities, psychological distancing and stereotyping, religiously inspired sanctification and demonization, entrapment of leaders (and followers) in confrontational positions, polarizing emotionalism and economic underdevelopment.

Ryan pointed out how in Cyprus – but the Northern Ireland resonances are clear – in over two decades of 'peace-keeping' UN forces had, by separating communities, made achieving a positive peace if anything harder. And, as for the UN's 'peace-making' efforts there, the destructive processes had not been directly addressed 'because this strategy is concerned with mediation efforts involving the leaders of the various communities'. The peace-building he advocated 'involves attempts both to change the negative attitudes that the parties to the conflict have of each other and to address problems in the socio-economic environment which feed destructive behaviour'. Ryan here itemized forgiveness and reconciliation, developing overarching common goals, economic development, confidence-building measures, education for mutual understanding and prejudice reduction as key 'peace-building' tasks. Within civil society in Northern Ireland the reconciliatory work of peace and ecumenical groups, the integrated schools and the EMU schools programme, 'prejudice reduction' workshops and 'anti-sectarian' training – assisted by the establishment in 1989 of the Community Relations Council – have made important progress in recent years.

From adversarialism to cooperation

But progress on common goals, economic development and confidence-building depends on elaborating the political, economic and human rights institutions we argue can only be advanced through repositioning Northern Ireland in the context of the new Europe.

The pragmatic sense of regional identity referred to by both Thompson and Ascherson has been reflected in cooperation between the normally adversarial parties in Northern Ireland on European concerns. Leading figures in the four main constitutional parties were instrumental in the establishment a few years ago of the Northern Ireland Centre in Europe, which acts as both a listening post and a regional voice for Northern Ireland in Brussels. And, despite the failure of the Brooke and Mayhew talks, here is one area of potential common ground. The following comments appeared in 1992 Westminster election material: 'We ... have always believed in a Europe of the regions. ... We in Northern Ireland must seek to play the fullest part in the growing regional dimension of European affairs. ... The concept of regionalism, especially in the European context, is gaining ground and we see in that further justification for a full return of democratic accountability to our people'.

Actually, this is from two manifestos – the first two sentences in that of the SDLP, the last that of the UUP (though this also contained more Eurosceptic comments). Moreover, the Alliance party is strongly identified with the European Liberal and Democratic Reform Group. And, while the DUP retains a strong Europhobia, it is an electorally declining force. Sinn Féin, meanwhile, is increasingly talking about a role for the EC, albeit undefined, in addressing the Northern Ireland conflict.

Partly, this emerging pragmatism is based on practical reality – indeed, already-existing practical experience. Following on from the comment by Cornelius O'Leary, that 'one of the great weaknesses of much learned discussion about the Northern Ireland problem is the absence of any reference to the European dimension', the political scientist Elizabeth Meehan has pointed out: 'In Northern Ireland, as elsewhere – for example, Strathclyde, Lombardy, the French provinces, the German *Länder* – there is extensive participation by public agencies, professional bodies and voluntary associations in trans-European networks that deal with culture, poverty, employment, training, urban and rural regeneration and sex equality'. And she went on to suggest that: 'a new kind of citizenship is emerging that is neither national nor cosmopolitan but which is multiple in enabling the various identities that we all possess to be expressed, and our rights and duties exercised, through an increasingly complex configuration of common institutions, states, national and transnational interest groups and voluntary associations, local or provincial authorities, regions and alliances of regions'.[10]

The economic imperative

That this tendency to involvement in inter-regional and sectoral networks will grow is driven by exigency, particularly in the context of the completion of the single market. The Northern Ireland Economic Council's report, *European Community Structural Funds in Northern*

Ireland, asserted: 'While relatively few industries in the Province are highly vulnerable to the removal of non-tariff barriers it is clearly the case that there are insufficient firms occupying high growth niches in the market to generate an above average economic performance by European standards. As a result, unless action is taken to restructure the local economy, there is a danger that Northern Ireland will be among those regions which lag even further behind the Community average in performance'.[11]

A dynamic public authority with a commitment to regional development – as against a direct-rule administration, implanted in the region, pursuing (failed) UK-wide policies – is a prerequisite of real economic progress. Kevin Morgan points out in *Innovating-by-Networking: New Models of Corporate and Regional Development*, a comparative study of regional innovation in Baden Württemberg (a successful German region) and Wales: 'Stimulated by the threats and opportunities of the new industrial order, and anxious to make the most of an integrated Community, Europe's regional authorities are becoming much more pro-active. They are trying to orchestrate their internal resources as never before. On the external front they are forging alliances with like-minded regions in other Community countries. In each case the aims are the same, namely, to spread the burden of innovation, to tap a wider "collective intelligence", in short to network themselves better at home and abroad'.[12]

It is widely accepted that – whatever its post-unification problems – Germany's exceptional post-war economic performance was linked to the decentralized constitution imposed upon it by the Allies. This gave the *Länder* important powers to secure regional economic development. The *TSB Business Outlook and Economic Review* has identified the economic potential of a wider European-wide decentralization for Northern Ireland: 'There can be no realistic prospect of a serious resolution of Northern Ireland's economic and social problems under the present administrative and economic policy regime, irrespective of whether the Conservative or Labour Parties hold the ring at Westminster. ... The issue of subsidiarity could ... be of immense significance to Northern Ireland. Subsidiarity effectively means the devolution of decision making down to the most efficient and effective level'.[13]

Popular participation

Northern Ireland, however, also lacks an appropriate European institutional culture in discussion of regional development. In part, this is because of the refusal of unionists to accept the pluralistic, coalition type of administration widely practised elswhere in European administration which could marshal all the resources and talents of civil society to a dynamic, developmental project. It is also because the market reliance of government during the Thatcher/Major 'miracle' years is in fact quite 'out of synch' with the way more modern administrations in more successful economies have involved the social partners in planning and regulating economic development. The latter is linked, moreover, to schemes for worker participation and social entitlements, such as those expressed in the European Social Charter from which the UK has opted out.

At the leading edge of this thinking is a further step, widening the concept of social partnership beyond employers and trade unions to involvement of the voluntary sector and community organizations. This has been a particular point of attention for the vice-president of the European Anti-Poverty Network, Quintin Oliver (director of the Northern Ireland Council for Voluntary Action), and the EC Poverty 3 Project in Craigavon. The latter's success hinges on drawing community organizations, government agencies and local political representatives into a fruitful multi-partner partnership of this type. There are plans for a conference this year which would explore the potential of this model of participatory decision-making to address the democratic deficit of the region as a whole.

The idea of a 'Europe of the regions' holds out the prospect, then, of a new, more modern Northern Ireland, in which pluralist, democratic and participatory institutions could acquire legitimacy, traditionally withheld by nationalists because of its association with the 'unionist aspiration', through pragmatic acceptance of its status as the Northern Irish region of the evolving Europe. Moreover, a European identity for Northern Ireland could help kickstart it out of its position, the product of so many decades of unionist conservatism, as a continental backwater into the mainstream of European debate. There would also be notable practical advantages, as indicated by the establishment of the Northern Ireland Centre in Europe, for a disadvantaged region like Northern Ireland in having a direct voice in European institutions, rather than being dependent on the UK permanent representation.

Breaching the border

Similarly, the process of European integration has the potential to make the 'nationalist aspiration' less unpalatable to unionists. For it becomes possible, in this context, to present closer relations between north and south as pragmatically desirable in a single-market Europe without frontiers, where people, goods and capital move freely across former barriers. Such a focus could help modernize nationalist politics on the island in the process, away from the traditional emphasis on border change and territorial unity towards a stress on the unity of peoples, of 'hearts and minds'.

Striking progress has indeed already been made in this regard. In spring 1990, the then Taoiseach, Charles Haughey, visiting Belfast in his capacity as president of the Council of Ministers during the republic's Euro-presidency, called for economic convergence between the two parts of Ireland within European union. This met a warm response, and only muted unionist protests. Later that year, the then presidential candidate, Mary Robinson, told an audience at Queen's University that the new Europe meant that closer cooperation across the border was simply common sense and required 'no ideological strings' to be attached.

She stressed throughout her campaign how she wanted to 'extend the hand of friendship' to the north. Since her election, a host of civil-society groups – community, women's and voluntary bodies – from the north have travelled to Aras an Uachtarain to meet President Robinson and their southern counterparts, forging people-to-people links and breaking down stereotyped enemy images. Ms Robinson, in turn, has reciprocated with highly successful, cross-community visits to Belfast and Derry.

Recently, from the opposite direction, the chair of the Ulster Bank, George Quigley, has excited considerable interest with his plan for the development of an island economy and a Belfast–Dublin economic 'corridor', through enhanced trade, joint marketing and the kind of collaboration on research and development, design, technology transfer and so on that the 'Four Motors' inter-regional project in central Europe espouses. And he has argued for a specific EC budget for allocation of enhanced structural funds to the island as a whole, to be distributed by the two governments. Dr Quigley argues that this should not be read through a political lens which assumes a nationalist agenda – indeed, he points out that to be effective it presumes new democratic institutions in Northern Ireland. Such an assembly, he points out, would thereby also acquire a direct say in the European institutions. The former Taoiseach Garret FitzGerald has advanced a similar argument.

The former president of the European Commission, Jacques Delors, was known to look very favourably on cross-border cooperation in Ireland, which he was anxious to support. Neal Ascherson's advocacy of 'porous' borders around crumbling nation-states is echoed by the Irish commentator and historian John Bowman, who has used it to describe his aspiration that the 'hard' border separating the two jurisdictions be progressively rendered a 'soft' one. It is the struggle between one nation-state, represented by the army, and an aspirant to another, represented by the IRA, which for the moment ensures that the border at Newry is the only Checkpoint Charlie remaining in the new Europe. It is fondly to be hoped that, like the traffic that informally bypasses it, history, too, will shortly pass it by.

Beyond centralist government

Much of the debate about the future of Northern Ireland over the last seven years has been a sterile argument over the merits/demerits of the Anglo-Irish Agreement. In reality, the most significant point about the agreement is that the indices of the conflict have been hugely unaffected by it. As Dennis Kennedy has pointed out, 582 died in Northern Ireland as a result of the 'troubles' in the seven preceding years, and 563 have died in the ensuing seven.[14]

Why so? What we would hope to have demonstrated is that the agreement, by prioritizing the relationship between the two governments, neither addressed the key feature of the conflict identified by the literature – the internal relationship between the 'two communities' – nor explored the crucial aspect of a new paradigm and of a new resolution: the European context. Indeed, we would argue that the British and Irish states are two of the least appropriate in Europe to guide a region like Northern Ireland to a consensual, peaceful future.

For us, the Committee of the Regions envisaged in the Maastricht Treaty is one aspect of the way forward for Northern Ireland. Yet the former European Parliament president Enrico Crespo Baron told one of us that the four countries most in favour of the committee were those which already had effective regional government (Spain, Germany, Belgium and Italy), while the two least eager were the UK and the Republic of Ireland.

The two states are, in fact, quite distinctive in the modern Europe – in particular in their high degree of centralization. Indeed the Free State was essentially copied from the structure of the British state. As the first president of the Free State, Douglas Hyde, put it: 'The English are the people we love to hate and never cease to imitate'. Both states have been, relatedly, among Europe's worst economic performers this century; both are relatively blind to European innovations in government and elsewhere, as Lee so excoriatingly demonstrated in relation to the

Republic in Ireland 1912–85.[15] Both states have difficulties in recognizing the principle of pluralism, whether politically (the UK) or socially (the Republic). Both have a very poor record on human rights issues, with neither as yet having bothered to incorporate the European Convention on Human Rights into domestic law.

In this context, the deliberations of the Scottish Constitutional Convention become of obvious relevance to Northern Ireland – indeed, in introducing its 1990 report, the convention's joint chairs, Harry Ewing and Sir David Steel, said they believed its proposals would 'in years to come serve as a model for other parts of the United Kingdom as centralised government comes more and more to be unacceptable'. But its purview was by no means confined to the UK, as was made clear in the report's distinction between establishing a new Scottish nation-state (as advocated by the SNP) and pursuing a more nuanced Euro-regional vision: 'The Scottish Parliament will look not only to Westminster, but also to Brussels and Strasbourg. An effective Scottish voice in the EEC [*sic*] is a pressing priority. This does not mean struggling to re-establish a nation state at the very time Europe is moving away from this narrow concept. The mood in Europe is very different with the German *Länder*, Spanish autonomous regions and the Italian provinces coming together to press common claims. . . . In this context the Convention recognises the rapid pace of change as the European Community moves towards closer economic and political union. Developments within other member states towards decentralised decision-making to regional and provincial Governments are seen as parallel moves to the Convention's own proposals. . . . The Scottish Parliament would, as an immediate priority, establish a representative office in Brussels to put clearly and directly Scottish interests'.

Conclusion

It is our view that a repositioning of Northern Ireland in a set of European contexts, guaranteeing democratic participation and minority rights, economic development and cultural diversity, offers a way out of the current impasse. Not one in which conflict ends, but one in which it is rendered non-violent, indeed becomes a healthy feature of a pluralist and democratic society.

A Europe of the regions is not to be confused with a *Europe des éthnies*. The federal framework we envisage, with recourse to pan-European courts of law and rights, could ensure that – unlike the unionist *ancien régime* whose reconstruction nationalists reasonably fear – each region fully respected the rights of minorities and resisted any tendency towards ethnic chauvinism.

Above all, we would centrally argue that this is the only way forward on the crunch issue of sovereignty over Northern Ireland. Speaking at the opening of the Northern Ireland Centre in Europe in Brussels in October 1991, Jacques Delors rightly appreciated the symbiosis between addressing the internal conflict and the European context. Mr Delors said then: 'Northern Ireland must look outwards as well as inwards. . . . The solutions must come primarily from within. I am, however, concerned that the European Community can, and should, be an ingredient in the overall process. It can, at least, help to ensure that the problems are not seen only in the context of a zero-sum game. Adding a wider dimension means that one person's gain is not necessarily another person's loss'.

The logic of our argument is that a new constitution is required for Northern Ireland to address its democratic deficit in a modernizing, egalitarian and participatory way. The aim would be to reconstitute it as a region exercising maximum subsidiarity within the UK and thereby able both to develop to the full the special relationship with the Republic and play its wider part in the new Europe.

This scheme would have to be legislated for at Westminster, with the agreement of the government of the Republic. But its impetus would come from within Northern Ireland, being the subject of widespread discussion and debate. Crucially, the legitimacy of the new arrangements would be internationally secured through endorsement by the Council of Ministers and/or the European Parliament, and by the Conference on Security and Cooperation in Europe and/or the Council of Europe, subject to regular review. The government of the Republic would, in particular, have a right to appeal against continued endorsement. If this were to be forfeited, Northern Ireland would revert to direct rule from Westminster, as qualified by the Anglo-Irish Agreement.

Key features of new democratic structures for Northern Ireland would be: (i) a popularly accessible assembly elected by proportional representation, with a high degree of autonomy enshrined in powers similar to those sought for Scotland by the Scottish Constitutional Convention, allowing strategic intervention in the economy and other policy arenas, with the ability to represent Northern Ireland directly to the institutions of the European Community, in particular the European Commission, and in effect 'opting in' to the European Social Charter; (ii) removal of all barriers occasioned by the border to the closest possible relationships in Ireland between north and south,

through people-to-people contacts, economic networking and cooperation across a range of policy areas – in particular, the 'island economy'
and allocation of enhanced EC structural funds – without prejudice to
UK inter-regional relationships but as part of a wider framework of
EC inter-regional cooperation, supported by the European
Commission and the new Committee of the Regions; (iii) in-built guarantees of pluralism in government, such as the requirement that an
executive sustain weighted-majority support in the assembly or through
a PR election of that executive from the assembly, with the requirement
regularly to report to, and with a right of appeal (including by the
Republic's government) to, the European Parliament; (iv) a commitment to embrace cultural diversity within the region, through an innovative and permissive cultural policy, including such areas as support
for the Irish language in the context of EC policy on lesser-spoken
languages, and across the island as a whole through coordinated support for cultural expression of the range of identities encapsulated in
the phrase 'varieties of Irishness'; (v) entrenchment of individual and
minority rights, through a bill of rights for Northern Ireland, such as
already drafted by the Committee on the Administration of Justice,
monitored by the Standing Advisory Commission on Human Rights
and the High Commissioner for Minorities of the Confederation on
Security and Cooperation in Europe, and with effective rights of inter-
cession conferred upon the Republic's government; (vi) extension of
democracy and participation through a constitutional requirement to
contract elected representatives, representatives of statutory authorities, employers' and trade union organizations, and the community and
voluntary sectors in multi-partner partnerships, with the assistance of
the European Commission; and (vii) recognition of sub-regional diversity through properly resourced local government, itself developing its
own relations with European and southern institutions and assuming
otherwise regional powers on an *à la carte* basis as appropriate, the
latter depending on demonstrated commitment to the constitutive principles of the region and subject to the same requirements of compliance
with the bill of rights.[16]

Towards a Council of Islands of Britain and Ireland

Richard Kearney and Robin Wilson (Proposal to the Forum for Peace and Reconciliation, Dublin Castle, January 1995)

In the wake of the paramilitary ceasefires (August and October 1994) and the considerable EU commitment to Ulster at the Essen Summit (December 1994), it is perhaps timely to reconsider some long-term 'European' options for helping to resolve the Northern Ireland conflict.

A model especially worth attention, at this point in time, is, we believe, a Council of Islands of Britain and Ireland (CIBI). This could issue from a patient and pioneering evolution of four existing bodies into a large-scale transinsular framework: (1) the Anglo-Irish Intergovernmental Council, (2) the British–Irish Intergovernmental Conference, (3) the Forum for Peace and Reconciliation, and (4) the development of all-party talks at Stormont (involving Sinn Féin and the ex-paramilitary loyalist parties). Such a coalescence of bodies would profit not only from the current momentum for a lasting peaceful solution (unprecedented in recent history) but also from the need for radical alternatives to the old models of nation-state government which have so dramatically failed to address the Ulster problem. The entry of Sinn Féin and the Progressive Unionist Party (and UDP) into discussions also calls for fresh thinking, as does the high-profile support for the peace process in the USA, and, more importantly, the European Union.

Indeed, Europe has a suggestive model to offer us in this regard. The entry of Sweden and Finland into the Community in 1995 may serve to focus our attention on the effective working of the Nordic Council. This council, comprising five nations and three autonomous regions, has been operating as a parliamentary and ministerial body since it was established in 1952 to resolve a number of territorial disputes in the Scandinavian peninsula. This former conflict-zone has, thanks to the close cooperative work of the Council, now been transformed into a highly successful network of transnational communities. Of particular relevance has been the establishment of Europe's first two 'demilitar-

ized' zones – the Spitsbergen Islands and the Aland Islands (once bitterly contested by Sweden and Finland). If something of an analogous
Council could be developed on these islands(Britain and Ireland),
might there not be a pressing case for declaring Northern Ireland
Europe's *third* such demilitarized zone? A neutral region in a new Irish–
British Council?

This might assuage one of the most vexed issues for loyalist and nationalist communities – security; and it might also encourage movement
beyond outworn ideologies of indivisible sovereignty. One of the roots
of the Ulster problem, as is widely acknowledged, is the irreconcilable
clash between two mutually exclusive claims for sovereignty over the
same territory.

It is now evident that absolutist sovereignty claims have no place in
negotiations on the North. And in this sense, a United Kingdom is as
unworkable in the long term as a United Ireland. Hence the timeliness
of the Framework Document debates on the revision of Articles 2 and
3 of the Irish Constitution and the amendment of the 1920
Government of Ireland Act.

Surely, the most logical, lasting solution is for both governments to
agree (1) to effectively cede or supersede their respective claims to unitary sovereignty, and (2) to work towards a Council embracing the
'totality of these islands' (the resonant phrase which initiated the process of Anglo-Irish *rapprochement*). Such a Council would require appropriate forms of decentralized regional government – where, arguably, the North might take its place on an equal footing alongside
Scotland, Wales, the Republic and England (itself regionalized into
North and South?). Each would function as a quasi-autonomous, albeit
interconnected, region under the overall aegis of the Council. At the
same time, each would retain and reaffirm its existing identity because
of increased levels of participatory democracy in local and regional
government.

What would be required, however, is a shifting of power from the
nation-state – *downwards* to more local goverment (subsidiarity) and
outwards to the transnational Council. Not a surrender of power, therefore, but a genuine sharing of power between mutually interdependent
regions.

While this may sound like a new political arrangment, it actually has
some precedents. As scholars like Daniel Binchy and Proinsias McCana
remind us, the Celts who originally inhabited these islands had no
notion of *politically centralized* sovereignty. (Ireland, for example, functioned in the form of five provinces – the famous *Pentarchy* which Eoin
McNeill argued was the 'oldest certain fact in the political history of

Ireland'. Another Celtic scholar, John Toland, went even further arguing that bardic/druidic Ireland was predicated upon principles of 'republican egalitarianism'!) The local kingdoms or *tuatha* were the basic
nexus of Irish society, and the concept of 'high-kingship' was a late and
largely spurious phenomenon according to Binchy. Political centralization was originally forced upon these islands, argue certain scholars, by
the need to respond to invasion from without – especially from the
Romans, Norsemen and Normans. The importance of these precedents
was not lost on James Connolly and his supporters, nor, more recently,
on certain strands of more progessive unionism.

But one doesn't have to invoke the 'Celtic model' to question the
inviolability of centralized political sovereignty. The phenomenon of
the centralized nation-state, founded on principles of absolute and
indivisible sovereignty, is a relatively modern concept – finding its
ideological proponents in thinkers like Bodin, Hobbes and Rousseau
(between the sixteenth and eighteenth centuries), and its most notorious political implementation at the hands of figures like Louis XI,
Napoleon and Bismarck. In the context of a new European
Community – simultaneously committed to greater integration and
greater regionalization – the model of the nation-state is fast becoming
redundant.

To recognize the implications of this for a settlement in Ulster will
require courage of all political leaders on these islands. But they may
take solace from the fact that there are numerous parallels already
operative in Europe. Not only is there the case of transnational cooperation within the Nordic Council cited above, but we find highly
successful regional networks at work within existing EC countries –
the 16 federated *Länder* in Germany, the 20 *regioni* of Italy, the 17
autonomias of Spain (largely resolving the separatist demands of
Basques and Catalans) and the two federated regions of Belgium.

As the European Community expands northwards and eastwards in
the coming years – with three countries joining in 1995 (Austria,
Sweden, Finland) and perhaps nine more before the turn of the century
(Poland, Romania, the Czech and Slovak Republics, Bulgaria, Estonia,
Latvia, Lithuania, not to mention Malta, Cyprus and Slovenia) – the
need for a decentralized federalist network will become even more
acute.

The prospect of over twenty nations governed by a single bureaucracy in Brussels by the turn of this century, with a population of up to
three hundred million citizens, is unfeasible. The infamous 'democratic
deficit' will have to be met.

The Nordic experience has also something to teach us here, in a curious sense. Denmark's 'no' to Maastricht and Norway's 'no' to membership are signal, if stern, reminders that the EU as it stands has simply not done enough to meet the legitimate demands of regional and local democracy. People want a more direct say in the governing of their own lives – and if it takes the doubting 'conscience' of our Nordic Hamlets to recall this, so be it. Europe needs such questioning voices to keep it asking itself how 'to be or not to be'. An EU of unanimous 'yes-men' would be undesirable in the extreme. Centralized rule from a single source of power is no longer tolerable or tenable.

The model of the Nordic Council could here provide a helpful clue not only for the British–Irish framework but, in time perhaps, for the Community at large. Thus we might find Europe eventually evolving into a network of regionalized Councils, e.g. Nordic, British–Irish, Iberian, Benelux, Mediterranean, Franco-Swiss, German, Middle-European, Baltic, etc. A sort of Federation of Federations – with each Federal Council based on practical principles of geographical, cultural and historical proximity. This would entail that the 'pooled sovereignty' principle, ratified by the SEA, be radically developed into a workable process of pluralist sovereignty (as debated in the North American context) or, quite simply, *post-sovereignty*.

The idea of a Council of British and Irish Islands requires a paradigm shift in our political imagination. And it requires patience. But while these things take time, we must not completely forget the words of that Scots regionalist *avant la lettre*, Lady Macbeth : 'If it were done, when 'tis done, then 'twere well it were done quickly!' Northern Ireland has already waited long enough.

Part II
Culture

6   The fifth province
Between the local and the global

When one speaks of the 'Irish community' today, one refers not merely to the inhabitants of a state, but to an international group of expatriates and a subnational network of regional communities. This triple-layered identity means that Irishness is no longer co-terminous with the geographical outlines of an island. The diaspora both within and beyond the frontiers of Ireland (over seventy million claim Irish descent) challenges the inherited definitions of state nationalism. But it does not condemn us to endless fragmentation. It is possible for Irish people today – indigenous or exiled – to imagine alternative models of identification. One such model, I submit, might be that of the ancient Fifth Province where attachments to the local and the global find reciprocal articulation. But what is this Fifth Province? In our editorial of the first issue of *The Crane Bag* (1977), we ventured the following interpretation:

> Modern Ireland is made up of four provinces. And yet, the Irish word for a province is *coiced* which means fifth. This fivefold division is as old as Ireland itself, yet there is disagreement about the identity of the fifth. Some claim that all the provinces met at the Stone of Divisions on the Hill of Uisneach, believed to be the mid-point of Ireland. Others say that the fifth province was meath (*mide*), the 'middle'. Both traditions divide Ireland into four quarters and a 'middle', though they disagree about the location of this middle or 'fifth' province. Although Tara was the political centre of Ireland, this fifth province acted as a second centre, which if non-political, was just as important, acting as a necessary balance. The present unhappy state of our country would seem to indicate a need for this second centre of gravity. The obvious impotence of the various political attempts to unite the four geographical provinces whould seem to warrant another kind of solution . . . one which would incorporate

the 'fifth' province. This province, this place, this centre, is not a political or geographical position, it is more like a disposition.[1]

This place, I submit, is not a fixed point or centralized power. It is not the source of some 'unitary and indivisible sovereignty'. If anything, it may be re-envisaged today as a network of relations extending from local communities at home to migrant communities abroad. The fifth province is to be found, if anywhere, at the swinging door which connects the 'parish' (in Kavanagh's sense) with the 'cosmos'. The answer to the old proverb – 'where is the middle of the world' – remains as true as ever: 'here and elsewhere'. We are speaking not of a power of political possession but of a power of mind. The fifth province can be imagined and reimagined; but it cannot be occupied. In the fifth province, it is always a question of thinking *otherwise*.

THE GLOBALIZATION OF IRISH CULTURE

A few words first about the global dimension. The internationalization of Irish identity is not only a matter of the extended Irish family abroad. It bears more generally on the self-understanding of the Irish as an island community. Being surrounded by water has always been viewed in one of two ways: as an insulating device against alien influences or as an open exchange with other peoples and places. The latter was traditionally celebrated in Irish maritime literature, which spoke of a perpetual coming and going between Ireland and the wider world. The ancient Irish voyage tales or *Immrama* – from *Mael Duin* to the *Navigatio Sancti Brendani* – record the migrations of Irish men of learning to the European Continent and the New World in search of the Isle of the Blessed (a pseudonym for the fifth province?). And Irish cultural history has witnessed successive waves of migration to foreign shores: e.g. Columbanus and Gallus to France, Switzerland and Italy in the seventh century; Eriugena, Marcellus and Sedulius Scotus to the courts of Carolingian Europe in the ninth; Catholic clergy and scholars to Irish Colleges in Paris, Salamanca, Prague, Cracow and Rome from the sixteenth century onwards; Toland, Berkeley, Burke, Cantillon, Tyndall and other thinkers to the European and/or American continents between the seventeenth and nineteenth centuries; and writers such as Joyce, Wilde, Beckett, McGreevy and Stephens to Continental cities in the twentieth century. Each successive wave was a confirmation of the Irish determination (outlined by Joyce in his Trieste lecture) to 'Hibernicise Europe and Europeanise Ireland!'.[2]

But what was true of Ireland's historical culture is even truer of its contemporary culture. The internationalization of Irish art is now a common phenomenon: the Chieftains, Van Morrison, Sinéad O'Connor, U2 in music; Jordan and Sheridan in cinema; Heaney, Muldoon, Banville in literature; Friel or Riverdance on stage. Each of these cultural forms has shown how the most indigenous of materials can be combined with an innovative cosmopolitanism. Neil Jordan is correct, I believe, when he states that the greatest danger for ideological nationalism is 'the pretence to be a self-enclosed and unconfused nation . . . to believe we could be at home in a single nation'.[3] Contemporary Irish identity is most at ease with itself, it appears, when the obsession with an exclusive identity is abandoned. Irish culture rediscovers its best self, not self-consciously, not self-regardingly, but in its encounter with other cultures – continental, British, American, etc. For as long as Irish people think of themselves as Celtic Crusoes on a sequestered island, they ignore not only their own diaspora but the basic cultural truth that cultural creation comes from hybridization not purity, contamination not immunity, polyphony not monologue. By reminding us of the many migrant minds which make up its heritage, Irish culture reveals that the island of Ireland is without frontiers, that the surrounding seas are waterways connecting it with 'foreigners', that the *navigatio* towards the other presents the best possibility of coming home to itself.[4]

The globalization of Irish culture is, needless to say, intrinsically bound up with the new communications technology. As Joyce correctly foresaw in *Finnegans Wake*, Shem the Penman (the traditional man of letters) is becoming increasingly inseparable from Shaun the Postman (the postmodern man of communications). With the European Space Agency's and other satellites now linking Ireland to information networks throughout the world, it is no longer feasible to think of Ireland as a land apart. And this expansion of cultural frontiers beyond the nation-state is paralleled by analogous amplifications of the economic and political spheres, as indicated by the passing of the Single European Act in 1988 integrating Ireland and Britain into a community of almost three hundred million citizens. The implications of this for a rethinking of the old chestnut of sovereignty are evident. As Roy Foster aptly observes in 'Varieties of Irishness' (1989), 'the very notion of indivisible sovereignty is now being questioned' and the 'concepts of dual allegiance and cultural diversity are surely associated'. In contrast to the unfortunate history of conflating cultural and political identities, Foster argues that 'cultural self-confidence can exist without being yoked to a determinist and ideologically redundant notion of unilaterally-declared nation-statehood'.[5] Following the accelerating movement beyond the exclusive identity of the nation-state, it is to be hoped that the inhabitants of Ireland will soon consider themselves citizens not only of states but of Europe and the world.

REGIONAL IDENTITY AND THE 'DEMOCRATIC DEFICIT'

The drift towards a more *global* understanding of identity calls for a countervailing move to retrieve a sense of *local* belonging. The new cosmopolitanism needs, I believe, to be complemented by a commitment to regionalism. Without the active exercise of 'participatory democracy' at local level, the 'representative democracy' of transnational government exposes a 'democratic' deficit – an untenable gap between power and people. In the Irish context, this would mean that the old centralized models of state (British and Irish) are merely replaced by an equally centralized Euro-state. A mere changing of the guards without any improvement of democracy.

But there are precedents for such participatory forms of social and cultural democracy in Irish history. In 'Notes on the Early Irish Concept of Unity', Proinsias MacCana reminds us that the Celts had no notion of centralized government. For the ancient Irish the basic unit of identity was the local region or *tuath*. 'In the primitive Irish view of things political cohesion and centralism were not in themselves necessarily a social good. . . . The underlying principle was one of coordination rather than consolidation. Overkings there were, and provincial kings, but the king *tout court* was the king of the petty or tribal kingdom, the *tuath,* and he and his kingdom constituted the central nexus, both ritual and political, in Irish society. One's *tuath* was one's *patrie*'.[6] Up to the time of the Vikings, Irish civil organization was marked by a cellular, un-centralist structure. It was, in fact, resistance to the Norsemen that provoked the need for a model of high-kingship to overcome the indigenous tradition of political disunity. Thus, as D.A. Binchy points out, the rise of the Tara monarchy in Ireland found a striking parallel in the rise of the national monarchy in England as the house of Wessex also sought to resist the Danes. In other words, it was largely the Norse invasions of Britain and Ireland that evoked among the native populations 'that sense of "otherness" which lies at the basis of nationalism'.[7] Binchy concludes accordingly that the political reality of high-kingship is relatively late, superseding the long tradition of the Pentarchy or 'Fifth Province' which conceived of unity as a spiritual–cultural rather than political–governmental phenomenon.

In Celtic culture, unity was an imaginary concept to be safeguarded by *fili* (poets) rather than political leaders. It was figural, not literal. This discrepancy between the cultural concept of unity and the reality of political disunity defied the modern equation of sovereignty with the state. And for as long as Gaelic society remained relatively intact, 'so long could the combination of spiritual unity and political disunity continue without serious risk'.[8] It was the collapse of this subtle equilibrium between cultural cohesion and political segmentation which, according to MacCana, 'marks the end of traditional Irish society and – from the ideological point of view – the reversion from order to chaos'.[9] In other words, it was not until the emergence of political nationalism from the eighteenth century onwards that sovereignty became identified with the *Volk* (a concept which, according to MacCana, figures hardly at all in Irish tradition) and later again with the nation-state. Whence the 'curious contradiction between the traditional view that cultural unity could dispense with political unity and the modern nationalist view which glorifies unity irrespective of cultural disparities'.[10]

But despite the centralizing tendencies of both British imperialism and Irish nationalism, several experiments in decentralized participatory democracy continued to make a mark (however modestly and exceptionally) on modern Ireland. The Vandaleur communites in Ralahine and the rural cooperatives initiated by Horace Plunket and George Russell ('AE') towards the close of the last century were cases in point. James Connolly and his colleagues also shared a vision of local democracy inspired by the ancient Celtic model; as did Alfred O'Rahilly and Sean MacBride, government minister and Nobel Peace Prize winner, in subsequent years. 'The unitary state is not the only option', wrote MacBride. 'The time has come to take another look at our system of government and to recognize the wisdom of a decentralized Irish federation of counties (as first proposed by Alfred O'Rahilly in the 1930s). Do we want centralized bureaucracy? Would we not be better off with four regional or even 32 local parliaments? There could be an overall coordinating body which (if like the Swiss government) would be like a board of directors, proportionately representing all parties. But each canton would remain in control of its own decision-making'.[11] To prevent such local councils falling into the trap of local chauvinism – what Kavanagh called 'provincialism' – it would be desirable to ensure a supervisory role for transregional bodies such as a British–Irish council or European court to protect minority and individual rights within each region. In the absence of such a higher court of appeal, the devolved self-governing communities could run the risk of relapsing into isolated communes where the local chiefs reign unchecked.

This is why I believe the most likely mode of regional democracy to succeed in contemporary Ireland is one established within the context of a Europe of equal regions. John Hume proposed as much in his influential *Report on Regional Policy*, unanimously approved by the European Parliament in 1987. This ground-breaking blueprint has been consolidated by various measures ratified by the European Council and Community to ensure proper provisions for regional culture and government: the Report on a Community Charter of Regional Languages (1981); the Kuijper Resolution on Minority Rights (1987); the Martin Proposal for a second Chamber of Regions – to replace the inter-governmental Council of Ministers (1988); the Single European Act's provision for 'social cohesion' and a pooling of sovereignties in Article 23 (1988); the Maastricht Treaty provision for a Committee of Regions, which might eventually evolve into a Second Chamber of regions (1993).

It is becoming evident that the best prospect of overcoming the sovereignty dispute in Northern Ireland is in the context of a European federation of regions.[12] And what the continuing debate on European regionalism brings home, again and again, is that if regional power without European integration runs the risk of neo-tribalism, an integrated Europe without devolution to the regions runs the risk of neo-imperialism. Both extremes are equally undesirable, and equally avoidable, if the proper balance between international and subnational association is to be struck.

A EUROPEAN FEDERATION OF REGIONS

The Europe of Regions model poses a radical challenge to the *status quo* in Ireland, north and south. The proposal for a new regional development policy for both parts of the island indicts the top–down government of both states. It recommends, for example, that EU regional funding be administered directly from the regions rather than through the central finance departments of London and Dublin. Such a dramatic decentralization would go a long way to restoring the electorate's loss of confidence in local government – a loss manifest not only in the erosion of democratic accountability but in a basic disaffection from the practice of representative politics. A European Charter of Regions would seek to respond to this sense of local powerlessness, giving people a direct say in the running of their localities. To this end, it would be necessary for regional councils and authorities to take an active role in 'ground–up' government regarding education, taxation, manufacture, transport, employment and social services. To keep looking to nation-state capitals or some European supercapital like Brussels to solve one's problems is to revert to the old colonial servility of the *béal bocht* (poor mouth) – tugging the forelock with one hand while extending the begging bowl with the other.

Genuine European interdependence can only come about through negotiations between regions that are sufficiently autonomous and free to consent to a sharing of their sovereignty. Surely the Irish Republic and United Kingdom have now sufficient confidence in their national independence to agree to a pooling of sovereignties – (i) between each other, (ii) between each other's internal regions (Ulster, Scotland, Wales, etc.) and (iii) with the other EU member states? Surely such a three-tiered repartition of powers offers the best solution for Northern Ireland – one of the most long-suffering wounds in the European body politic. That pioneering Irish mind, James Fintan Lalor, anticipated this many years ago when he said that 'a federal union must be the result of negotiation and agreement between the federating parties. . . . But in order to negotiate, the parties must stand on equal terms and each be independent of the other. . . . The steps are independence, negotiation, federal union'.

The golden mean, in short, between the absolute independence of the nation-state and the absolute dependence of a Euro-state lies in a European federation of interdependent regions. To achieve such a federation means implementing a Regional Charter (with teeth) capable of granting direct power to local councils, balancing representative democracy with participatory democracy. European regionalism offers the best promise for both communities of a divided Ulster, pointing a way beyond the nationalist/unionist endgame of exclusive sovereignty.

LOCAL AND COSMOPOLITAN IDENTITY

In conclusion, I would like to cite the example of two Northern Irish poets – John Hewitt and Seamus Heaney – who have addressed the traumas of their province by cultivating a sense of region that is at once lived and imagined.

Already in the 1940s, Hewitt, a native of the North and curator of the Ulster Museum, acknowledged regionalism as an answer to the identity conflict of his province. He chose to resolve his own dual identity at national level (Irish–British) by declaring additional allegiance to Ulster at regional level and to Europe at transnational level. In *The Bitter Gourd* (1947) he wrote with customary percipience: 'To return for one moment to the question of "rootedness", I do not mean that a writer ought to live and die in the house of his fathers. What I do mean is that he ought to feel that he belongs to a recognisable focus in place and time. How he assures himself of that feeling is his own affair. But I believe he must have it. And with it, he must have ancestors. Not just of the blood, but of the emotions, of the quality and *slant* of mind. He must know where he comes from and where he is: otherwise how can he tell where he wishes to go?' Two years later in *Regionalism: The Last Chance* (1949), Hewitt turned his attention to some of the larger political implications of regional identity. Most significantly, he recognized the necessity for regional fidelities to remain open to a universal dimension: 'Ulster considered as a Region and not as the symbol of any particular creed, can command the loyalty of every one of its inhabitants. For regional identity does not preclude, rather it requires, membership of a larger association. And whatever that association be . . . there should emerge a culture and an attitude individual and distinctive, a fine contribution to the European inheritance and no mere echo of the thought and imagination of another people or another land'.

Seamus Heaney elaborates on the idea of regional identity in an essay entitled 'The Sense of Place', first delivered as a lecture in the Ulster Museum in 1977 and later published in his collection of prose essays, *Preoccupations* (1980). Taking his tune from Kavanagh's poem 'Epic', which compares a local skirmish between Duffys and McCabes with the 'bother' caused by the *Putsch* in Munich, Heaney explains how in this poem – and presumably in most poetry – 'the local idiom extends beyond the locale itself'. More exactly: 'Munich, the European theatre, is translated into the local speech to become bother, and once it is bother, it has become knowable, and no more splendid than the bother at home. Language, as well as gods, makes its own importance – the sense of place issues in a point of view, a phrase that Kavanagh set great store by and used always as a positive. He cherished the ordinary, the actual, the known, the unimportant'. So does Heaney. And one feels he is equally partial to Kavanagh's view, cited later in the lecture, that 'parochialism is universal'. But Heaney is also cognizant that forty-odd years passed between Kavanagh's poem and his own lecture. The sense of belonging to a more amplified space is incontrovertible, even if it does not diminish the search for one's own place. 'We are no longer innocent', concludes Heaney, 'we are no longer just parishioners of the local. We go to Paris at Easter instead of rolling eggs on the hill at the gable. "Chicken Marengo! – it's a far cry from the Moy", Paul Muldoon says in a line depth-charged with architectural history. Yet those primary laws of our nature are still operative. We are dwellers, we are namers, we are lovers, we make homes and search for histories'.[13]

The fact that Hewitt hails from Protestant planter stock and Heaney from a Catholic nationalist background doesn't prevent either from finding common ground in an Ulster regional identity – Hewitt's Antrim, Heaney's Derry – interconnected with the wider world. Both gravitate towards a 'bottomless centre' bespoken to a more global circumference. Both subscribe to the Joycean version of a 'post-nationalist home' celebrated by fellow poet, Jacques Darras: 'The concept of a birth-place, a homeland, which has nourished European nationalism for the past two centuries, has done more evil than good, carrying as it does notions of territoriality and conquest, of segregation and exclusion. . . . Joyce clearly believes there is no better birthplace than the one we are travelling *towards*. The journey may end where it started; but what a wealth of experience is gathered *en route*'.[14]

The linking of a local identity with a cosmopolitan identity is, I believe, the best route beyond the British–Irish conflict in Northern Ireland. It points in the direction of a cultural pluralism which, in the evolving framework of a postnationalist Europe of Regions, may lead to the affirmation and acceptance of differences.

7   Myths of motherland

What role does myth play in Irish nationalism? More particularly, how does the mythology of sovereignty relate to the discourses of martyrdom and motherland which have informed Irish republican ideology? In Chapter 4 I talked of the need to explore the cultural and political *imaginary* of Irish society. In what follows I propose to interrogate the roots of this *imaginary* in two modes of discourse: (i) the prison discourse of martyrdom, and (ii) the poetic discourse of motherland. The interrogation will disclose a common *myth of sacrifice* underlying both.

THE CONTEMPORARY ROLE OF MYTH

We begin, however, with a more general question: how does myth relate to society today? Most contemporary nations and states invoke indigenous myths which provide a sense of 'original identity' for their 'people'. The symbolic or ritualistic reiteration of these myths is thought to redeem the fractures of the present by appealing to some foundational acts which happened at the beginning of time and harbour a sense of timeless unity. Such mythic origins are frequently connected to figures of motherland (or fatherland) – potent symbols for reanimating the power of 'dead generations' and restoring a conviction of unbroken continuity with one's tradition. Such figures generally lie at the root of national myths of sovereignty. Mircea Eliade describes their functioning thus: 'Myth is thought to express the absolute truth because it narrates a sacred history; that is, a trans-human revelation which took place in the holy time of the beginning. . . . Myth becomes exemplary and consequently *repeatable*, thus serving as a model and justification for all human actions. . . . By *imitating* the exemplary acts of mythic deities and heroes, man detaches himself from profane time and magically re-enters the Great Time, the Sacred Time'.[1] When it comes to myth, the past is never past.

Foundational myths disclose the original meaning of tradition – *tradere* – carrying the past into the present and the present into the past. So myths of tradition may be said to defy the normal logic of *either/or* by conflating not only opposite time-scales but also such opposed orders as living and dead, divine and human, redeemed and damned. Here we are confronted with another logic – that of imagination and dream – where laws of contradiction and causality no longer operate. 'The alternative *either-or* cannot be expressed in the process of dreaming. Both of the alternatives are usually inserted in the text of the dream as though they were equally valid'.[2]

This basic law of the unconscious imaginary is dramatically evident in myth, as Lévi-Strauss notes in *Structural Anthropology*. Here we have to do with a logic of analogy (*la pensée sauvage*) quite as rigorous and purposive as scientific logic. With this major difference: myths are concerned with wish-fulfilment and reversal, with making possible at an imaginary level what is impossible in our real or empirical experience. Lévi-Strauss argues accordingly that myth is concerned with 'the fantasy production of a society seeking passionately to give symbolic expression to the institutions it *might* have had in reality', if the socio-political conditions of that society had been conducive to the solution of its problems. But since the remedy is lacking in reality, the community finds itself unable to fulfil its desires of sovereignty and so begins to 'dream them, to project them into the imaginary'.[3] In short, myth can serve as an ideological strategy for inventing symbolic solutions to problems of sovereignty which remain irresolvable at a socio-political level.

Contemporary thinkers have been divided on this function of myth. Followers of Eliade and Jung, for example, tend to defend myth as an inherent dimension of our mythopoetic unconscious, expressing a genuine need for collective rootedness and identity. 'Myth itself', this thinking goes, 'never quite disappears from the present world of the psyche – it only changes and disguises its operations'.[4] If not acknowledged as an indispensable part of our lives, the mythic unconscious tends to find perverse outlets in profane experience (e.g. the secular cult of fascist, totalitarian or charismatic figures). Hence the deep suspicion of myth expressed by many modern theorists. Girard, for instance, sees myth as a scapegoating mechanism: the sacrifice of the victim, on whom the evils of society are projected, being mythically experienced as a means of purging and restoring the community to unity. Theologians like Bultmann and Moltmann call for a radical 'demythologization' of the Judaeo-Christian tradition, which they believe has been infiltrated by magico-mystery rites of saviour cults, epitomized in myths of pagan deities (Hellenic, Orphic, Celtic).[5]

An initial résumé of this contemporary conflict of opinions might run something like this – myth is neither good nor bad but *interpretation* makes it so.

MARTYRDOM AND MOTHERLAND

So how does this debate on myth relate to Irish nationalist ideologies of martyrdom and motherland? The first (martyrdom) I will approach through the prison discourse of republicanism; the second (motherland) through the poetic discourse of the Celtic Revival. Both, as we shall see, express an underlying 'political unconscious' which finds explicit articulation in a mythology of sacrifice.

The most dramatic instance of the myth of sacrificial martyrdrom in recent times has been the hunger-strike campaigns of republican prisoners in Northern Ireland, culminating in the death of Bobby Sands. The hunger-strikers in the H-Block at Long Kesh were driven by politics but inspired by myth. The distinction is, I believe, important. If asked why they were doing what they were doing, the prisoners would invariably reply – to defeat the British. But if asked why they saw the self-infliction of suffering and hunger to the point of death as a way of doing this, they would point to mottoes by Pearse or McSwiney on their cell walls. The republican hunger-strikers sought to escape their actual paralysis by realigning their plight with a mythico-religious tradition of *renewal-through-sacrifice:* a tradition stretching back through the 1916 leaders, Terence McSwiney, O'Donovan Rossa and the Fenian martyrs to the timeless personae of Cuchulain on the one hand and Christ on the other.

The invocation of this sacrificial rhetoric was to become a conspicuous feature of the Long Kesh campaign. But it was something which operated largely as a pre-reflective password of the tribe, frequently escaping critical analysis. The IRA's ideology of martyrdom inverted what went by the name of normal political logic (at a parliamentary or military level); it subscribed instead to a mythic logic which claimed that defeat is victory, failure is triumph, past is present. This mythic logic, as we already observed, is not some irrational reflex action, impervious to analysis. It is a highly structured and strategic method of combining contraries which secular reason keeps rigidly apart.

The IRA's ideology was sacrificial to the degree that it invoked, explicitly or otherwise, a 'sacred' memory of death and renewal which provided legitimation for present acts of suffering by grafting them onto paradigms of a recurring past. It thus afforded these acts a timeless and redemptive quality. By insisting in 1978 that their prison campaign was 'not ten years old but sixty years old',[6] the IRA were clearly identifying with the long nationalist tradition of the 1916 and Fenian martyrs. On the one hand, to be sure, the Provisionals presented themselves as a highly modernized and pragmatic paramilitary movement. But on the other, they confessed to taking their 'inspiration and experience from the past', that is, 'from the native Irish tradition' founded on 'our Irish and Christian values'.[7]

Taking a cue from this referral to tradition, we find obvious precedents for the sacrificial myth of martyrdom in the discourse of the 'past' generations of Republicans: Pearse's funeral oration at O'Donovan Rossa's grave in 1915; the reply by the volunteers in 1916 to the British call to surrender, that they 'had gone there to die not to win'; the victory achieved by the rebels not when they shot *at* the British from the General Post Office but when they were shot *by* the British in Kilmainham jail; and the celebrated maxim of Terence McSwiney, Sinn Féin Lord Mayor of Cork who died on hunger strike in 1920: 'It is not those who can inflict the most, but those who suffer the most who will conquer'.[8] All of these confirm the appeal to, and the appeal of, sacrifice.

The modern IRA were not unmindful of the mythopoetic power of this sacrificial heritage. They commemoratively exploited it to secure widespread sympathy (*sym-pathein*, to suffer with) for their prison campaigns. So while it is true that the Provisionals were hard-nosed, feet-on-the-ground activists who wanted nothing better than to achieve military victory over the British Army, it was equally true that once faced with imprisonment (precluding military action), they readily subscribed to McSwiney's view that those who suffer the most will ultimately prevail.

The IRA had long memories. William McKee, a noted Belfast Republican, declared that that was why the war would be won 'in the prisons'. A Maze prisoner reiterated this sentiment in 1980 when he wrote on the wall of his cell: 'I am one of many who die for my country . . . if death is the only way, I am prepared to die'. The *many* here refers to the long litany of martyrs whose sacrificial death for the nation was translated into the 'sacred debt' of the 'freedom struggle'. And one of the most popular responses to this sacrificial debt was, interestingly, the spread in the 1970s and 1980s of rhymes, graffiti, snatches and ballads which – like the myths of martyrdom they repeat – were authored by nobody, yet known to everybody.[9]

The extraordinary power of this mythic logic was not lost on the IRA leadership. They had impressive evidence to suggest, after all, that support for the 'cause' increased in reaction to sacrificial suffering more than to military aggression. Hunger-strikes were better recruiters than bomb-strikes. Quite apart from christening the murder of 14 Derry civilians by the British Army in 1972 as 'Bloody Sunday' (the same term attributed to the shooting of civilians by the British Army in Croke Park, Dublin in 1920), Sinn Féin did not hesitate to present the H-Block campaigns in the late 1970s and 1980s in mythic idioms of martyrdom. The Blanket-men and hunger-strikers were depicted in popular posters wrapped in loin-cloths. While wall-drawings showed battered and emaciated prisoners in Christ-like posture, the wire of Long Kesh transformed into crowns of thorns. And it was this success in identifying the IRA as sacrificial victims (rather than terrorist aggressors) which succeeded in providing the 'movement' with a tacit base of support in the Catholic nationalist community, North and South.

Just as Padraig Pearse, leader of the 1916 Rising in Dublin, had identified with the blood sacrifice of Christ in the poem 'A Mother Speaks', written on the eve of his execution, the death of the hunger-strikers in Long Kesh was seen in analogous terms. While the military wing of the movement often cited the idioms of revolutionary socialism (e.g. liberation of the oppressed from imperialist exploitation), the 'prison wing' invoked the more mythic idioms of Catholic nationalism. Daily Mass in Long Kesh became, by the prisoners' own account, a major source of sustenance by enabling them to identify with the Gethsemane agonies of the great national martyrs. The prison priests, Fathers Murray and Faul, introduced their H-Block document of Christmas 1979 with a drawing of the Pope blessing the kneeling prisoners and quoted the Pontiff's Drogheda statement of the same year that the 'Law of God stands in judgment over all reasons of state'. The American Jesuit, Daniel Berrigan, spoke of a '... hieroglyph (sacred writing) being spelt out' by the prisoners who smeared themselves with their own excrement during the 'dirty protest'. Irish classes also became a regular feature of life in Long Kesh. And one could hardly find a more apt description of the psychological force of the sacrificial language of the tribe than in Cardinal O'Fiach's statement after his visit to the prisoners in July 1978. 'In the circumstances I was surprised that the morale of the prisoners was high', said the Cardinal. 'From talking to them it is evident that they intend to continue their protest indefinitely and it seems they prefer death rather than submit to being classed as criminals. Anyone with the least knowledge of Irish history knows how deeply rooted this attitude is in our country's past. In isolation and perpetual boredom they maintain their sanity by studying Irish. It was an indication of the triumph of the human spirit over adverse material surroundings to notice Irish words, phrases and songs being shouted from cell to cell and then written on each cell wall with the remnants of toothpaste tubes'.[10]

The impact of the prison protest was not confined to the prison. Nor was it meant to be. Bobby Sands, Owen Carron and Gerry Adams were elected to Westminister less because they represented a quasi-Marxist guerrilla movement than because they articulated a tribal voice of martyrdom, deeply embedded in the Catholic tradition. This was surely why Adams, for example, was so embarrassed by Republican offensives (particularly if they involved civilian casualties) during his election campaign. Which is not to deny that there was double-think at work in both elected and electorate. But it was precisely because of this double-mindedness that it was simplistic to equate a vote for Sinn Féin with a vote for violence. Unless, that is, one meant a vote for violence 'suffered' more than violence 'inflicted'. That the IRA themselves subsequently interpreted this vote as an endorsement of their military offensive is undeniable. But that did not diminish the initial ambivalence in the mind of the voter.

The operative word here is ambivalence. As the prison campaign showed, the Republican-nationalist movement operated in terms of two distinguishable, if not always distinct, discourses: on the one hand, the secular discourse of military action and social struggle; on the other, the mythic discourse of sacrificial martyrdom.

MYTHOLOGIZING AND DEMYTHOLOGIZING IN IRISH LITERATURE

Irish literature also displayed two different attitudes to the nationalist idea of myth. While Yeats and the literary revivalists championed it, Joyce and other cosmopolitan modernists such as Beckett, Flann O'Brien and McGreevy challenged it.

Yeats offered the myth of Mother Ireland as symbolic compensation for the colonial calamities of history. The mythological motherland served as a goddess of sovereignty who, at least at the imaginary level, might restore a lost national identity by summoning her sons to the sacred rite of renewal through sacrifice. So doing, the Irish people might re-enter the sacred time which transcends historical time, thereby undoing the wrongs of history. Where reality indicated division and dispossession, myth provided an answering poetics of unity and sovereignty.

More specifically, Yeats sought in myth an idealized Celtic paganism *pre-existing* the colonial rupture of Ireland into sectarian denominations. This pre-historical religion of the pious Celt would, Yeats argued in *The Trembling of the Veil* (1922), provide the segregated Irish people with a common currency of 'holy symbols' – eternal archetypes first bestowed 'by God to the bright hearts of those long dead'. Accordingly, Yeats affirmed that a mythic religion founded on the Collective Unconscious of the race would recollect the fragmented communities of the land in the form of a 'memory beyond all individual memories': an *anima mundi* which is not deliberately chosen by us but 'comes into the mind from beyond the mind'. His true vocation, Yeats declared in 1898, was to form a 'company of Irish poets' whose 'religious philosophy' would transform both poet and non-poet into 'ectstatics and visionaries'. Thus we find Yeats openly confessing to the Fenian leader, John O'Leary, that 'the mystical life is the centre of all that I think and all that I write' – presuming, no doubt, to have hit upon a visionary mythology shared by poet and politician alike.

Yeats was convinced, it seems, that the religious *Unity of Spirit* could be translated into a corresponding *Unity of Image*. This would enable us to see 'all life as a mythological system' and thereby serve as the 'originating symbol of a national literature' (*The Trembling of the Veil*). Yeats was deeply disappointed by the fact that the Irish Literary Revival inaugurated by himself, Synge and Lady Gregory had been spurned by the Catholic middle classes, the Gaelic Leaguers and many of the republican nationalists. Pearse, for example, in a letter in the journal *An Claidheamh Soluis* in 1899, had declared that 'If we once admit the Irish-Literature-is-English idea, then the language movement is a mistake'. And he goes on: 'Against Mr. Yeats personally, we have nothing to object. He is a mere English poet of the third or fourth rank and as such he is harmless. But when he attempts to run an "Irish" Literary Theatre it is time for him to be crushed'. The recourse by Yeats and Lady Gregory to the legendary images of Celtic mythology may thus be read as an attempt to make peace between the opposing interests of class, creed and language. It was a plea for a unifying notion of identity and sovereignty, based upon an 'ancient Irish sect' which preceded all contemporary dissension. In its way, it was an endorsement of Wolfe Tone's ideal of a non-sectarian Irish tradition.

Finally, at a political level, we find Yeats contriving to transmute the violent conflicts of the National Struggle into the salvific myth of a 'terrible beauty'. In his poem, 'Easter 1916', Yeats admits that the rebel leaders whom he had previously dismissed in a 'mocking tale or gibe' have been 'transformed utterly' by the mythic rite of blood-sacrifice. The motley crew of disparate individuals have been metamorphosized into a visionary sect – 'Hearts with one purpose alone'. They have, in short, been redeemed from the contingencies of history and become magically contemporaneous with the mythic personages of the Holy Beginning. Thus Pearse is transposed into the heroic Cuchulain. 'When Pearse summoned Cuchulain to his side', asks Yeats in *The Statues*, 'what stalked through the Post Office?' His quarrel with Pearse in life is resolved in myth. They find common cause outside of time. By means of the ritualistic repetition of blood-sacrifice, Pearse and his fellow signatories cease to be historical individuals opposed to the Anglo-Irish Ascendancy, becoming one with it in the timeless tradition of 'dead generations'. This is why Yeats can ultimately embrace Pearse's myth of an 'enduring nation' revivified by the ritual sacrifice of sons to the sovereign and indivisible motherland: 'For Padraig Pearse has said / That in every generation / Must Ireland's blood be shed'.

*   *   *

But modern Irish writers were not all of one mind. Beckett, for example, repudiated Yeats's mythologizing as sanctimonious posturing. He abhorred the idioms of collective continuity and community, declaring his intention to explore the 'rupture of the lines of communication'. Beckett rejected myth as an illusory compensation for one's own anguish. Individual misery could not be converted into some external system of universal meanings. There could be no communication, he bluntly insisted, 'because there is nothing to communicate'.

Not surprisingly, therefore, Beckett had nothing but contempt for the myth-making of the Irish Literary Revival which he discarded, in an essay on 'Recent Irish Poetry' (1936), as the 'altitudinous complacency of the Victorian Gael'. In opposition to such 'antiquarian' writers as Yeats, Clarke and Corkery, who endeavoured to 'flee from self-awareness' by retrieving the lost traditions of some 'hidden Ireland', Beckett promoted a counter-tradition of Irish authors who espoused a modernism of self-reflection. In this latter category he included (besides himself) such fellow expatriates as Coffey, Devlin and McGreevy. What these writers shared was the admission that they belonged 'nowhere'. They possessed no motherland. They refused to drop through the escape-hatch of myth whereby the 'self is either most happily obliterated or else so improved and enlarged as to be mistaken for the decor'. Like Beckett, these cosmopolitan exiles began with their own nothingness and wrote about the impossibility of ever translating this nothingness into something else. Here was an art of 'pure interrogation'. Question without answer. Misery without myth. Existence without essence. The very idea of a National Mythology was itself denounced as myth. Which is why Beckett commended O'Casey's anti-nationalism in

Juno and the Peacock, interpreting his send-up of tribal mythologies – particularly blood-sacrifice – as testimony to the collapse of consoling shibboleths: 'mind and world come asunder in irreparable dissociation – *chassis'*.

But Beckett's most sustained attempt to demythologize the Irish cultural Revival is recorded in his first novel, *Murphy*. Here he parodies the literary nationalism of authors like Yeats and Clark in the personage of Austin Ticklepenny, a 'pot poet' who felt it his 'duty to Erin to compose' verses 'bulging with as many minor beauties from the Gaelic prosodoturfy as could be sucked out of a mug of Beamish's porter'. For Beckett the Filthy Modern Tide had dissolved all nationalist sureties; it had to be confronted head on by each solitary self. That is why Beckett emigrated to Paris and resolved to stay on there in the 1940s, preferring, as he put it, France at war to Ireland at peace.

Joyce too revolted against the use of myth to sacrifice the creative individual to tribal cults. By debunking what he saw as the fetish of the motherland, he hoped to emancipate the self from the constraints of the past. To this extent, Joyce shared not only Beckett's preference for exile but also his abhorrence of insular nationalism, which he derided as a 'pale afterthought of Europe'. But Joyce differed from Beckett in that he was not content to simply abandon myth for modernism, swopping Dublin for Paris or his own language for a foreign one (French). After several months in exile, Joyce wrote that he wished not only to 'Europeanise Ireland' but to 'Hibernicise Europe'. He wanted to blend a fidelity to his local origins with a counter-fidelity to the culture of the Continent. He wanted, as it were, Ireland to become more universal and Europe to become more particular. To this end, Joyce did not hesitate to have recourse to myth – albeit myth in a new sense.

In *Ulysses*, Joyce deploys one kind of myth to demythologize another. Molly, for example, is the antithesis to the 'Mothers of Memory' which Stephen equates with the paralysing 'nightmare of history'. Her passionate affair with Blazes Boylan contrasts with the self-sacrificing Virgin of *Mother-Church*; she has not a word of the *Mother-Tongue*; and she commemorates the sensual Andalusian maidens of Gibraltar rather than the Celtic Goddesses of the *Mother-Land* (e.g. Roisín or Caitlín). Yet Molly is both mother and memory – as the final soliloquy testifies. And, as such, she does achieve the proportions of a mythic figure whose double commitment to the singularities of everyday experience *and* to the universality of European mythology (she is Penelope of the Odyssey) enables her to debunk the stereotypes of tribal sovereignty. As Joyce explained in a letter to Valery Larbaud: 'Penelope has the last word'. By playing archetypes off against stereotypes in this way, Joyce was suggesting that we can be liberated from pre-established narratives of identity without capitulating to the modernist cult of solipsism.

Joyce was attracted to the Hellenic mythology of Ulysses/ Penelope/Telemachus because of its *foreignness* – its ability to offer us alternative models of universality whose very otherness to our indigenous models would enable us to redefine experience in a new way, untrammelled by pieties. Accordingly, Molly is for Joyce a distinctively *Irish* woman precisely because she has been freed from those clichés of Irish womanhood which would have prevented her expressing herself as she *really is*. And yet by identifying her with the open-ended persona of Penelope, Joyce is allowing this Irishwoman to be Everywoman. In short, Joyce seems to be saying that myth is good when it opens the familiar to the foreign, bad when it reduces the foreign to the familiar.

This does not reflect a bias against Irish mythology *per se* in favour of Greek or any other kind. If Joyce had been born in Athens he might well have chosen Caitlín ní Houlihán as his liberating model! Moreover, in *Finnegans Wake*, Anna Livia Plurabelle represents a universal mother figure drawn from both non-Celtic and Celtic mythologies (Anna or Anu was the ancient Celtic goddess of sovereignty and Livia derives from Liffey). In this respect, we might say that Joyce is brushing indigenous sovereignty myths against the grain, enabling them to coalesce with alien ones. He is, as it were, deconstructing his tradition from within by exposing it to heterogeneous traditions. *Finnegans Wake* teaches us that Dublin is 'Doublin' – itself and not itself. It suggests that tradition is not some pre-ordained continuity which makes us all the same. Myth is revealed as history, history as myth.

Joyce thus shows that our narrative of self-identity is itself a fiction – an 'epical forged cheque' – and that each one of us has the freedom to re-invent our past. Far from being a liquidation of historical individuals, Joyce shows that myth actually requires the multiple reinterpretations of different writers in order to recreate itself. At its best, myth is *recreation* – in both senses of the word. This is why Joyce presents Anna Livia Plurabelle as a model of *unity in plurality*: a 'bringer of plurabilities' who is 'every person, place and thing in the chaosmos of alle . . . moving and changing every part of the time'.

MOTHER IRELAND'S SACRIFICIAL SONS

A common motif emerging from our analysis of the prison discourse of martyrdom and the literary discourse of myth is that of motherland. Thus far, I have treated the political and literary discourses separately but they frequently overlap. The writings of Pearse are a good example. In the name of a national Revival, Pearse sought to retrieve foundational myths of sovereignty which, he believed, would help break the colonial dependency on Britain. These foundational myths would enable the orphaned children of Erin to return to the security of their maternal origins: the mother church of Catholic revival; the motherland of national revival; and the mother tongue of Gaelic revival. In the opening and closing sentences of the Easter Proclamation of 1916, for instance, we find an implicit conflation of these revival idioms. Opening with a ceremonial address to *Poblacht na hEireann*, the text reads: 'In the name of God and the dead generations from which she receives her old tradition of nationhood, Ireland, through us, summons her children to her flag and strikes for freedom'. In this and related phrases, we witness a rhetorical correlation between (i) the Catholic symbolism of mystical reunion with martyrs through the sacrifice of the Mass, and (ii) the mythological idea of Mother Ireland calling on her sons to shed their blood so that the nation be restored after centuries of historical persecution.

Elsewhere, Pearse is more explicit in his conjugation of Catholic and mythic idioms of sacrifice. In his farewell poem from his death cell in Kilmainham, he identifies his own martyrdom with that of Christ who also 'had gone forth to die for men'. The poem is appropriately entitled *A Mother Speaks* and ends with the poet comparing his own mother's faith in his powers of renewal with Mary's faith in the resurrection of Christ – 'Dear Mary, I have shared thy sorrow and soon shall share thy Joy'. And in Pearse's play, *The Singer*, we find the hero McDara conflating his resistance to the impious enemy with Christ's suffering at the hands of the Romans: 'I will stand up before the Gaul as Christ hung naked before men on a tree'. Nor did Pearse have any difficulty eliding the martyred Christ and the martyred Cuchulain as a means of translating the defeats of historical time into the victory of mythic timelessness. It is surely within this context of filial sacrifice for the motherland that we must understand Pearse's claim that 'life springs from death' and that 'bloodshed is a cleansing and a sanctifying thing'.[11]

These sentiments were by no means confined to Pearse and the poets. They epitomized the overall *mythos* of the 1916 Rising which gained common currency in the 'popular imaginary' – particularly after the signatories were executed. Posters appeared on the streets of Dublin showing Pearse reclining pietà-like on the bosom of a seraphic woman brandishing a tricolour: a mixture of Mother Ireland, the Virgin Mother of Christ and the Angel of the Resurrection.

Is it possible that such idealized *imagos* of womanhood might be related to the social stereotypes of the Irish woman as pure virgin or son-obsessed mother? In the historical evolution of Irish religious ideology, we witness a shift away from the early Irish Church which was quite liberal in sexual matters and assigned an important role to women, to a more puritanical religion which idealized women as other-worldly creatures of sublime innocence. And it is perhaps no accident that this shift coincided in some measure with the colonization of Ireland. The more dispossessed the people became in reality the more they sought to repossess a sense of identity in the imaginary. Since the women of colonized Ireland had become, in James Connolly's words, the 'slaves of slaves', they were, in a socio-political sense at least, the perfect candidates for compensatory elevation in the order of mystique. The cult of virginity undoubtedly corroborated this process of sublimation. Woman became as sexually intangible as the ideal of national sovereignty became politically intangible. Both became imaginary, aspirational, elusive.

Thus it might be argued that the transposition of Irish women into desexualized, quasi-divine mothers corresponded in some manner to the ideological transposition of Ireland from a fatherland (the term *an t-athardha* was often used to denote Ireland in much bardic poetry up to the seventeenth century) into idioms connoting a motherland. As psychoanalysis reminds us, the mother has always been a powerful unconscious symbol for forfeited or forbidden origins.

The idealization of Irish womanhood was reinforced in the late nineteenth century by the counter-reformational cult of the Virgin Mary (mariolatry) witnessed in the rise of confraternity and abstinence movements which championed sexual purity. Indeed, it is interesting how elements in the Irish hierarchy – which offered women no real power – increasingly came to equate Ireland with a virginal motherland best served by safeguarding the native purity of 'faith and morals' against the threat of alien culture.[12] To traduce these national ideals was, as Bishop Harty remarked early in the century, to 'bring shame on the Motherland'. The more colonially oppressed the Irish became in history the more spiritualized became the mythic motherland. To see this one need only contrast the redemptive Mother Eire of 1916 – the decently clad Caitlín who preferred her sacrificial sons and lovers dead rather than alive – with the barebreasted carnal maiden of the French *République*. Unlike Marianne, Caitlín ní Houlihán was less a creature of the living present than a memory of the mythic past.

But the most formative factor in the development of these myths of motherland remains, arguably, the political invasion of Ireland. After the plantations of the seventeenth century, Ireland became more frequently identified with a vulnerable virgin ravished by the aggressive masculine invader from England: the *Sasannach*. In the *Aisling* poems of the eighteenth century, the 'hidden' Ireland was thus personified as a visionary daughter or *spéirbhean* threatened by the alien marauder (or inversely, following the same logic, as a shameless hag – *meirdreach* – who lifted her skirts for the invader's pleasure).[13] In the nineteenth and twentieth centuries, the passive daughter seems to assume the more militant guise of a mother goddess summoning her faithful sons to rise up against the infidel invader so that, through the shedding of their blood, she might be redeemed from colonial violation and become pure once again – restored to her pristine sovereignty of land, language and liturgy.

If the mutation of mythic *imagos* mirrors, however obliquely, the nation's political unconscious, is it not reasonable to conjecture that the identification of Ireland as dispossessed daughter/mother might represent a symbolic projection of a prohibited sense of possession? Deprived of sovereignty in the present, might not the poets of the nation have sought compensation in the idealized 'female' personifications of a pre-colonial past?[14]

THE DIALOGUE OF MYTH AND HISTORY

The discourse of poets and prisoners is there to remind us that myth often harbours memories which reason ignores at its peril. Myths of motherland are more than antique curiosities; they retain a purchase on the contemporary mind and can play a pivotal role in mobilizing sentiments of national identity. Sometimes, this serves the legitimate interests of national liberation or resistance. Other times, it plays a more sinister role. Julia Kristeva remarks on this in her critique of the collusion between sacrificial terrorism and what she calls the 'myth of the archaic mother'. She explores in particular the anthropological and psychological motivations underlying the alliance between idealized motherland and messianic violence. Her conclusion serves as both a summary description of her argument and a warning: 'If the archetype of the belief in a good and pure substance, that of utopias, is the belief in the omnipotence of an archaic, full, total englobing mother with no frustration, no separation, no break-producing symbolism . . . then it becomes evident that we will never be able to defuse the violences mobilised through the counter-investment necessary to carrying out this phantasm, unless one challenges precisely this myth of the archaic mother. It is in this way that we can understand the warnings against the recent invasion of the women's movement by paranoia, as in

Lacan's scandalous sentence "there is no such thing as Woman". Indeed, she does *not* exist with a capital "W". Possessor of some mythical unity – a supreme power, on which is based the terror of power and terrorism as the desire for power'.[15]

Myth is a two-way street. It can lead to perversion (bigotry, racism, fascism) or to liberation (the reactivation of a genuine social imaginary open to universal horizons). If we need to demythologize, we also need to remythologize. And this double process requires a discrimination between authentic and inauthentic uses of myth. For if myths of motherland are often responses to repression, they can also become repressive in their own right. That is why it is necessary to see how myth emancipates and how it incarcerates, how it operates as an empowering symbol of identity and how it degenerates into a reactionary idol. At best, myth invites us to reimagine our past in a way which challenges the present status quo and opens up alternative possibilities of thinking. At worst, it provides a community with a strait-jacket of fixed identity, drawing a *cordon sanitaire* around this identity which excludes dialogue with all that is other than itself.

Without mythology, our memories are homeless; we capitulate to the mindless conformism of fact. But if revered as ideological dogma, and divorced from the summons of reality, myth becomes another kind of conformism, another kind of death. That is why we must never cease to keep mythological images in dialogue with history. And that is why each society, each community, each nation, needs to go on telling stories, inventing and reinventing its mythic imaginary, until it brings history home to itself.

8   Myth and nation in modern Irish poetry

Yeats and the Celtic Revival looked to myth for a story of continuity which history denied them. They invoked narratives whose prehistoric integrity might compensate for the ruptures of Irish history and resolve its endless quarrels. Here – as noted in the preceding chapter – were timeless creatures from an antique world, healing memories older than the scars of conflict, a heritage of 'national sovereignty' for all the tribes of Erin. In this manner, myth was often deployed as emblem for a new Ireland proudly restored to pristine wholeness. As has been argued at some length in Chapter 7, Yeats and other revivalists believed that myths were prime movers of history. And this belief was confirmed, first, by leaders of the 1916 rebellion who identified with the mythological heroes of blood sacrifice, and, second, by the patrons of the new Irish state who erected a statue of Cuchulain in the GPO in Dublin at the very place where Pearse had proclaimed a free Ireland.[1]

The revivalists, as we saw, saw myth as a means of overcoming divisions in Ireland. A revived mythology of 'national sovereignty' would provide a Unity of Culture which might in turn galvanize a Politics of Unity. But many modern Irish poets invoked myth in a quite different manner. Instead of interpreting it as a token of unbroken heritage, they treated it as an agency of critique. Instead of seeing it as a means of restoring the nation to its proper place – thereby fulfilling its ancestral destiny – they took their cue from Joyce, redrafting myth as a subversion of fixed identities, a catalyst of disruption and difference, a joker in the pack inviting us to free variations of meaning. Hence we find many of the stock legendary characters being recast in modern Irish poetry as actors of liberty and fun, iconoclasts of sacrosanct origins transmitted uncompromised from the ancient past.

This latter approach to myth I call *utopian*. In contrast to the ideological use of myth to reinstate a people, nation or race in its predestined 'place', utopian myth opens up a 'no-place' (*u-topos*). It emancipates the imagination into a historical future rather than harnessing it to the hallowed past.

IDEOLOGY AND UTOPIA

As I use the terms here (in a way common since Mannheim),[2] ideology refers to that complex of myths and images which serve to maintain the status quo; utopia refers to the deployment of myths and images to challenge and transform the status quo. Utopia can accordingly be equated with that unconquered power of imagination, that surplus of symbolic desire which resists the closure of ideology. Utopia has to remain *critical*, lest it congeal into a new ideology subordinating the catalysing power of dream to the literal demands of propaganda. In principle, utopian myths are oppositional, ideological myths conformist:

> For a specific, homogeneous utopian vision would be a betrayal of radical utopian discourse and would only end up serving the instrumentalisation of desire carried on by the present structures of power. There can be no *utopia* but there *can* be utopian expressions that constantly shatter the present achievements and compromises of society and point to that which is not yet experienced in the human project of fulfilment and creation.[3]

To view poetry in terms of a dialectic between ideological and utopian uses of myth recognizes its role as a significant part of the social process of discourse – that is, as an expression of a 'cultural unconscious' which harbours a desire for a realm of freedom in a world transformed. Utopian myth is thus predicated upon an operation of estrangement. It alienates us from the inherited state of affairs and engages in the imagining of an alternative community, other ways of seeing and existing. This commitment to radical otherness sometimes produces an experience of 'uncanniness'. While mythology generally provides us with what is most familiar, utopian myth re-presents stories in an unfamiliar guise, with a twist in the tail, a shock of alterity at the heart of the habitual.

This is certainly true of Joyce's re-reading of myth, as outlined in the preceding study. But it is equally true of several works by modern Irish poets. Kavanagh, Heaney, Kinsella, Durcan, McGuckian, Muldoon and others, I will argue, provide us with examples of this 'defamiliarizing' process. Each succeeds in rediscovering home away from home, in rereading native myths of sovereignty from an other place – unchartered, unhomely, *unheimlich*. So compelling are the myths of Irish revivalist culture that they can only be approached anew from a *foreign place* – Heaney's other North, Jutland; Durcan's other home, Russia; Mahon's other Belfast, Delft. The utopian imagination of these poets exercises an *analogical* role. It evokes the importance of being elsewhere. It provokes new spaces in us by juxtaposing dissimilar images and idioms. And it is surely for this reason that Fredric Jameson recommends that we consider utopian discourse in literature as an 'object of meditation, analogous to the riddles or Koan of the various mystical traditions or the aporias of classical philosophy, whose function is to provoke a fruitful bewilderment and to jar the mind into some heightened but unconceptualisable consciousness of its own powers, functions, aims and structural limits'.[4] So doing, the critical myths of utopia stand in stark opposition to the limiting ideology of nation-state sovereignty – republican or unionist.

POST-REVIVAL DEMYTHOLOGIZERS

After the Revival it became necessary to dismantle myth in order to save it. Yeatsian mythologizing was so imposing that it soon became part of a new cultural orthodoxy. The next generation of Irish writers felt it necessary to escape from his shadow. They had to bury their revivalist fathers in order to create anew. Beckett followed Joyce into exile in Paris and dismissed the native revival as so much 'cut and dried sanctity'.[5] Several young authors joined him – in particular McGreevy and Coffey – while others stayed at home and resolved to undermine the revivalist movement from within. Patrick Kavanagh was no doubt the most dramatic example of the latter. In his famous *Self-Portrait* (1962), he declared his total repudiation of what he termed 'this Ireland thing'. Kavanagh saw the Literary Revival as a trap sprung by the 'Celtic Twilighters'. The Ireland 'patented by Yeats, Lady Gregory and Synge' was, he declared acerbically, a 'thoroughgoing English-bred lie'.[6] He rejected the revivalist shibboleths of genuine peasant and aristocrat. 'Irishness', he quipped, was no more than 'a way of anti-art',[7] a means of playing at being a poet without actually being one. To the mythologizing spirit of the Revival, Kavanagh opposed what he called the 'comic spirit':[8] an attitude which scorned the self-importance of Grand Narrative, preferring the carelessness and ordinariness of the immediate. This deflation of posturing he described as the 'difficult art of not caring'. Only a fidelity to the parochial and local, to experience in the lower case, could hope to arrive at that highest because simplest of all conditions – 'complete casualness'.[9]

If Kavanagh championed the parochial, he had no time for the pro-vincial. In 'Dark Ireland' he regrets the insular mentality of the new bourgeois state: 'We are a dark people, / Our eyes ever turned / Inward'. The provincialism of middle-class Catholic Dublin – as Kavanagh dis-covered when he tried to launch his journal *Kavanagh's Weekly* there in the 1950s – was quite as inimical to art as the aesthetic elitism of the fashionable Ascendancy. The mean-minded materialism of the former class was simply the obverse of the effete spiritualism of the latter. Both shared an unseemly devotion to sentimental myths of the Revival. Whenever Kavanagh himself chose mythic figures – which was rare enough – he generally drew from Greek rather than Celtic mythology, and always with a view to showing how the Grand Narratives of myth are inextricably bound up with the vicissitudes of everyday life. Thus in 'Pegasus' he compares his soul to an old horse hawked 'through the world / Of Church and State and meanest trade' until, freed into the simplicity of things – the 'grazing of the sun' – it grows wings upon its back and rides through every land of poetic imagination. In 'Pygmal-ion' the ancient goddess is cast in the form of a 'stone-proud woman. . . . Engirdled by the ditches of Roscommon'. And in 'Epic' the poet contrasts world-shattering events with the neighbourly dispute be-tween Duffys and McCabes – 'Till Homer's ghost came whispering to my mind / He said: I made the Iliad from such / A local row. Gods make their own importance'. Finally, in his own parody of the *Iliad* entitled 'The Paddiad', Kavanagh compares the Devil to a patron of Irish letters whose 'forte's praise for what is dead'. His inventory of revivalist stereotypes is a damning account of the Celtic Twilight:

Paddy Whiskey, Rum and Gin
Paddy Three sheets in the wind;
Paddy of the Celtic Mist,
Paddy Connemara West,
Chestertonian Paddy Frog
Croaking nightly in the bog.
All the Paddies having fun
Since Yeats handed in his gun.

Seamus Deane assesses this aspect of Kavanagh's poetic contribution perceptively:

He is at odds with the spiritual heroics of the foundation period of the State and is perfectly in accord with the general desire to climb down from the dizzy height of mythology, the glories of battle, elab-orate readings of tradition and labyrinthine pursuits of Irishness and to concentrate instead on the stony grey soil of his native Monaghan and the actualities of living the here and now.[10]

Another Ulster poet much indebted to Kavanagh, John Montague, makes this point laconically when he praises him for allowing a new generation of Irish writers to be 'liberated into ignorance'.[11]

Kavanagh was not the only demythologizer of the revivalist posture. After the Second World War, during which Ireland had been neutral, a young group of writers emerged in Dublin; they were committed to modernist forms and practised a mode of comic satire which reflected disillusionment with the reactionary ideology of the 1950s. Prominent amongst this emerging group were Flann O'Brien, Seán Ó Faoláin and Anthony Cronin. Cronin's memoir *Dead as Doornails* graphically captures the oppressive sense of malaise which dominated this period – a time when censorship was rife, clericalism rampant and the world war no more than a 'ghastly unreality'. While poets such as Coffey and Devlin had followed Beckett into exile, and Austen Clarke had striven nostalgically for an impossible synthesis of Celtic lore, Catholic mystery and pagan sensuality, the demythologizing Dublin set of Cronin, Kavanagh and O'Brien developed an adversarial stance. Their work cultivated wit, iconoclasm and a deliberate estrangement from accredited wisdoms. They wiped the domestic slate clean. They served as a middle generation cutting through the lush vegetation of tradition to clear spaces where new voices might be heard.

REPOSSESSING IRISH MYTHOLOGY

Among the most eloquent voices of the post-1950s dispensation of Irish poetry must be numbered those of Thomas Kinsella, John Montague and Seamus Heaney. These poets would return to questions of myth. But they were to do so with a discriminating eye, having passed through Kavanagh's demythologizing detour. The *via negativa* had opened up a utopian reappropriation of myth.

*   *   *

Kinsella's reprise of myth was critical and considered. He was influenced not only by Kavanagh's unsanctimonious attitude to Celtic myths, but also, during the 1950s and 1960s, by the modernist aesthetic of American poets such as Pound and William Carlos Williams. The international culture of modernism provided him with a way to break out of the 'smug peripherality of Irish experience and face up to the violent heritage of the post-war world'.[12] But, as the horizon of world experience expanded, the horizon of personal experience retracted. The apocalyptic implications of global history – after Auschwitz and Hiroshima – were being poetically registered in the fragile idiom of private nightmare. Kinsella needed a larger canvas to frame his sentiment of breakdown. And so, in the 1970s, he returned to motifs of Irish mythology and Jungian psychology in an effort to achieve a new equilibrium between the claims of historical disorder and poetic order. In volumes such as *Notes from the Land of the Dead, Song of the Night, The Messenger* and *One*, we find him exploiting the psychic resources of myth in a selective and utterly unsentimental fashion. His aim? To reconstruct an architecture of images from the debris of post-war experience.

Kinsella's repossession of Irish mythology was, in his own words, 'nursed out of wreckage'. He had no time for the Yeatsian romanticizing of myths and museums. The archetypes of mythic memory are invoked to cope with nausea, not nostalgia. Instructed by his journeying through the international idioms of post-war modernism, Kinsella feels himself in a position to retrieve selectively the energies of his native myths. There are several allusions to early Celtic literature (in particular *The Book of Invasions)* in his *Notes from the Land of the Dead*, a poem in which the recurring patterns of myth – birth and death, invasion and appropriation – exemplify the cyclical turns of Kinsella's sense of collective and personal history. The experiences of rupture and disinheritance are forever present in his mythic retelling of inner loss. The biblical myth of the Fall becomes a narrative overlay for the defeats of Irish history and the Kinsella family; while the Gaelic narrative of invasions provides an analogy for the contemporary sense of conflict, both *politically* in Ulster and *linguistically* in the 'divided mind' of a literature ghosted by the silence of a lost tongue.

Reviewing the traditions of his ancestral civilization, Kinsella refuses the triumphal enthusiasms of the Celtic Twilight. His vision of the mythological past is one of homelessness and dispossession. This is evident in his translations of the Gaelic poems in *An Duanaire* and the *Tain*, and also in the following statement in his formative essay 'The Divided Mind' (1972): 'I recognise a great inheritance and simultaneously a great loss. The inheritance is certainly mine but only at two enormous removes – across a century's silence and through an exchange of worlds. . . . I recognise that I stand on one side of a great rift and can feel the discontinuity in myself. It is a matter of peoples and places as well as writings – of coming from a broken and uprooted family, of being drawn to those who share my origins and finding that we cannot share our lives'.[13]

But, if Kinsella is never at ease with native myth, neither can he find a home in the English language. 'An Irish poet has access to the English poetic heritage through his use of the English language', he observes, 'but he is unlikely to feel at home in it'.[14] This double charge of homelessness is intrinsic to Kinsella's negotiation of myth. But it also allows him a certain kind of detachment – a poetic liberty to draw re-creatively from a variety of traditions: the modernist tradition of Pound and Joyce as well as the mythological tradition of his Gaelic heritage. And in this Kinsella, it could be said, anticipates postmodernist experiments with radical eclecticism and double coding.[15]

*   *   *

John Montague's reappropriation of myth takes a different turn – less archetypal than humanist. Myth is now seen as a way back into history rather than as a time that existed before it. The prehistory of psyche or nation does not preoccupy Montague, as it did Kinsella in such poems as 'Finistere'. What concerns him is the use of myth to reimagine an eclipsed place of history – what he terms his 'forgotten Northern landscape'. In one of his most famous early poems, 'Like Dolmens round my Childhood, the Old People', he recounts the pressures exerted upon his imagination by the 'rune and the chant' of 'Ancient Ireland'. The conclusion of the poem is an exorcism whereby the old people who had haunted his childhood exit from the shadowy world of dreams and pass 'into the dark permanence of ancient forms'. In this way he faces his ancestral memories.

Montague shares with Kinsella an enthusiasm for international (and especially American) modernism, and also feels a sense of guilt at Ireland's non-participation in the Second World War (see 'Auschwitz, Mon Amour'). The realities of contemporary and cosmopolitan life, experienced during his childhood in Brooklyn and his first marriage in Paris, are sobering ingredients in his poetic menu. As places 'other' than ancestral Ulster, they serve as negative utopias affording the poet a certain critical measure. Thus, when, in 'The Wild Dog Rose', he returns to confront his mythic *cailleach,* he does so with the irony of New York and the scepticism of Paris. The mythological goddess is humanized into a presence of solitude and fear.

A similarly chastening strategy is employed in another late poem, *The Dead Kingdom*, where Montague returns to his homeland in Tyrone – The Black Pigs Dyke – on hearing the news of his mother's death. As he drives northwards from Cork, he encounters his 'homely Ulster swollen

/ To a plain of Blood'. But this initial shock is soon earthed by the affections of his father and mother. The myths of motherland and fatherland are replaced by the real and tender particularities of his own parents. And so we find the part of Montague's imagination which is tempted by the 'fomorian fierceness' of the old mythic gods – Cuchulain, Ceres, Dis and Gautama in *The Dead Kingdom* – giving way to a more contemporary experience of loss, dislocation and exile (even after his return 'home' to Ulster). In this way, Montague obliges myths to 'drink / from the trough of reality'. And yet he himself is simultaneously obliged to myth for offering him a distance from the immediacies of the overheated instant. Myth estranges his experience at the same time as he humanizes myth into experience. In poems such as 'The Sean Bhean Bhocht', 'Old Mythologies' and 'Virgo Hibernica', Montague struggles to address the 'legendary elements of his past, trying to take the weight of it in his verse without being bent low by it. History is important, but to be manageable it has to be shaped and stylised into images. The image thus becomes more than a representation of the past; it is also a mark of the poet's triumph over it. It is familiarised into his own idiom'.[16]

In the heel of the hunt, myth plays the role of witness to something absent. The mythological homeland of Tyrone is, for the poet, a ruined landscape, a ravaged recollection, the severed head of mute Gaeldom. If myth can be given voice again it is only as a testimony to contemporary homelessness. Montague's myths gravitate not towards collective ideology but towards incorrigible isolation.

*   *   *

Seamus Heaney is also obsessed with dreams of 'loss and origins'. Here again, the myths of origin – be they Neolithic, Celtic or Gaelic – can only be remembered as lost. Or else they are approached obliquely through an alien mythology. One encounters the memories of home away from home. The Nordic myths of Jutland provide an analogy for the myths of Heaney's native North. As he puts it in 'The Tollund Man', out there in the man-killing parish of Jutland he felt 'lost, unhappy and at home'. In an essay in *Preoccupations* Heaney unpacks this analogy. He tells of how he came across P.V. Glob's book *The Bog People* in 1969, the same year as the killing started in Ulster. The book is concerned with the discovery, in the bogs of Jutland, of the preserved bodies of men and women who had been strangled in a sacrificial ritual back in the Iron Age. The famous Tollund Man – to whom Heaney dedicates a poem in North – was just such a victim sacrificed to the mother goddess of the earth, who required the blood of new bride-grooms each year to renew her fertility. Heaney adds this telling comment: 'Taken in relation to the tradition of Irish political martyrdom for that cause whose icon is Cathleen Ni Houlihan, this is more than an archaic barbarous rite: it is an archetypal pattern. And the unforgettable photographs of these victims blended in my mind with photographs of atrocities past and present, in the long rites of Irish political and religious struggle'.[17]

Heaney fully recognizes the sacramental charge of Irish history, but he usually prefers to approach native mythologies through non-native ones. The Viking model is present, the Greek and Roman also. The mythic gods Heaney invokes as tutors are Terminus (god of boundaries and borders) and Janus (god of double vision). And he also draws from classical myth to exemplify the struggle in his own psyche between the god of reason (Hercules) and the god of ancestral memory (Antaeus). 'Hercules represents the balanced rational light while Antaeus represents the pieties of illiterate fidelity. The poem ['Hercules and Antaeus'] drifts towards an assent to Hercules, though there was a sort of nostalgia for Antaeus. . . . This is a see-saw, an advance–retire situation'.[18] This dialectic of advance–retire is equally evident whenever Heaney chooses examples from Irish myths. Sweeney is a case in point. And it is significant, I think, that Heaney opts for a figure of popular legend – the exiled madman of *Sweeney Astray* – rather than one of the heroes of mythology (Fionn, Cuchulain, Cormac, Fergus, and so on). Moreover, Sweeney is a largely comic figure transposable into contemporary mock-heroic settings – as in the third part of *Station Island* (the book) with its humorous play on 'Sweeney'/'Heaney'.

In short, Heaney approaches indigenous myths either indirectly, through borrowed myths (Nordic, Greek, Roman,) or through the detached eye of the 'inner emigré'. Joyce and Kavanagh are his guides here, rather than Yeats and the revivalists. And in the final visitation of 'Station Island' (the poem), we find Heaney replacing the archaeological myth of the bog – whose 'wet centre is bottomless' – with the more utopian myth of the sea. The wise and blind Joyce counsels Heaney to abandon the 'subject people stuff' of tribal grievance in favour of an imaginative leap:

It's time to swim

Out on your own and fill the element
With signatures of your own frequency . . .

Elver-gleams in the dark of the whole sea.

DUAL RESIDENTS

While Heaney found a mythic correlative of his native Ulster in the Nordic images of Jutland, Derek Mahon finds one in a Dutch painting of a courtyard in Delft. There is also a denominational inflection at work. Where the ritual sacrifices of the people to the earth goddess correspond to the sacrificial motifs of Heaney's cultural traditions (notably Catholicism and nationalism), the puritan orderliness of the painting – its 'chaste/precision' – provides Mahon with a utopian analogy for his Protestant Ulster tradition. What fascinates Mahon is the contrast between the elegantly 'pale light of that provincial town' and the violence of his own Belfast – a contemporary Irish legacy of the victory of the Dutch imperial forces of William of Orange. The painting of Delft by Pieter de Hooch in 1659 counterpoints the Battle of the Boyne waged by King Billy in 1690. But this image of what the Protestant ethic of civilization – as exemplified in the Dutch masterpiece – *could* have been for Ireland is shattered by the realization of what it actually produced: a band of sectarian marauders 'smashing crockery, with fire and sword'.

If Delft was to be something of a geographical utopia for Mahon's imagination, the aesthetic of modernism was to be his poetic utopia. In this, his mentors were Louis MacNeice and Samuel Beckett. Reminding him of the isolation of the artist in contemporary Ireland, these Irish modernists opened a path for Mahon which led him to such metaphysically minded authors as Cavafy, Villon, Pasternak, Rimbaud and Lowry. Here Mahon finds a community and a continuum denied him in his native province. He becomes a world citizen of letters, a provincial turned cosmopolitan. And in collections such as *Lives, Night-Crossing* and *The Hudson Letter* the poet's inability to find a home in either of the competing mythologies of North and South, Catholic and Protestant, nationalist and unionist, is celebrated as a token of liberty.

Mahon's 'dual residence' in a divided Irish culture is transformed on occasion into a virtue of 'non-residence'.[19] But Mahon never fully subscribes to this vocation of absentee wordlord. The ruined cityscape of Belfast continues to haunt his imagination. In the opening poem of *The Snow Party* (1975), Mahon confesses that no community of aesthetic minds has the right to turn its back on the pain of history. He adds ruefully:

Perhaps if I'd stayed behind
And lived it bomb by bomb
I might have grown up at last
And learnt what is meant by home.

A similar fidelity to the ravaged and forgotten people of history is registered in the final poem of this collection – 'A Disused Shed in Co. Wexford'. Based on a novel by J.G. Farrell about the Irish Civil War, called *Troubles*, it concludes with a plea from the silenced voices of the past not to be left in oblivion:

> They are begging us, you see, in their wordless way,
> To do something, to speak on their behalf
> Or at least not to close the door again.

Mahon ends a poem to the 'rubbled city' of Derry – written in 1979, ten years after the troubles broke out – with this curious image: 'A Russian freighter bound for home / Mourns to the city in its gloom'.

*　　*　　*

Paul Durcan – one of the most innovative and iconoclastic of the younger generation of Irish poets – begins his utopian quest where Mahon left off. In *Going Home to Russia* (1987), Durcan rejects the nationalist myth of motherland, vowing instead to discover in that snow-bound otherland of Russia the utopian home he could not find at home. Svetka, his contemporary Russian lover, replaces the ancestral Caitlín ni Houlihán at the heart of his poetic affections. Russia, that no-place of broken dreams and betrayed revolutions, becomes the true counterpoint to the cosy, comfortable middle-class life Durcan leaves behind in Ireland. Durcan discovers in this land of dissident poets not only the old birthplace of God ('God was born in Russia') but a new birthplace for himself. Surrendering to the sexual warmth of Svetka, Durcan is reborn into a new poetic identity and pleads with his adopted lover-mother to give him a name:

> To live again with nature as before I lived
> In Ireland before all the trees were felled
> Again collecting leaves in Moscow in October,
> Closer to you than I am to myself.

> My dear loved one, let me lick your nose;
> Nine months in your belly, I can smell your soul;
> Your two heads are smiling – not one but both of them -
> Isn't it good, Svetka, good, that I have come home?

> O Svetka, Svetka, Don't, don't!
> Say my name, O Say my name!
> O God O Russia! Don't, don't!
> Say my name, O say my name.

The critic Peter McDonald has remarked that, while Durcan's Russian poems are 'not reports from Utopia by any means, they are affirmative poems in which an escape is an escape into an unconstrained self, able to face up to its own obsessions and fears'.[20] This is true, if we are referring to Utopia with a capital U. But one of the greatest strengths of Durcan's collection is precisely the way it upsets our pre-conceptions about the meaning of such terms as 'utopia' and 'home'. If the Russian nation is a utopia betrayed and the Irish nation a utopia delayed (until the reunification of North and South), then, Durcan is saying, we must have done with the ideologies of nations. Durcan feels a foreigner in his native land and a native in foreign lands. His utopian images stem from a basic ambiguity towards sovereign homelands. As he puts it in the Russian sequence, 'Should there be anyone in the world who has not got mixed feelings?'. In Russia, Durcan feels home away from home. In Ireland he feels away from home at home. For Durcan, 'uncertainty is one way of defining any proper "home" for the imagination'.[21]

But Durcan does not confine his utopian glance to the role of born-again Russian. The critical powers of utopian imagination – as negation and affirmation – are also glimpsed in earlier collections such as *O Westport in the Light of Asia Minor* and *Berlin Wall Café*. In the former, he revisits his ancestral homeland in Westport, County Mayo – as Montague, Heaney and Mahon revisited their homelands before him – by way of detour through an alien land. Not Jutland, Brooklyn or Delft this time, but Asia Minor. Indeed, it could be said that Westport and Asia Minor have about as much in common as the umbrella and the sewing-machine which chanced to meet on Duchamps's surreal operating-table. And yet from the yoking together of these discordant places, Durcan opens up an imaginary no-place. In *Berlin Wall Café*, Durcan draws on the analogy of a divided Europe to provide an object-ive (geographical) correlative for the break-up of his marriage and his home. Through this analogy, and because of the avoidance of self-indulgent narcissism, the figure of his wife, Nessa, suggests 'mythical precedents'. Derek Mahon, for example, identifies her with Eurydice. But whether one agrees with him or not, it is clear that she is no Caitlín ni Houlihán and Durcan is no Cuchulain. The Pearsean passion is over. The temptation of martyrdom is resisted. One cannot imagine Mother Ireland saying to Pearse what wife tells husband in 'The Pietà's Over':

A man cannot be a messiah for ever,
Messiahing about in his wife's lap,
Suffering fluently in her arms,
Flowing up and down in the lee of her bosom,
Forever being mourned for by the eternal feminine. . . .
Painful as it was for me, I put you down off my knee
And I showed you the door.
Although you pleaded with me to keep you on my knee
And to mollycoddle you, humour you, within the family circle . . .
I would not give you shelter if you were homeless in the streets
For you must make your home in yourself, and not in a woman.
Keep going out the road for it is only out there -
Out there where the river achieves its riverlessness -
That you and I can become at last strangers to one another . . .

If sovereignty exists at all, it is not in rarefied mother figures or
motherlands but in the desolation of one's inner self. The *via negativa*
of family breakdown was not the only chastening influence on
Durcan's imagination The early collections already bore witness to a
scrupulous and unrelenting resolve to demythologize. In 'Fat Molly'
Durcan transmutes the sanitized Caitlín ni Houlihán of the Revival
into a carnivalesque big mama who taught him the 'perfectly useless'
'art of passionate kissing'. Celtic lore and *Book of Kells* calligraphy are
invoked in a parody of sexy Motherland:

Sweet, warm, and wet, were the kisses she kissed;
Juicy oranges on a naked platter.
She lived all alone in a crannog
which had an underwater zig-zag causeway
And people said – and it was not altogether a fiction -
That only a completely drunken man
could successfully negotiate Fat Molly's entrance;
Completely drunk, I used stagger home
And fall asleep in the arms of her laughter.

The demystification of Mother Ireland is also pursued in poems such
as 'Charlie's Mother', where the poet beseeches her to 'take her purple
veined hand out of my head'; and 'Ireland 1972', with its bitter evoca-
tion of tribal carnage:

Next to the fresh grave of my beloved grandmother
The grave of my first love murdered by my brother.

But it is probably in his satire 'Before the Celtic Yoke' (echoing Kavanagh's satire of the 'Irish thing') that Durcan's debunking of ideological myths finds most cogent expression. Imagining a time in Ireland before the Celtic yoke – 'before war insinuated its slime into the forests of the folk' – Durcan pleads for a prelapsarian language which might name without violence, praise without prejudice. Once again, as in Heaney's appeal for signatures like 'elver-gleams in the dark of the whole sea', the utopian tongue is associated with the maritime images of free passage, unencumbered by racial or imperial divisions:

> Elizabethan, Norman, Viking, Celt,
> Conquistadores all: . . .
> Thrusting their languages down my virgin throat . . .
> But I survive, recall
> That these are but Micky-come-latelies
> Puritanical, totalitarian, by contrast with my primal tongue:
> My vocabularies are boulders cast up on time's beaches;
> Masses of sea-rolled stones reared up in mile-high ricks
> Along the shores and curving coasts of all my island . . .
> In Ireland before the Celtic yoke I was the voice of Seeing
> And my Island people's Speaking was their Being.

In 'Ireland, 1977' Duncan professed himself a 'native who is an exile in his native land'. In view of his repudiation of the Celtic Revival and his gravitation towards the hinterlands of Russia, Berlin and Asia Minor, one can see what he means. It is not that Ireland gave him nothing. The Irish modernists opened novel horizons for him as they did for many other poets of his generation. 'James Joyce or Patrick Kavanagh', he writes, 'I believe in them'. But where Durcan differs from most of his contemporaries in Irish poetry is arguably in his postmodern collation of high art and popular culture. Thus one finds allusions to Dylan, Morrison, television and cinema alongside references to Pasternak, Voznesensky, Titian or Dali. Durcan is not afraid to mix the waters. Traditional ideologies are turned on their head, conventions flouted, expectations defied. And it is this polyphonous perspective in his work which allows the reader's imagination to conjure up new images from the flotsam and jetsam of the old. This is where his utopian impulse originates. Derek Mahon puts it well: 'If Durcan reads strangely to us, it's because we haven't got there yet – or rather, because we never can. He doesn't write out of a future where we have yet to arrive, for that would be merely to anticipate. He writes from lateral imaginative zones ... [and] it's the laterality, the sideways look (not, despite his degree in archaeology and medieval history, the "backward look"), the simultaneous presence of alternative modes of perception, that characterises his vision'.[22]

CRITICAL-UTOPIANS

In conclusion, I want to make brief mention of the critical-utopian approach to myth in the work of three additional contemporary poets: Medbh McGuckian, Brendan Kennelly and Paul Muldoon.

*   *   *

Medbh McGuckian ironizes the myths she uses, substituting her own personal meanings for orthodox public ones. This is especially evident in McGuckian's deployment of the myth of motherland. Invoking the conventional figure of woman as land, she subverts two standard associated tropes: (i) the militant goddess summoning her sons to bloody sacrifice; and (ii) the virginal maiden violated by the invading enemy. The refiguration of the traditional equations of woman and land has significant consequences, particularly for women writers' relation to nationalism. Challenging the stock appeal to the feminine figure of Ireland as a claim to some totalizing Irish identity, McGuckian debunks the 'essentialist' connection between language and land. For McGuckian, the mythology of motherland is transformed into a genealogy, a history which can only be experienced and recorded through an exploration of her own experience as a woman. It is her felt experience of contemporary Irishwomen's lack of authoritative roles which testifies to the falsity of the stereotypes of virgin or virago. The recovery of the history of Irish women is translated accordingly through the prism of private witness – through lived metaphors of body, sex and childbirth.[23] So doing, McGuckian contrives to bring private life into conflict with public myths. She exposes the codes – decoding and recoding women's sense of themselves. Rewriting thus the genesis of Irish womanhood, McGuckian discloses its indeterminability, its freedom to perpetually accrue new meanings.

In her poem 'Dovecoat', for example, McGuckian examines the nationalist response to the hunger strike of 1981 through the trope of the female body and childbirth. The poem is at once an account of (a) the private attempt of a woman to restore self-identity of body and mind after giving birth to the child which had occupied her body; and (b) the attempt of the Catholic community in Ulster to recover its sense of self-definition during the Long Kesh campaign. 'The Dovecoat becomes a symbol both of the woman's body which after childbirth "returns again to straight", and of the desire of the woman, and the Irish community, to be "one" and undivided: it reminds her "how seldom compound bows are truly sweet".'[24] For McGuckian the hunger-strikers are at 'the mercy of their own people' who used them to consolidate Ireland in its 'boat-shaped' insularity. The doves are described as innocent victims circling in on their treacherous home, instead of striking out on their own journey. 'The retreat into selfhood in the final stanza after the splitting of the body and the spirit in pregnancy, is imaged in terms of a rainfall (perhaps waters breaking), which enables her body to return to its former well-defined and self-sufficient shape. But this recovery of self-definition is at the expense of the doves whose hovering trustfully over the dovecote was described as a "cloud that never rains". Self-definition for both the woman and the Catholic community is achieved by "letting go" of the child/Strikers who were dependent on them for nurture.'[25] The poem insists on viewing the public myth of martyrdom through the prism of subjective experience – the response to the sacrificial rite of hunger-striking serving as analogy for the understanding of the personal experience of childbirth. The myths of national history are thus read back into the annals of personal history. They are internalized, 'privatized', restored to the lived traumas from which they first emerged.

Nowhere is this deconstructive gesture more obvious than in McGuckian's rewriting of the myth of motherland. The canonical mythology of Mother Ireland is radically reconsidered in the light of women's reproductive capacities. In contrast to the culturally debilitating emblems of the Sean Bhean Bhocht, Mother Eire or Caitlín ní Houlihán, McGuckian re-empowers the image of Irish women as sexually complex. The 'virginal-maternal' orthodoxy is destabilized so as to prevent the myth of motherland being used as a facile national symbol. Thus in poems like 'The Heiress' and others in *The Flower Master*, McGuckian may be said to occupy a 'displaced or marginal position in relation to a tradition in which she as a woman can only exist as the ground of nationalist "speculations". Because of this, her exploration of private and personal life must be read in terms of her attempt to reveal the complex nature of the female figure which has been used to bolster a narrative of the Irish nation'.[26] McGuckian repudiates the sublimating complicity between the sexual intangibility of women (as quasi-divine mothers or daughters) and the political intangibility of the nation. Woman finds herself in a place where she is of no use to the ideological agenda, nationalist or imperialist. Women's fertility becomes unappropriable for male mythology. Using a mix of grammatical asymmetry and surreal illogicality, McGuckian's language mimes this gesture of non-appropriation. And this linguistic *via negativa* is in turn complemented by a positive emphasis on both words and children as embodiments of constant growth – a perpetual genesis of meaning that can never be fixed in one position. Words and women revitalize the *idées fixes* of myth by giving birth to an unpredictable, utopian future.

Like other contemporary Irish poets – Eavan Boland, Eiléan ní Chuilleanáin and Nuala ní Dhómhnaill – McGuckian reconfigures myths of motherland, rejecting the use of 'Woman' as emblem for the idealized nation: an abstraction which objectifies women, depriving them of real, historical experience. Against such reductionism, McGuckian explores the positive metaphor of women as agents of genesis and futurity, refusing to treat them as figures for 'something else'. But it would be wrong to think of McGuckian repudiating her native tradition altogether. The target of her poetic irony is the simplification of the female figure as passive ornament or projection of male consciousness. Her aim is to 'reach back further into the Gaelic tradition, and to retrieve from the mythic and early Irish past an image of woman as sexually and socially active, desiring and powerful – an active figure which was progressively desexualized through the nineteenth century, through the twin pressures of Catholicism and celticism'.[27]

The result is a merging of archaic sexualized femininity with contemporary lived experience. The idealized *aisling* figure is replaced with the disruptive voice of women's experiential testimony – a testimony which transcends ideological myth and opens up new possibilities of language and life.

*   *   *

In *Cromwell* (1987) Kennelly sets out to unravel the competing myths which inform the collective memory of Cromwell. A more fitting emblem for the divided interpretations of British–Irish history could hardly be found. Cromwell is a redemptive hero for one ideological community, a satanic marauder for the other. What Kennelly does in this long poem is allow his own imagination to serve as an asylum – in both senses of that word – where the conflicting faces of Cromwell may show themselves, the masks of stereotype slipping off to reveal the underlying psychic energies which have mobilized people into political action. Kennelly can only exorcise himself of these ghostly and ghastly stereotypes by allowing them to rise up within himself as archetypes of his own unconscious. The antithetical figures of Cromwell and his alter ego, Buffún, thus serve as 'prisoners on parole from history, / Striving to come alive as I think I am'. But, in order to dispossess himself of the atavistic past, the poet must first allow it to enter his inner being. 'The butcher walked out the door of my emptiness, straight into me', as he puts it. The imagination knows no censorship. In mythology all is permitted. The poet is obliged accordingly to let go of his personal ego, with its built-in defence strategies. The conscious will must be suspended so that the *poiesis* of the unconscious may have its say. 'I do not want this dream', admits the poet, 'but it dreams me'.

This translation of Irish mythology into poetic psychodrama allows for a new sense of freedom to emerge. The stereotypes of political ideology are liberated into archetypes of utopian imagination. Demythologization becomes the precondition of remythologization. The primary object of critique is the fetish of Celtic purity which has obsessed so many advocates of the Revival. Kennelly is especially trenchant in his deflation of the sentimental quest for the Holy Grail of identity:

> I sing tragic songs, I am madly funny,
> I'd sell my country for a fist of money . . . .
> I am a home-made bomb, a smuggled gun.
> I like to whine about identity,
> I know as little of love as it is possible
> to know, I bullshit about being Free . . . .

Douglas Hyde put his finger on a crucial paradox in the Irish psyche when he observed that 'the English are the people we love to hate yet never cease to imitate'. This is the tangle of self and anti-self which Kennelly seeks to unwind in his imaginative variation of the different guises which Cromwell assumes in us. 'All his faces' are passed in review – puritanical priest, drunken doctor, boastful philanderer, sadist, even a battle-weary emperor pleading to be entertained by his fanciful slave, 'Fatuus Homunculus Hibernicus'.

Passing thus through the psychic purgatory of self-analysis, disclosing the ideological memories which drive us to fury and despair, Kennelly is finally in a position to explore a utopian dimension of myth which points beyond the ruins of the past. Having debunked the demons of Cromwell and Buffún – by transmuting them into mock-heroic fictions – the poet imagines the possibility of another kind of home in history. 'I am an emigrant in whose brain / Ireland bleeds and cannot cease / to bleed till I come home again.' Once he has stripped the 'old man', 'swaddled in lies' of his false mythology, Kennelly is liberated into a positive ignorance, free to reconnect with foreclosed dimensions of being. The dissolution of orthodox myth releases new energies for the re-creation of utopian myth. Having tranversed the 'dirt road' in his own mind, the poet eventually emerges in another place, untrammelled by undergrowth, guided by sea-light, echoing with 'children-words'. The maritime metaphor returns once again to capture the sense of this utopian homecoming:

This could be home, God knows, strange territory,
A glimpsed lit strip of sea, shifting . . .

Kennelly's poetic myth-making brings us to the edge of the sea. But he does not set sail. He leaves the voyaging to each one of us.

* * *

There is a recurrent motif of sea voyage in Irish legend. This is most powerfully evident in the *immram* chronicles of expedition and adventure, written mainly between the seventh and ninth centuries. This is the material from which the Northern poet Paul Muldoon forges his poetic utopia in *Why Brownlee Left* (1980). To avoid the temptation to sentimentalize the myth of voyage in some kind of revivalist gesture – after all, the *immram* tales feature some of Ireland's most revered saints and scholars – Muldoon deploys a postmodern device of collage, blending old Celtic quest motifs with contemporary Raymond Chandler idioms.

Parody abounds in this poetic parable. The author's own name, Muldoon, is a contemporary homonym of the ancestral wanderer Mael Duin, protagonist of the most famous *immram* tale. The original version recounts how Mael Duin set out on a journey to avenge his murdered father, Ailill, only to encounter (at least in the Christian rewriting of the pagan version) an old hermit who counsels forgiveness. Muldoon's *immram* begins with the narrator's claim that his 'old man was an asshole' and his mother an addict. Indeed, this desacramentalizing of fatherland and motherland itself recapitulates an earlier poem of Muldoon's, 'Aisling', where the maternal figure of Dark Rosaleen is recast in the persona of Anorexia. From the outset, Muldoon's quest hero, who goes by the whimsical name of Golightly, is a 'foster' son who plays about in an urban 'pool-hall' – a possible reference to his hybrid heritage, conflating idioms of high and popular culture. Similarly, Muldoon's hermit is modelled on a Californian Howard Hughes, and the wandering islands of the ancient legend take the form of heroin joints, strip clubs, penthouse suites, skyscraper hotels, hallucinatory morgues and evangelical missions. The writing itself features a multilayered pastiche of previous literary versions of the voyage motif – from Shakespeare, Spenser and Byron to Tennyson, MacNeice and Chandler. In this sense, Muldoon's 'Immram' could be seen as a poetic counterpart of Joyce's parody of the genesis of English prose narrative in the 'Oxen of the Sun' episode in *Ulysses*. Indeed, Joyce's 'Ithaca' crops up here too, but now transported from Dublin in the 1900s to New York in the 1980s.

There is, however, an even more immediate Irish precedent for Muldoon's parody of the voyage tale – and that is Louis MacNeice's version of the *immram* in 'The Mad Islands'. It is instructive to compare the two. MacNeice concludes his modernist rendering of the myth with the voyager returning to a 'house / he could not remember seeing before'. Having found forgiveness, 'he raised his hand and blessed his home'. Muldoon's postmodernist reading also ends with absolution and homecoming; but there is a twist. Muldoon himself describes the conclusion of his poem as a 'whimsical dismissal by the bane of both their [father's and son's] lives. 'I forgive you . . . and I forget'.[28] Home is located not in a 'house' but in the flow of life in Main Street.

Muldoon takes more liberties than MacNeice in his rewriting of the original *Immram Mael Duin*. His rendering is more brazen and 'whimful' (to cite one of his favourite neologisms). His imagination more attuned to the broken and often hysterical voices of post-1969 Ulster. Muldoon's utopia is hard-won. 'My poem', he concedes, 'takes the episodes and motifs of the original and twists them around, sometimes out of all recognition'.[29] The reverent attitudes of hagiography – traditionally associated with the legends of missionary saints – mutate into attitudes of hallucination and humour. The Irish-American expert Brendan O'Leary serves as consultant for Muldoon's postmodern narrator, alluding to both the 1960s LSD guru Timothy O'Leary, and to the fakery of Irish-American sentimentalism for a lost homeland – *Brendan O'Leary's / Grand-mother's pee was green, / And that was why she had to leave old Skibbereen'.*[30]

Muldoon's use of maritime and cosmopolitan idioms deterritorializes the inherited equation of national sovereignty with land. But Muldoon does not jettison the energies of myth altogether. There is a powerful labour of remythologizing going on in Muldoon's rewriting of the *immram* legend. A utopian horizon of free passage between multiple islands opens before us. The two-way flow of life in Main Street alludes to a frontierless seascape where people may be as mixed up and 'mulish' as they wish. The acceptance of difference is an integral part of Muldoon's dream. Culture is not purity but fusion. Literature is not a

continuum but a matter of 'singleminded swervings'. The end of his art
– and of the utopian revisions of myth which he and several of his
contemporaries have undertaken – is not the recovery of some long-lost
'original' identity, but peace.

Part III
Philosophy

9　George Berkeley
We Irish think otherwise

My father introduced me to Berkeley's philosophy at the age of ten.
Before I was even able to read or write properly he taught me to
think. He was a professor of psychology and every day after dinner
he would give me a philosophy lesson. I remember very well how he
first introduced me to Berkeley's idealist metaphysics and particularly his doctrine that the material or empirical world is an invention
of the creative mind: to be is to be perceived / *esse est percipi*. It was
one day after a good lunch when my father took an orange in his
hand and asked me: 'What colour is this fruit?' 'Orange', I replied. 'Is
this colour in the orange or in your perception of it?' he continued:
'And the taste of the sweetness – is that in the orange itself or is it the
sensation on your tongue that makes it sweet?' This was a revelation
to me: that the outside world is as we perceive or imagine it to be. It
does not exist independently of our minds. From that day forth, I
realised that reality and fiction were betrothed to each other, that
even our ideas are creative fictions.[1]

The author of these words is not Irish, but the Argentine fiction writer
Jorge-Luis Borges. There are, I suspect, few, if any, Irish citizens who
could boast of assimilating Berkeley's metaphysics with their father's
postprandial oranges. Berkeley is not a household name in Ireland as
Descartes or Sartre are in France, Kant or Hegel in Germany, Locke or
Mill in England, or Kierkegaard in Denmark. This is not altogether
surprising when one considers that, even at university level, Berkeley's
philosophy has usually been relegated to specialized courses on 'British
Empiricism' rather than included as a central component of any general course of Irish Studies. Although Berkeley is one of Ireland's most
distinguished philosophers, along with John Scotus Erigena and John
Toland, his name adorns no major Irish institution (unlike the famous
Berkeley college in California). In recent years, this conspicuous neglect

of Berkeley in the land of his birth has been partially remedied, thanks in large part to the pioneering research of a handful of scholars – most notably Luce, Bracken and Berman.[2] The decision to name the new library in Trinity College, Dublin after Berkeley and to commemorate his bicentenary in 1985 with a special stamp bearing his portrait are perhaps further signs of Ireland's belated willingness to properly acknowledge one of its foremost thinkers.

In a number of passages in his *Philosophical Commentaries*, Berkeley explicitly identifies himself as an Irishman. He refers to Newton as a 'philosopher from the neighbouring nation' and rejects the argument of the English empiricist, John Locke, with the celebrated retort: 'We *Irish* think otherwise'. Variations of this formula are repeated at several key points in the *Commentaries* and can be variously interpreted. Berkeley himself, however, affirmed an Irish dimension to his thought which the official annals of our cultural history have been slow to acknowledge, for reasons discussed in our studies of Toland and Tyndall below.

What exactly did Berkeley mean by the phrase: 'We Irish think otherwise'? This question may be answered by assessing the 'Irish' dimension of Berkeley under three main categories: (1) biographical; (2) philosophical; and (3) ideological.

BIOGRAPHICAL CONSIDERATIONS

The basic minimum requirement for calling Berkeley an 'Irish' philosopher is that he was born and educated, lived and worked in Ireland.[3] This biographical dimension is uncontroversial.

Berkeley was born near Kilkenny on 12 March 1685. He first attended Kilkenny College (the Alma Mater of Swift and Congreve) before matriculating at Trinity College Dublin in 1700 at the age of 15. Berkeley's association with Trinity was to last 24 years. He received his BA Degree in 1704 and was elected Fellow in 1707, lecturing in Greek and Hebrew and also serving as College Librarian for a time. In 1710 Berkeley was ordained a priest of the Church of Ireland and was made a Doctor of Divinity in 1721. He was later appointed Dean of Derry (1724) and finally Bishop of Cloyne (1734) where he pursued an isolated career devoted to local pastoral concerns until he left for Oxford in 1753 where he died six months later.

Berkeley also spent several years outside of Ireland. Between 1713 and 1721, he made a number of important journeys to Britain and the Continent. In Paris in 1713, he met Malebranche, one of the most renowned Cartesian Idealists of the time. In London he became a close associate of Addison, Steele, Swift and Pope (who was to pay him the generous tribute – 'To Berkeley every virtue under Heaven'). Berkeley's most famous voyage was undoubtedly his expedition to Rhode Island in America in 1729 where he spent three years campaigning to establish an international college in Bermuda to educate the American colonists and train missionaries for the conversion of the Indians. The project ultimately failed due to a series of broken promises by London financiers and parliamentarians; Berkeley College in San Francisco bears commemorative witness to the idealism of 'the first great Irish-American' (as Berman calls him), an Irishman whose unbridled humanitarianism and pioneering zeal made as much impact internationally as nationally.

Most of Berkeley's writings were produced in Ireland and some were directly about Ireland. During his formative years in Trinity (1704–7), Berkeley developed his famous 'immaterialist' philosophy in his *Philosophical Commentaries*. (This was later reformulated in his magnum opus, *The Principles of Human Knowledge* (1710) and his somewhat more polemical *Dialogues* (1713).) Other writings of Berkeley address themselves explicitly to contemporary Irish matters, religious, social and economic – in particular his late works, *The Querist* (1737), *Siris* (1744) and *A Word to the Wise* (1749). We shall return to the ideological background of Berkeley's later writings on Ireland in the third section of this chapter.

PHILOSOPHICAL CONSIDERATIONS

If it is indisputable, therefore, that Berkeley was 'Irish' from a biographical point of view, the question remains as to whether there is anything 'Irish' about his thinking – any intellectual characteristics or concerns which might in some way distinguish Berkeley as an Irish mind.

When Berkeley used such phrases in the *Philosophical Commentaries* as 'We Irish think otherwise', or 'We Irish do not hold with this' or 'We Irishmen cannot attain to those truths' (entries 392, 393, 394, 398, etc.), he was clearly counting himself Irish in a way that dissociates his thinking from the 'philosophies of the neighbouring island' – i.e. the empiricist and mechanist theories of Locke and Newton.

Most philosophical commentators of Berkeley have simply ignored such phrases; however they are interpreted, they subvert the orthodox view of Berkeley as one of the founding fathers – along with Locke and Hume – of what is commonly known as 'British empiricism'. This official view, habitually advanced by the Oxford and Cambridge tradition of philosophy, has been challenged by a number of scholars in recent years – most notably A.A. Luce and Harry Bracken.

In a note on the 'We Irish' entries in the *Philosophical Commentaries*, Luce claims that 'we need not read a political reference into the words. Berkeley certainly regarded himself as an Irishman . . . but when he writes "we Irishmen", he simply means "we ordinary folk", shrewd judges of fact and commonsense'.[4] Such caveats notwithstanding, Luce proceeds to challenge the commonplace interpretation of Berkeley as a mere disciple of Locke and the British empiricists, arguing that the 'way to the heart of Berkeleyianism lies through Malebranche' (the Continental Idealist of the anti-empiricist tradition).[5]

In a study entitled 'George Berkeley: the Irish Cartesian', Harry Bracken pursues a stronger version of this thesis. He writes: 'Berkeley's classification (along with John Locke and David Hume) as *British empiricists* helped create the picture of him as an outsider to Irish intellectual currents. Berkeley's arguments ought to be taken more seriously in their own right, rather than be forced into a preconceived abstract framework. One stands a better chance of understanding Berkeley if one reads him as an Irish Cartesian than as a "British Empiricist"'.[6]

Bracken makes clear that his claim that Berkeley is an Irish Cartesian is in no way committed to a political thesis about the role of a national culture. Bracken convincingly demonstrates the profound, if habitually ignored, differences between Berkeley's *philosophy* and that of the British empiricists.

Berkeley was intimately versed in the continental idealism of Descartes, Malebranche and Bayle (access to whose works was available through Archbishop Marsh's well-endowed library in Dublin). In stark opposition to Locke, Berkeley subscribed to the idealist thesis that the mind has an intellectual vision which is irreducible to materially caused sensations. Endorsing the 'immaterialism' of Malebranche, he sought to replace ephemeral sensory ideas with 'tough substantial ideas' ultimately sustained by Divine Vision.

Berkeley's preference for the idealist rather than empiricist model of understanding is most evident in his numerous refutations of Locke. He categorically rejects the Lockean notion that ideas of qualities are related directly or indirectly to patterns which exist in material objects. Locke's empiricist doctrine of material substance is, for Berkeley, conceptually absurd (for if our ideas of secondary qualities such as colour or warmth do not actually *resemble* the material things themselves, as Locke himself admits, then it is impossible to compare our mental ideas with the material substances which supposedly cause them; or, what is more, to know whether our ideas of them are therefore true or false). In brief, Berkeley contended that Locke's attempt to sustain an atomistic and mechanistic relationship between mind and matter is false, and ultimately vulnerable to scepticism. To offset such scepticism, Berkeley argues instead for a radical immaterialism which holds that ideas cannot exist without a mind to perceive them. Hence his famous *esse est percipi* (to be is to be perceived). For something to exist it must be perceived by an immaterial mind – human or divine. This conclusion that ideas stand in a necessary relation to minds is radically non-Lockean. Equally so is Berkeley's further conclusion that since some ideas are independent of our human will, they must depend on some other Mind or Spirit – i.e. God.

Berkeley considered his discovery of immaterialism as a radical break with the dominant theses of British empiricism, dissolving at once the appearance / reality dichotomy which lay at the root of scepticism and affirming the existence of a substantial immaterial self and of a divine Mind. Indeed Berkeley's philosophical contemporaries did not see him as an empiricist (the 'British empiricist' schema of Locke–Berkeley–Hume did not come into prominence for another century). One French reviewer of the time referred to Berkeley as a *Malebranchiste de bonne foi*. And the celebrated continental Idealists, Leibniz and Wolff, hailed him as a 'kindred spirit'.[7]

Berkeley was by no means the only Irish philosopher of his time to engage in the great European philosophical debates of the eighteenth century, or to champion the cause of continental Idealism against the theories of British Empiricism. A host of other distinguished Irish thinkers – including Clayton, Hutcheson, Swift, Burke and Skelton – shared Berkeley's position on a number of crucial points. But here we begin to touch on the 'ideological considerations' of our final section.

IDEOLOGICAL CONSIDERATIONS

Our analysis above has suggested that Berkeley may be legitimately called an "Irish thinker" in the sense (1) that he was born and educated, lived and worked in Ireland, and (2) that his philosophy amounted, in significant measure, to a refutation of the dominant British philosophy of the time (i.e. Berkeley was an Irish Idealist not a British Empiricist). This might be called the 'minimalist' argument for Berkeley's 'Irishness'. The 'maximalist' argument goes further in claiming that there is something specifically Irish about the character and content of Berkeley's writings.

Sometimes this claim takes the form of positing some metaphysical cast of mind developed over the centuries. Jorge-Luis Borges makes such a supposition when he observes that 'as an outsider looking on successive Irish thinkers', he has been struck by a number of 'unusual and remarkable repetitions'. He offers the following examples:

> Berkeley was the first Irish philosopher I read, from the *Principles* and the *Three Dialogues to Siris*, and even his messianic poem about the future of the Americas: 'The course of Empire takes its sway . . . etc.' Then followed my fascination for Wilde, Shaw and Joyce. And finally there was John Scotus Erigena, the Irish metaphysician of the 9th century. I loved to read Erigena, especially his *De Divisone Naturae*, which taught that God creates himself through the creation of his creatures in nature. I have all of his books in my library. I discovered that Berkeley's doctrine of the creative power of the mind was already anticipated by Erigena's metaphysics of creation and that this in turn recurred in several other Irish writers. In the last two pages of the foreword to *Back to Methuselah*, we find Shaw outlining a philosophical system remarkably akin to Erigena's system of things coming from the mind of God and returning to him. In short, what Shaw calls the life-force plays the same role in his system as God does in Erigena's. I was also very struck by the fact that both Shaw and Erigena held that all genuine creation stems from a metaphysical nothingness, what Erigena called the 'Nihil' of God, which resided at the heart of our existence. I doubt that Shaw ever read Erigena; he certainly showed very little interest in medieval philosophy. And yet the coincidence of thought is there. I suspect it has less to do with nationalism than with metaphysics.[8]

On other occasions, however, the affirmation of an Irish dimension to Berkeley's thought does assume a markedly nationalist character. This is certainly true of Yeats, for example, when he hails Berkeley's statement about 'We Irish thinking otherwise' as the 'birth of the national intellect'. Yeats enthusiastically endorsed Berkeley's defence of visionary powers of mind against the narrow mechanistic reductionism of British empiricism. He declared himself 'attracted beyond expression' to Berkeley's idealist championing of the 'intellectual fire' of imagination, thereby liberating the mind from its servility to material reality into a quasi-divine creativity.[9] Locke's empiricism had 'taken away the world', wrote Yeats, and 'given us excrement instead'. Or as Yeats put it in another famous stanza: 'Locke sank into a swoon, the Garden died / God took the spinning jenny out of his side' (i.e. Locke's denial of the creative powers of the mind was the occasion of the second 'fall' from the spiritual Garden of Eden into the mechanistic and dehumanizing Industrial age). But Yeats did not see Berkeley as an isolated defender of spiritual vision against the mechanism of Newton and Locke. He went much further and developed his reading of Berkeley in conformity with the Revivalist ideology of a continuous Irish intellectual tradition counting among its members Swift, Goldsmith, Sheridan and others. 'Born in such a community', wrote Yeats, 'Berkeley with his belief in (spiritual) perception, that abstract ideas are mere words, Swift with his love of perfect nature, of the Houyhnhnms, his disbelief in Newton's system and every sort of machine, Goldsmith and his delight in the particulars of common life that shocked his contemporaries, Burke with his conviction that all states not grown slowly like a forest tree are tyrannies, found in England the opposite that stung their own thought into expression and made it lucid'.[10]

It has been argued that Yeats's retrospective invocation of an Irish intellectual tradition constituted a 'mythologizing' of the historical past which suited not only Yeats's *nationalist revivalism* (his need for an unbroken continuity between tradition and the present) but also his *Ascendancy conservatism*.[11] By positing the myth of a unifying intellectual continuity between past and present, Yeats was in fact denying the political discontinuities – ruptures, conflicts, discordances – of Ireland's colonial history. In this respect, it is telling that all of those included by Yeats in his privileged intellectual pantheon – with the exception of Burke – belong to the Anglo-Irish Protestant Ascendancy. And one suspects, moreover, that it is to this same tradition that Yeats refers when he invokes the lineage of 'We Irish' in his poem, *The Statues:*

> We Irish, born into that ancient sect
> But thrown upon this filthy modern tide
> And by its formless spawning fury wrecked
> Climb to our proper dark, that we may trace
> The lineaments of a plummet-measured face.

But if this is how Yeats employed the term 'We Irish', can the same be said of Berkeley? It would certainly be a gross anachronism to suppose that Berkeley shared Yeats's commitment to revivalist nationalism. But there is some evidence to support the view that Berkeley was (in Raymond Houghton's phrase) a 'patriotic, if colonial, nationalist'. When Berkeley's writings do touch on Irish political or social matters (e.g. *The Querist, Siris, A Word to the Wise*, etc.), the notion of 'We Irish' often assumes the form of an identification with the interest of the Anglo-Irish Ascendancy as distinct from *both* their imperial British neighbours *and* their subordinate Catholic compatriots. Berkeley clearly saw Protestant Ireland as a separate nation with a separate parliament (indeed he was himself a member of the Dublin parliament). Englishmen belonged to the 'neighbouring nation'. But within this Irish nation Berkeley observes a distinction between the Protestant interests of 'We Irish' and the subordinate interests of what he refers to, on occasion, as 'our poor Irish' (or the Catholic 'natives'). For the most part, Berkeley campaigned for social and economic reforms which would benefit all Irish communities. And there can be little doubt that he was motivated here by a profound humanitarian compassion for all his fellow countrymen. But whenever the interests of these two communities enter into conflict, Berkeley's allegiance to the Protestant position is paramount.

Let me take some examples. While it is true that Berkeley was never actively involved in Irish parliamentary politics – though a member of the Dublin parliament, he never participated in its legislative debates – he did in his later years as Bishop of Cloyne (in County Cork) publish several important writings on Irish matters of social concern. In a parish where Catholics outnumbered Protestants eight to one, Berkeley was confronted daily with the suffering and poverty of his Catholic compatriots. But while the overall tone of *The Querist* (his most significant text on the national question) was one of deep preoccupation with the Catholic Irish, the details of his social analysis almost invariably remained within the prevailing framework of Protestant policy. Unlike Swift, Berkeley was never prepared to radically challenge this policy. And what reforms he did recommend, although quite progressive, were almost always couched in terms likely to preserve the interests of his Ascendancy class.

(a) On the *land question*, when Berkeley asks in *The Querist* whether allowing 'Roman Catholics to purchase forfeited lands would not be a good policy', he adds significantly '. . . as tending to unite their interests with that of the Government'. In his later work *A Word to the Wise,* Berkeley revokes this moderate strategy. In response to the argument that for those who possess no land of their own, 'there is no small encouragement . . . to build or plant upon another's land, wherein they have only a temporary interest', Berkeley offers the condescending reply 'that life itself is but temporary'.

(b) On the *language question*, Berkeley was something of an exception in counselling his Protestant countrymen to learn Irish. But his primary reason for such counsel is, once again, revealing: it may well be 'the most practicable means for converting the natives'. This allusion to the 'natives' is illustrative of the illiberal pragmatism underlying much of Berkeley's liberal preaching. Indeed one might recall here

Berkeley's advice to the reluctant colonial planters in Rhode Island that they convert their black slaves to Christianity since 'their slaves would be better slaves for being Christian'.[12]

(c) On the *political question*, Berkeley's position remained that of an Ascendancy conservative. The climate of Irish politics in Berkeley's time was tumultuous, or at best uncertain. James II had been defeated by William of Orange at the Boyne, Queen Anne had no heir, and her half-brother (the 'Old Pretender') was hovering menacingly in the background. The question of legitimate authority and compliance was, therefore, a foremost consideration for Berkeley when he wrote his three sermons on *Passive Obedience*. 'With Anne having no child of her own', as Raymond Houghton remarks, 'The Protestant Ascendancy in Ireland was highly anxious over the question of succession and seeking to assure their continued control. It could hardly be said that Berkeley's writings were restricted to abstract themes. It was the equivalent of the most learned of contemporary philosophers commenting on the present political state of Northern Ireland'.[13] In his sermons on *Passive Obedience*, delivered at the Trinity College chapel in 1712, Berkeley extrapolated from Romans (XIII, 2): 'Whoever resisteth the power, resisteth the ordinance of God', warning that rebellion is a 'breach of the law of nature' which can easily terminate in 'anarchy'. Thus, even though it was rumoured that Berkeley had a certain sympathy for the Jacobite cause, there is little evidence to support this suspicion. Indeed, Berkeley published two letters against the second Jacobite rebellion of 1745 and also raised and equipped a troop of horses.[14]

(d) On the *economic question*, Berkeley's identification with the prevailing Protestant ideology is once again apparent. While he made an innovative proposal that Ireland should establish her own national bank, as part of a long-term cure for the basic economic ills of the country, there can be little doubt that he envisaged the ownership rights of such a bank's residing with the ruling class. In his influential pamphlet, *A Word to the Wise*, subtitled, *An Exhortation to the Roman Catholic Clergy of Ireland*, Berkeley appeals to the Catholic Church to improve the economic lot of the Irish poor by conquering what he terms their 'innate hereditary sloth'. Berkeley is prepared to acknowledge the existence of certain 'obstructions' to such improvements in the social order such as the exclusion of Catholics from civil employments and the occasional 'hardness of the landlord'. But he insists nonetheless that the 'discouragements' of these and other Penal Laws should not prevent the humbler Catholics from achieving a modest prosperity. The most fundamental obstruction to such prosperity, Berkeley submits, is the inherent laziness of the Irish Catholics themselves. Accordingly, the real remedy for poverty resides not with the government but with the active involvement of the Catholic clergy. For 'our poor Irish', explains Berkeley, are 'distinguished above all others by sloth, dirt and beggary'.[15]

Though some members of the Catholic clergy returned their 'sincere and hearty thanks to the worthy author' of *A Word to the Wise* for his useful advice, others were less acquiescent. One Northern clergyman composed *An Answer to the Bishop of Cloyne's Exhortation to the Roman Catholics* in which he pointed out that 'sloth and idleness are no more peculiar to our countrymen, than they are to any other people on earth, and that those who are now remarkable for their industry (e.g. the Dutch, French, etc.) would in our circumstance be whatever we are'. This clergyman concludes that Berkeley's advice amounts in fact to an 'obloquy thrown upon us by those whom self-interest has biased against us ... and whose determined resolution it has been for many years past, and still is, to render us poor and miserable'.[16]

(e) Finally, the *religious question*. Even though Berkeley supported inter-Church cooperation in his local parish and was in frequent dialogue with his Catholic countrymen, he never radically departed from the view that such cooperation best serves Christian charity by also serving Protestant interests. Berkeley was before his time, for example, in urging that Catholics be admitted to Trinity College without obliging them to attend Chapel, catechism or divinity lectures, 'in imitation of the Jesuits in Paris, who admit Protestants to study in their colleges' (*The Querist*). But the reasons he actually gives for providing well-off Catholics with education in Ireland are that such a move might: (1) 'keep money in the Kingdom'; and (2) 'prevent the prejudices of a foreign education'. Berkeley certainly had no great love for the Jesuits and showed himself extremely suspicious of their conspiratorial 'popery'. Indeed, he even maintained in *Alciphron* (1732) that the 'Emissaries of Rome are known to have personated several other sects, which from time to time have sprung up amongst us'. The conspiracy theory, as David Berman has demonstrated, was also shared by other prominent intellectuals of the Anglo-Irish Ascendancy at that time – most notably Swift and Skelton. It was directed particularly against the free-thinking 'republican' philosophy of John Toland, born a Gaelic-speaking Catholic in Donegal but subsequently a convert to dissenting Presbyterianism and finally to his own brand of humanist Deism. Toland was variously denounced by the Ascendancy thinkers as a 'Jesuit', 'an Irish priest' and 'the son of an Irish priest'. And when faced with the logical objection that Toland's principal work *Christianity not Mysterious*, actually condemned the 'principles of popery and superstition', the advocates of the campaign against Toland replied: 'That's nothing: for Jesuits to unsettle us will even preach against their own religion!'.[17] We shall return to this theme in the study of Toland which follows.

The great flowering of Irish thought between 1692 and 1757 which produced such extraordinary intellectuals as Berkeley, Swift, Burke, Skelton, Brown and others, was generally characterized by a counter-Enlightenment tendency. This philosophy, as David Berman argues in 'The Irish Counter-Enlightenment', was ideologically informed, in part at least, by the need of the Irish Ascendancy to justify their privileged position as a governing elite against both the free-thinking trends of the Enlightenment and the Jacobite sympathies of the Catholic population. It is in such a context that we can better appreciate how Toland became a scapegoat for Berkeley and his Protestant colleagues in so far as his Catholic formation and Enlightenment views (though, in several respects, theologically incompatible) were seen as conspiring allies in the attempt to subvert the Establishment. In *Christianity not Mysterious*, Toland had proposed a free-thinking, rational and tolerant religion (Latitudinarianism) which would reconcile all religious creeds and communities. Swift denounced Toland as the 'Great Oracle of Anti-Christians' in *An Argument against the Abolishing of Christianity* (1711), endorsing Berkeley's view that the acceptance of Enlightenment Deism would be the 'readiest course we can take to introduce popery'.

In *Alciphron*, Berkeley himself counters Toland's call for a rational or unmysterious religion with the argument that since religion is an 'emotional' rather than 'cognitive' act, the mysteries of the Christian faith are sacrosanct. Berkeley also defends here the views of fellow Irish Anglicans (King, Brown and Synge) that God's mystery is unassailable since He is 'an Unknown Subject of Attributes absolutely unknown'. One of the main reasons for the attack by these Counter-Enlightenment Irishmen against such pro-Enlightenment Irishmen as Toland, Emlyn and Clayton is, Berman suggests, that if the nation no longer believed in Christian mysteries there would no longer be a sound theological justification for the existence of *different* Christian religions – and by extension no sound reason for upholding the Penal Laws in Ireland which safeguarded the privileges of the Anglican Ascendancy. In short, the Counter-Enlightenment character of most Irish philosophy in the eighteenth century was at least partly motivated by the fear of the ruling class in Ireland that 'free thought as a tolerant, enlightening and counter-divisive force, could insidiously undermine the privileged status of the Ascendancy. . . . The Christian mysteries were needed by the Irish Anglicans to divide, explain or (as some would say) mystify'.[18]

CONCLUSION

The fact that Berkeley's writings sometimes reflected, consciously or otherwise, the dominant ideology of Irish Protestantism does not invalidate the genius of his philosophy or the central role it played in the 'golden age' of Irish thinking. More to the point, Berkeley's close identification with the intellectual tradition of the Irish Anglicans, while not always endearing, does not make him any less *Irish*. And this Irish dimension is evidenced in a number of key facts: (1) Berkeley's birth and life in Ireland; (2) his long and intimate association with Trinity College, where he first developed his theory of immaterialism against the empiricist thinkers of the 'neighbouring nation'; (3) his active intellectual involvement with political and economic matters of national import; and (4) his participation in the Counter-Enlightenment movement of Irish thought, a movement deeply informed by the particular ideology of Irish Anglicans in the eighteenth century.

One is compelled to conclude, however, that Berkeley's Irishness was more complex than that of mere apologist for his Protestant planter class. While Berkeley's patriotism occasionally reads (as it does in Swift) as a form of 'colonial nationalism',[19] it was at bottom, more generous than this. His repeated protestations against English injustice were as inspired by concern for the suffering 'poor Irish' as by interest to promote his own Anglo-Irish class. Moreover, Berkeley's pedagogical commitment to the Bermuda Mission in the Americas, and to the movement of Cartesian idealism on the European Continent, showed him to be above all else a 'cosmopolitan' Irish mind – like Toland before him and Tyndall after him.

10 John Toland

An Irish Philosopher?

John Toland was condemned by the Irish parliament and denounced from church pulpits all over Ireland after the publication in 1696 of his controversial book, *Christianity not Mysterious*. Threatened with arrest, Toland fled abroad (not for the first time). Then only 26, he was to spend the remainder of his years in exile, philosophizing, publishing and polemicizing on the burning issues of his time. On his death-bed in 1722, Toland signed one of his last books, *Pantheisticon*, with what he claimed was his original baptismal name Janus Junius Edganesius – a signature indicating his place of birth on the Inis Eoghain peninsula in Donegal in accordance with native Gaelic practice. Beside this baptismal name, he added the pseudonym *Cosmopoli*, meaning 'one who belongs to the world'.

But who was John Toland? Those who have tried to answer this question have generally given up in despair. Pierre des Maizeaux, who embarked on a biography shortly after Toland's death, found the materials insufficient. The intervening two-and-a-half centuries have not improved matters, as Robert Sullivan admits in his recent mammoth study of the man: 'Toland habitually covered his tracks, and the bulk of his papers have been destroyed. Coming across the order "burn this" on the charred fragment of a letter concerning Toland, a researcher must wonder how much [else] has been lost besides'.[1] Toland himself proposes some solution to this anticipated dilemma – 'If you would know more of him (he writes of himself) search his writings' (*caetera scriptis pete*).[2] But this, as we shall see, is no solution. Toland's final self-description, inscribed in a Latin epitaph on his grave in a Putney churchyard, declared that he would rise again, 'yet never to [be] the same Toland more' (*At idem futurus Tolandus nunquam*). But who, one is compelled to ask, is the *same* Toland? *Which* Toland are we talking about? Even in death, John Toland continued to tease and mystify.[3] He chose to remain an enigma.

A MIGRANT MIND

While no definitive portrait of Toland is possible, a rough identikit can be assembled from the odd records (and rumours) that have survived. Here is a list of some of the more salient features. Born an Irish-speaking Catholic in Donegal, Toland subsequently acquired nine other languages, and as many other religions, as he journeyed through Britain and the continent. A shepherd-boy until the age of 14, he was known locally as 'Eoghan na leabhar' (John of the Books). He became a scholarship student at Redcastle school in Derry and converted to Protestantism in 1686 before proceeding to study divinity at Glasgow University at the age of 17. After three years there, Toland travelled on to the Universities of Edinburgh (1690), Leyden and Utrecht (1692–94). But his philosophical and theological inquiries did not stop there. Toland's intellectual itinerary was also to take in such disparate centres of cosmopolitan learning as Hanover, Berlin, Dusseldorf, Vienna and Oxford. Toland spent much of his life seeking to restore, or reinvent, a noble genealogy for himself, going so far as to suggest that he was the descendant of old Gaelic aristocracy (the Ó Tuathalláin) and persuading Irish Franciscans in Prague to certify his story.[4]

Privately insecure, improvident and racked by self-doubt, Toland's public persona was one of bold self-assertion. His prolific publications soon made him a subject of international debate: Locke supported him, as did Leibniz who championed him as '*Un homme d'esprit et de savoir*'. Other luminaries of the period, including Swift, Berkeley and Defoe, became scornful adversaries. Denounced as a drunken braggart, apostate waif, spoiled Jesuit and subversive infidel, Toland became one of the leading 'free-thinkers' of his time, publishing over one hundred books, inventing the term 'pantheism' and establishing himself, into the bargain, as 'the founding father of modern Irish philosophy'.[5]

The enigmas do not end there, however. A strident spokesman for Republican virtue – publishing editions of Cicero, Milton, Harrington and the regicide millenarian Edmund Ludlow – Toland was, simultaneously, a darling of the royal court of Hanover. He was alleged to be a secret agent of the Prussian monarchy and amorous confidant of the Electress Sophia, who received him alone in her room for several hours a day and rewarded him with 'gold medals and other curiosities to a considerable value'.[6] A defender of English liberties against Jacobite plots, Toland was himself accused of Jesuit conspiracy and disloyal adventurism. Branded an atheist, he was obsessed with religious questions, displaying a particular proclivity for pantheistic, Rosicrucian and Latitudinarian movements (and spending considerable time studying the mystical doctrines of Giordano Bruno). A cosmopolitan idealist, Toland never abandoned his Irish roots and returned again and again to the claim that the ancient Irish Church of the Culdees was the most genuine form of Christianity. In fact, Toland was to devote several scholarly studies to the Gaelic tradition. These included (i) extensive research for an Irish dictionary conducted in Oxford in 1694; (ii) a compendious *History of the Druids*, published posthumously in 1726 and containing a Breton–Irish–Latin Dictionary as well as *A Critical History of the Celtic Religion and Learning*; and (iii) *An Account of the Druids, Vaids and Bards of the Ancient Gauls, Britain, Irish and Scots*. Toland's researches on the Gaelic traditions also comprised work on an old Irish manuscript, written in Armagh in 1138, stolen from the Bibliothèque Royale in Paris by a renegade priest called Jean Aymon who befriended Toland in Amsterdam in 1709.

This last text merits some comment as it contains revealing passages about Toland's attitude – however disguised in scholarly detachment – about his native culture. The full title of the text is *The Relation of an Irish Manuscript of the Four Gospels, as likewise a Summary of the Ancient Irish Christianity, and the Reality of the Culdees (An Order of Lay-religious)*. The manuscript was published as part of *Nazarenus* in 1718. Though originally catalogued in the Bibliothèque Royale as a Latin text with Anglo-Saxon glosses, Toland was able to correct the error and decipher the meaning of the Old Irish script. He concluded that it epitomized the tolerant free-thinking spirit of the *Céle Dé* (or Culdee) movement which Toland identified as the primitive form of Irish Christianity. Indeed, Toland appears to take mischievous pleasure in his commentary, quoting claims from certain ancient scribes which he himself could never advocate directly. For example, we find him citing the sentiment of the monk Cummian that 'Rome errs, Jerusalem errs, Alexandria errs, Antiochia errs, the whole world errs; but the Irish alone . . . are right!'.[7] Later in the same text Toland rehearses another ancient opinion to the effect that the Irish 'were to all others a harmless race, and to the English (whom they entertained, furnished with books and instructed gratis) a most friendly nation . . . the Saxons were indebted to them for their letters, no less than for their learning'.[8] An Irish cultural patriot *avant la lettre?*

It is certainly tempting to read a certain *apologia pro sua vita* in Toland's choice of opinion. And this suspicion intensifies when several pages later Toland identifies his own persecution with that of his compatriot and predecessor John Scotus Eriugena. Eriugena's book, writes Toland, 'was, by the authority of the Pope and the Council of Verceil, flatly condemned, [this being] the only way they had to confute it'. And

he adds, significantly, 'this method of answering is successively practised *to this day* by the promotors of error everywhere, and by those
who prefer interest to truth'.[9]

Lest there be doubts about Toland's own sentiments on the matter,
we need only turn the page to find him citing Eric of Auxerre's celebration of Irish scholars in exile: 'Why should I mention Ireland, not fear-
ing the danger of the sea, and removing almost all of it with a flock of
philosophers, to our shores; whereof of how much any one excels the
rest, he undergoes a voluntary exile; and by so much the readier is he to
stand before our most wise Solomon and to devote himself to his service'.[10] Toland makes plain here whom he counts among this ancient
flock of wise migrants – 'those ancient Irish monks [who] were of no
order, nor indeed men in Orders at all, famous over all the world for
their virtue, piety and learning; but particularly for their conventions
and the schools that they founded among the Picts, Anglo-Saxons,
Germans, Burgundians, Switzers and French: as who has not heard of
Sedulius, Columba, Columbanus, Colmannus, Aidanus, Furseus,
Kilanus, Gallus, Brendanus, Claudius, Clemens, Scotus Eriugena and
numberless others?'[11] These secular monks were, according to Toland,
'Western latitudinarians' before their time – anti-hierarchical and non-
sacerdotal, courageous of mind and adventurous of spirit.

It is little wonder that the exiled Toland should choose to identify
with these migrant Irish minds, just as the exiled James Joyce would do
two centuries after him in his famous Trieste Address.

IRISH AND NON-IRISH

In addition to the explicitly Irish dimension of Toland's biography and
bibliography, the question of whether he was an 'Irish' thinker might be
extended to some of his philosophical writings where no ostensible
Irish content is in evidence. We might ask, moreover, if it actually matters whether Toland is called an 'Irish' thinker or not? And if it is true
that Irish Bishops were calling for his books to be burnt in 1697, surely
things have changed in two hundred and fifty years? Yes and no.

Let me take an example. On 12 May 1985 the Bishop of Limerick,
Jeremiah Newman, delivered an address on the occasion of the
International Year of Youth. It was a nine-page typescript distributed
to the press and reported widely in the Irish media. In this address,
Bishop Newman singled out John Toland as a thinker who did not
'represent the Irish mind as such'. His rationalist scepticism regarding
church doctrine rendered him, in the Bishop's view, a more appropriate
listing for histories of 'English' philosophy. Newman proceeded to ex-

press indignation at 'what is going on at present in our country by way of changing . . . our Catholic inheritance' – citing as example the inclusion of Toland as an Irish philosopher in a book I had edited called *The Irish Mind*. The particular essay on Toland was, as Bishop Newman insinuatingly observes, written by a 'non-Irish contributor' – namely Dr David Berman, a self-confessed atheist of American-Jewish origin and expert on eighteenth-century Irish thought. The following is an extract from the Bishop's diatribe:

> [This book] purports to explore the intellectual traditions of the Irish people, that is us – yes us. Who else could claim to be Irish? But apart from one chapter on the medieval Catholic scholar, John Scotus Eriugena, this book is devoted almost entirely to a type of thinking that is *anything but typically and traditionally Irish*. In the sphere of philosophy, it manages to concentrate on figures with names such as Molesworth, Hutcheson, Clayton, Dodwell, Skelton and Toland. One has only to consult any thorough history of English philosophy to find most of these names included in it, which means or should mean that they do not exactly represent the Irish mind as such. Indeed, I could not but find annoying, as well as quite unscholarly, the statement by a non-Irish contributor to the book to the effect that the 18th-century rationalist John Toland is, quote, 'the father of modern Irish Philosophy'.[12]

This statement begs as many questions as it raises. In particular it recalls the controversial (and in my view untenable) distinction made by certain cultural nationalists between the 'Irish Irish' and the 'non-Irish Irish' – that is, between the real Catholic Irish and the rest. This is surely what Newman has in mind when he states that most of the thinkers mentioned in Berman's article belong to 'English' (not Irish) intellectual histories, and represent a threat to Ireland's genuine 'Catholic inheritance'.

This dual complaint sadly illustrates how 'exclusivist Catholic nationalism can go hand in hand with English cultural expropriation'.[13] The philosophers mentioned by Berman were each of them born, bred and published in Ireland. Their only allegedly non-Irish characteristic was their non-Catholicism. The one true 'Irish' philosopher the Bishop cites as typical of our 'Catholic inheritance' is John Scotus Eriugena – a thinker who had his books banned in Rome and was placed on the Index by successive Popes: the charge against him, ironically, was the same as that brought against Toland a thousand years later, namely, pantheism. Moreover, if we were to take the Bishop's equation of Catholic and Irish to its logical conclusion, we would have to say that

Toland was in fact 'Irish', for as long as he was Catholic (up to the age of 15, approximately), but became 'English' when he converted to Anglicanism and left Ireland for Glasgow University in 1687!

According to the rigid criteria of exclusivist Catholic nationalism, Toland is *both* Irish *and* non-Irish. In other words, he upsets the distinction itself and therefore cannot be tolerated. If he is not *pure Irish*, he must be English. Toland's complex Irishness, like that of most Irish thinkers of the period, defies a narrow logic of identity (A is A); it epitomizes the defiance of an excluded middle. Indeed, Toland himself seems to have been aware of the anomaly created by his hybrid character and playfully exploits his own self-presentation to his public. In addition to his puzzling epitaph, mentioned above, the question of his baptismal name – *Janus Junius* – also carries connotations of ludic doubleness. In a recent biography, Alan Harrison notes that Toland was christened a Catholic with the name *Janus Junius*. Toland himself was the origin of this assertion as reported by des Maizeaux; but Harrison suggests it is more likely he was christened Seán Eoin. Both these names occur in Irish and derive from different forms of John: *Seán* from the Norman-French Jehan and *Eoin* from the Latin Johannes. While distinguishable in Irish, the two names become identical in English: John John. Harrison concludes accordingly that *Janus Junius* 'may be an elaborate verbal joke on Toland's part, echoing the anglicized version of his own name and at the same time indicating qualities he considered important in his personality: *Janus* the two-faced god (very much a trickster symbol incidentally) indicating his propensity for looking at things in more than one way and for his sayings to be capable of more than a simple literal interpretation; and *Junius* recalling the name of Junius Brutus, the reputed founder of the Roman Republic which in terms of political philosophy, was Toland's ideal period'.[14]

The ploy of double-coding was no doubt a strategy of survival adopted by Toland to escape condemnation as a 'free-thinker'. Several commentators besides Harrison have recognized this, and Toland's acknowledgement of the esoteric/exoteric distinction in such works as the *Pantheisticon* (1720) and the *Tetradymus* (1720) confronts this. Fear of persecution, Toland states in the latter, leads authors to become 'supple in their conduct', 'reserved in opening their minds' and even 'ambiguous in their expressions'; a view already anticipated in *Letters to Serena* (1704) and in his claim in *Christianity not Mysterious* (1696) to 'propose his sentiments to the World by way of Paradox'.[15] This was, in fact, a practice adopted by many free-thinking minds of the age, from Locke to Voltaire, eager to avoid censure. But there is more to Toland's doubleness than a strategy of survival or *succès de scandale*. We also witness here what is perhaps a telling symptom of Irish intellectual culture since the seventeenth century. Perhaps one of the reasons why Toland presented himself as a *contradiction* (as Leibniz and others noted) was because the Irish mind was a cleft-mind? Not uniform but pluriform. Not homogeneous but diverse. Anglo *and* Gaelic. Catholic *and* Protestant. Native *and* planted. Regional *and* cosmopolitan.

I am not claiming that no other European cultures of the period experienced similar divisions, only that Ireland was arguably a more accentuated version of such conflict to the extent that it was at once a brutally colonized country (particularly since the introduction of the Penal Laws) and one of the most advanced centres of elite intellectual culture (especially in the Pale). Toland's doubleness was undoubtedly a general feature of persecuted Enlightenment rationalists – but it *also* bore the birthmarks of his cultural-historical origins. This is true of all thinkers, no matter how universalist or cosmopolitan their thought, and certainly true of Toland who was consciously aware of his 'Irish' identity and devoted several works to the study of it, most notably the *History of the Druids*. In short, while Toland's doubleness was not uniquely or exclusively Irish, it was Irish to *some* extent; and this extent is not insignificant.

THE DIVIDED MIND

Does this offer a supplementary perspective from which to review the ambiguities and duplicities that proliferate in Toland's writings? Does it help answer any of the following questions? Why did Toland deploy so many pseudonymous ruses that, in Sullivan's words, he is 'never able to assert his long-obscured person over his obscuring personas'?[16] Why does he conceal esoteric meanings behind exoteric modes of argument, saying indirectly what cannot be said directly? Why does he defend Enlightenment rationalism against religious sectarianism and superstition but devote several of his major writings to a defence of ancient Celtic Christianity? Why was he such a zealous supplicant of patronage from English, Dutch and German Royalty, while remaining a died-in-the-wool 'commonwealthman' whose heroes were invariably radical republicans – Brutus, Milton, Sidney, Ludlow and Harrington? Why, finally, was Toland able to support the Protestant Succession after the 1688 Revolution against Popish conspiracies yet proudly invoke his own Catholic descent and, when it came to the crunch, appeal to Irish Franciscans in Prague to authenticate his Gaelic origins? (The Latin certificate, dated 1708 and signed by the clerical superiors of the College, O'Neill and O'Devlin, would have offered Toland *carte blanche*

to visit other Irish Catholic colleges in Vienna, Rome and Louvain –
places where Irish learning was still fostered and where priests and
professionals were trained before they returned to Ireland to work for
the Catholic cause during the Penal times)?[17]

Several commentators have suggested connections between Toland's
strategic duplicity and his Irish background. Alan Harrison, for example, describes him as a 'threshold figure' in line with the Irish paradigm of the 'trickster'.[18] Stephen Daniel observes that Toland's ruses
are a version of anti-colonial deconstruction: 'On the periphery of the
English experience, Toland is the Irish anomaly, the spokesman for
alterity within national or linguistic unity'.[19] While David Berman relates Toland's critique of Christian mysteries to an attack upon the
Penal Laws imposed on Ireland by colonial rule. Toland's compulsion
to conceal his colonial subversiveness behind a veneer of respectability
would certainly explain his camouflaging of his real message behind an
ostensibly innocuous public pronouncement. Indeed, Toland's deployment of the esoteric/exoteric strategy ranks him, in Daniel's phrase,
'among the foremost eighteenth-century theorists of discretion'.[20] This
discretion derives at least in part from Toland's deep-rooted need to
develop hidden layers of meaning in order to challenge the official discourses of power which prevailed during his time. The hermeneutic
tricks deployed by Toland at the level of biblical, political and linguistic
exegesis were liminal strategies to out-manoeuvre the orthodox centres
of authority.

One wonders, moreover, if this strategy of wandering trickster, peripheral rebel, unpredictable Irishman-in-exile, was not in fact typical of
other Irish intellectuals in the eighteenth century and after? Does one
not find similar devices of duplicity, irony, subterfuge and satire in the
writings of Swift, Sterne, Burke and Congreve, or later again, of Wilde
and Shaw, Beckett and Joyce? Indeed is Joyce's description of *Finnegans
Wake* as a narrative hovering 'between twotwinsome minds', a double-
sided story inviting us to have 'two thinks at a time', not itself a
twentieth-century reinscription of that subversive Irish mind epitomized by Toland? Is it an accident that Toland's own experience of peripheral difference and exile issued not only in appeals for tolerance of
different perspectives, but also in his spirited defence of foreigners and
Jews in England?[21] This is a position which anticipates Joyce's own
empathy with outsiders and abhorrence of imperial conformity as
manifested in his choice of a Jew, Leopold Bloom, as central character
of his celebrated novel.

Toland was by no means the only Irish thinker of his time to exemplify the double role of Janus responding to crises of identity and

authority. The multiple divisions of Irish cultural life – Protestant and Catholic, Planter and Gael, native-speaker and English-speaker, con-formist and dissenter – were also evidenced in the controversies sur-rounding Irish philosophy for most of the eighteenth century. The 'golden age' of Irish philosophy stretching from 1690 to 1760 was, as mentioned above, deeply informed by questions of power and revolt in Ireland. To follow Berman's own genealogy, proponents of theological representationalism (the theory around which the dominant school of Irish philosophy developed) were responding directly or indirectly to the radical implications of Toland's rationalist critique of Christian mysteries in *Christianity not Mysterious* (1696). Such prominent thinkers as Edward Synge, William King, John Ellis, Philip Skelton and Thomas McDonnell felt obliged to respond (in different ways) to Toland's insinuation that the existing authorities – both clerical and political – had no fundamental basis for claiming that the Establishment 'represented' God's rule on earth. One immediate con-sequence of this was that the Penal Laws upholding Ascendancy power in Ireland were devoid of philosophical foundation. As Berman suc-cinctly points out: 'Toland's non-mysterious, tolerant Deism threatened the sectarian basis of the Ascendancy'.[22]

Irish philosophers responded in different ways to this challenge. Some, including theological representationalists like Berkeley and Swift, reacted negatively to Toland's argument – the latter even vilifying Toland as 'the son of an Irish priest' and 'the great Oracle of the anti-Christians'.[23] Burke too expressed considerable hostility to Toland, pre-ferring Berkeley's argument for an emotive rather than cognitive model of belief in his *Philosophical Inquiry into the Sublime and the Beautiful* (1757). Many other Irish minds, most notably Francis Hutcheson, Robert Clayton and Thomas Emlym, followed in Toland's footsteps. The point, however, is not to adjudicate between the sides, but to show how the key philosophical debates which raged in Ireland in the eight-eenth century betrayed a deep sense of cultural and political division within the island – and in its relationship to the neighbouring island. No matter what side of the divide one came down on, one could not but be aware that division existed. Thus while Swift, for example, may have railed against Toland, wearing his hat as a colonial Protestant, he railed against the injustices of English interference in Ireland wearing his hat as a colonial nationalist. This double stance was shared by Berkeley and other Irish thinkers of his time.

Irish intellectuals *since* the eighteenth century have also displayed ambivalence towards their identity. The recurring allusions to masks, mercurial allegiances, pseudonyms, esoteric codes and double-layered ironies in works from Swift and Congreve to Wilde and Yeats is not adventitious. This cleft mentality is a specific characteristic spawned by eighteenth-century Irish culture as Andrew Carpenter argues in his thesis of the 'double vision'. It may even have more ancient origins in Irish cultural history as suggested by Vivian Mercier in *The Comic Tradition* and Thomas Kinsella in 'The Divided Mind'. Either way, such a mentality is omnipresent in Toland's work, and is arguably a general feature of the 'golden age' of Irish philosophy running from the publication of *Christianity not Mysterious* in 1696 to Burke's essay on the *Sublime and the Beautiful* in 1757.[24]

MULTIPLE IDENTITIES

The choice of Burke as the major culminating figure of this period offers an opportunity, in conclusion, to comment upon the recurrence in his writings of the cleft mentality so prominent in Toland. In his biography, *The Great Melody*, Conor Cruise O'Brien argues that Burke's intellectual career was deeply informed by his native experience of 'doubleness', growing up in Ireland with his mother's Catholic family (the Nagles) in the Blackwater Valley in County Cork, yet obliged to hide this distinguishing birth-mark as he donned the official mask of Ascendancy Ireland in order to function, like his convert father before him, as a legitimate legal authority. This masking strategy was to become ever more pronounced as Burke became a leading public figure in English affairs.

Taking a metaphor from Seamus Heaney's *Cure of Troy*, O'Brien describes Burte's experience of doubleness as a 'Philoctetes wound'. He traces its scars through Burke's split allegiances in Trinity College (where he felt obliged to adopt debating strategies of irony and indirection to avoid exposure) to his tormented efforts to revoke a death penalty imposed on one of his Nagle relatives and, more generally, to support the Catholic Relief Act of 1778. But the most dramatic expression of Burke's Philoctetes complex was his famous speech against the Penal Laws in Ireland to the Bristol Guildhall in September 1780. This was an extraordinarily deft and passionate speech which carried with it a major threat to his seat in the House of Parliament. Referring to this event, O'Brien writes: 'This is the closest glimpse we get of the festering wound of Philoctetes. . . . When Burke speaks of "infection" and "corruption" in this context, he necessarily has his own family and personal situation most uncomfortably in mind. He loathes the Penal Laws, not merely for being unjust, but because of the false position in which the combined effects of the laws, and fear and worldly ambition, have placed the Burkes. This is what "frets him with feverish being"; and is clearly fretting him right there in the Guildhall, in the probably perplexed presence of the discontented burgesses of Bristol'. O'Brien goes on to suggest that a 'lesser person, circumstanced as he was, would have turned his back on Ireland altogether, and this would have been wholly to the advantage of his political career in Britain. It would have freed him from the "Jesuit" albatross, which he carried around his neck throughout his political career. It would almost certainly have saved his seat at Bristol, whose retention would have enhanced his consequences in the House of Commons'.[25] Above all, argues O'Brien, Burke would have been perceived as a more normal person by his English contemporaries if he had 'lived down' his Irish connections and not said anything to remind people of its importance. Such a suppression of his Irishness would have left him free to pursue high office undisturbed. 'Edmund Burke chose otherwise. He often spoke in the persona of an Englishman, but he never dropped Ireland altogether, which was the only way he could have induced Englishmen to take him seriously as one of themselves. Specifically, he failed to drop the cause of Irish Catholics, the most compromising, and the most disabling, by far, of all his Irish associations'.[26]

While such conflicts of allegiance may not have been as dramatic for most other Irish thinkers of the period, they were never very far from the surface and nowhere more so, in my view, than in Toland. Burke's Philoctetes complex finds parallels in the litany of split fidelities which ghosted the Donegal heretic's life. I rehearse them here by way of résumé. Toland was at once Irish and non-Irish, Gaelic-speaking and English-speaking, Catholic by birth and deist by choice, native and cosmopolitan, devotee of ancient Celtic sects and champion of Enlightenment reason, inventor of countless pseudonyms yet never forgetful of his original Irish name.[27] Born and bred on the Inisowen peninsula yet a traveller through eleven intellectual capitals of Europe. Speaker of ten languages yet forever fascinated by his native tongue whose ancient wisdoms he explored in numerous tracts. Sworn enemy of religious orthodoxy yet obsessed with the intellectual origins of religion. Author of *Christianity not Mysterious*, there was rarely a Christian more mysterious. In short, the Philoctetes wound of divided loyalties was as tormenting for Toland, the founder of the 'golden age' of Irish philosophy, as for Burke, its ultimate exponent.[28] Neither enjoyed the luxury of being able to say with Rousseau in Book 9 of *The Confessions*: 'I played no part: I became indeed what I appeared'.[29] Resembling and dissembling, masking and unmasking, the play between reality and appearance was to remain a hallmark of their Irish psyche.

So where does all this leave Bishop Newman's argument that to be *typically and traditionally Irish* means conforming to our 'Catholic inheritance'? I would have to say that, from such an extreme viewpoint, Toland is neither typical nor traditional. But then, was there *any* Irish thinker of major stature – including John Scotus Eriugena – who *is*? Certainly Newman's sectarian claim flies in the face of any generous definition of Irishness which embraces the numerous intellectual traditions of Catholic, Protestant and Dissenter.

In a telling if oblique way, John Toland *is* a typical Irish thinker in that his genius for dual forms of identity epitomizes a crucial feature of Irish culture, nowhere more dramatically manifested than in the eighteenth century. Perhaps the real form of Irish identity is a plurality of identities? Perhaps the essence of the Irish mind is to have no essence (in the sense of a single, homogeneous character)? Perhaps the Irish mind is at its best when differentiated into diverse minds, preferring complexity to uniformity? That such an hypothesis challenges the orthodoxy of narrow versions of Irish nationalism which seek to exclude scientists and philosophers from their essentialist category of belonging, is undeniable. But that is what the hermeneutic retrieval of historical and cultural memory entails – a *conflict* of interpretations as to who and what we are. These concluding studies on Berkeley, Tyndall and Toland offer an *interpretation* of historical facts which have a bearing on how Irish citizens understand themselves today. That such self-interpretation muddies the waters and blurs essentialist boundaries between Irishness and Britishness is a risk worth taking. All reminders that we are a hybrid, mongrel, mixed-up group of peoples are to be welcomed. Especially at the historical juncture at which we now find ourselves some three centuries after Toland.

These are some of the lessons to be learnt from that ambidextrous adventurer, John Toland, christened Janus Junius Edganesius in the parish of Clonmany, Donegal, in the year 1670, and, to this day, one of Ireland's finest philosophers.

11 John Tyndall and Irish science

THE SUBMERGENCE OF IRISH SCIENCE

For centuries philosophy and science were Siamese twins. From Thales and Aristotle to Hume and Kant, questions of philosophers were inextricably bound up with scientific inquiry into the workings of nature. Today an intellectual apartheid segregates science and philosophy. Even in third-level colleges, the natural world is analysed in 'Science Faculties', while matters of meaning and morality are exiled to 'Arts Faculties' – often located in separate buildings if not separate campuses.

This dissociation of inquiry has also taken its toll on the Irish intellectual scene. The creative dialogue between philosophical and scientific questioning which prevailed between the seventeenth and nineteenth centuries – from Toland and Berkeley to Hamilton and Tyndall – has virtually disappeared. The dynamic debates of the Dublin Philosophical Society, where issues of natural and moral knowledge were passionately discussed, are no longer to be heard. And it is almost unthinkable that any contemporary Irish scientist could provoke the sort of public controversy, at national or international level, which resulted from Tyndall's famous Belfast Address in 1874. It is regrettably true that few Irish citizens today have ever heard of Tyndall's achievements, not to mention those of other distinguished Irish scientists, for example: Rowan Hamilton's discovery of the 'Hamiltonian function' which plays a central role in quantum mechanics; Fitzgerald's contribution to special relativity; William Parsons's reflecting telescope; Richard Griffith's innovations in geological mapping; the decisive discoveries of Boyle, Boole or Molyneux in natural philosophy; Ernan McMullan's contributions to the philosophy of science, and so on. Ireland has a most impressive scientific tradition, especially in the nineteenth century which Gordon Herries Davies has nominated the 'golden age of Irish science', comprising the achievements of more than fifty scientists of world renown.[1]

A curtain of silence has descended on this scientific history. And the resulting eclipse has had unfortunate consequences for scientific research in Ireland. In 'The Case for Irish Culture' (1993), J.A. Slevin argues that the Irish view of science is contaminated by a 'syndrome of disinterest, apathy and even hostility formed largely by the cultural attitudes which have been historically dominant within the country's educational and political institutions. The traditional tensions which exist between the two cultures (arts and science) in other countries are benign by comparison with the very real schism which exists here in Ireland and the resulting malaise is, as far as science research is concerned, very much deeper'.[2] Unless this malaise is reversed, Slevin argues, Ireland will fail to develop its own ideas in science and to promote new indigenous industries in the high-tech area – with a resulting lack of economic growth leading to dependency on imported products. G. A. Fitzgerald spells out the practical consequences as follows: 'The impoverishment of scientific investment in Ireland is a silent crisis that will prove increasingly relevant to the number and nature of jobs created here. It is a crisis which has not been politically articulated, through a failure to understand the real potential and feasibility of creating internationally competitive research in Ireland, and a failure to appreciate the direct and indirect benefits which derive from doing so'.[3]

But Ireland had its own particular reasons for expelling scientists from its pantheon of 'national intellects'. As noted in preceding chapters, the agenda of cultural nationalism which informed the emerging ideology of the new state had occasional difficulties accepting what was not Catholic or Gaelic as 'genuinely Irish'. Irish science – a discipline largely, though not exclusively, developed by Ireland's Protestant class – was a casualty. Hence most Irish scientists from Molyneux and Kelvin to Tyndall and Hamilton have been considered 'English' and excluded from encyclopaedias of official Irish culture and syllabuses of 'Irish studies'. Ironically, this nationalist cliché found a perverse ally in the imperialist cliché of the Irish as exotic unthinking Celts. In matters of science, as in so many matters of politics, Irish nationalism and British nationalism conspired to implement a policy of mutual exclusion.

But where academia and ideology have often failed us, Irish writers have frequently insisted on the creative role that science can play in the life of the mind – from Shaw's fascination with political science to Flann O'Brien's invention of Dr Selby and John Banville's magnificent exploration of the great scientists – Kepler, Copernicus, Newton. Moreover, it was the poet and painter, AE, who made the following claim for a more inclusive definition of the Irish intellectual heritage: 'We wish the Irish mind to develop to the utmost of which it is capable, and we have always believed that the people now inhabiting Ireland, made up of Gael, Dane, Norman and Saxon, has infinitely great intellectual possibilities. . . . The union of races has brought a more complex mentality. Ireland has not only the unique Gaelic tradition, but it has given birth, if it accepts all its children, to many men who have influenced European culture and science, Berkeley, Swift, Goldsmith, Burke, Sheridan, Moore, Hamilton, Kelvin, Tyndall, Shaw, Yeats, Synge and many others of international repute' (*The Irish Statesman*, 1925).

STEREOTYPES OF IRISH MENTALITY

The studies of Toland and Berkeley have explored the two ideological prejudices most responsible for the eclipse of Irish minds in our cultural history: the 'colonial' and the 'cultural nationalist'. The first takes the form of the old imperialist view that if someone can think s/he cannot be Irish. In order to justify their campaign of colonial conquest, it was necessary for the English to deny that the Irish were capable of thinking for themselves. One of the earliest examples of this colonial stereotyping of the Irish as mindless irrationals was recorded in Giraldus Cambrensis's *History and Topography of Ireland*. Written in 1187, after the author's return from an invasionary expedition to Ireland with Prince John, Cambrensis delivered himself of this damning verdict of the Irish (despite praising their propensity for fantasy and magic!): 'They are a wild and inhospitable people. They live on beasts only and live like beasts. They have not progressed at all from the primitive habits of pastoral living. . . . For given only to laziness, they think that the greatest pleasure is not to work'.[4]

Clearly, the purpose of this tract was to vindicate a programme of political supremacy. The English conquerors had brains; the conquered Irish had not. But this designation of the Irish as brainless savages unfit to govern themselves was continued right up to the nineteenth century – and arguably beyond. In 1863, Disraeli, the Prime Minister of England, declared: 'The Irish hate our order, our civilisation, our enterprising industry, our pure religion. This wild, reckless, indolent, uncertain and superstitious race have no sympathy with the English character. Their ideal of human felicity is an alternation of clannish broils and coarse idolatry. Their history describes an unbroken circle of bigotry and blood'.[5] This colonial campaign of vilification was, of course, pursued in more popular fashion in the notorious *Punch* cartoons of the Irish as simian dullards and drunkards.[6]

Another less malign version of this colonial prejudice was witnessed in the romantic portrayal of the Irish as 'fanciful thoughtless Celts'. According to this version, there is indeed something called an Irish 'soul' but *not* an Irish 'mind'! The Irish, as Mathew Arnold and many of his Victorian peers believed, were best cultivated as 'dreamers of dreams'. Rational minds, capable of scientific rigour or political responsibility, were the prerogative of the Anglo-Saxon race. Accordingly, while Arnold could enthuse about the Celtic virtues of Irish fantasy, he opposed the Home Rule for Ireland Bill of 1886. As one commentator remarked, 'the Celts could stay quaint and stay put'.[7]

But the stereotype of the fanciful, thoughtless Celt was not alas confined to the colonizer. Many of the colonized also endorsed this portrait of themselves. They internalized the master's view, donning the masks of stage-Irishry with relish. The popular theatre of London was awash with Irish comedies at the same time as famished thousands back in Ireland queued for emigrant ships. Garret Barden, an Irish philosopher, has put it aptly: 'In the dialectic of master and slave, the slave's image of himself is precisely that – an image. His speech is taken from him not only by the master but by himself. . . . He is a slave because he identifies with his servile discourse'[8].

The irony is that when Ireland finally achieved her independence in the early decades of this century, the colonial prejudice against the existence of a thinking Irish mind was not immediately discarded. The anti-intellectualism of the newly emancipated republic was often in evidence, most notoriously in the censorship laws denounced by Samuel Beckett, Seán Ó'Fáolain and many other Irish writers. But it was not only the nudes of the national gallery that were veiled from public perception; it was also the works of our scientists and philosophers. Berkeley, Burke, Molyneux, Toland, Hutcheson, Clayton, Cantillon, Thompson, Kelvin, Tyndall. How many contemporary Irish schools and colleges teach the achievements of these thinkers? How many Irish Studies courses and Summer Schools feature them in discussion? More often than not, these names have been dismissed as not *really Irish* at all. While Irish mythology was being proudly restored by our Cultural Revival at the turn of the century (and rightly so), Irish science and philosophy were unconscionably ignored.

The tendency of many cultural nationalists to equate the 'real Irish' with those deriving from the Catholic and Gaelic traditions only served, curiously, to reinforce the old colonial stereotype by branding those who were not of this tradition – the majority of Irish scientists between 1650 and 1900 – as 'non-Irish'. In this manner, the colonial ploy of segregating Catholic, Protestant and Dissenter was carried over to a post-colonial ideology of anti-Britishness. The result was that most of Ireland's greatest scientists, being Protestant, were repudiated as 'English'. In short, the failure to recognize Tyndall and his like as in any sense 'Irish' scientists resulted not only from the *cultural imperialism* of the English, but also, in part at least, from a narrow *cultural nationalism* adopted by many of the Irish themselves.

Bishop Newman did not, it is true, mention Tyndall in his 1985 denunciation of thinkers who were 'anything but typically and traditionally Irish'. But there is no doubt that Tyndall's rationalist and Enlightenment caste of mind make him a perfect candidate for the Bishop's blacklist. It requires no great leap of imagination to conjecture what the Bishop would have thought of Tyndall's remarks on determinism and agnosticism in his Belfast Address. Certainly he would not have deemed his plea for absolute freedom of inquiry and his presentation of naturalistic philosophy as 'traditionally Irish'. Not to mention his argument that life and mind are latent in the cosmos; or his warning that religious sentiment is 'mischievous if permitted to intrude on the region of objective knowledge over which it holds no command'. Above all, one suspects that the Bishop of Limerick would have been horrified by Tyndall's bold claim for terrestrial life – 'By a necessity engendered and justified by science I cross the boundary of the experimental evidence, and discern in that Matter which we, in our ignorance of its latent powers, and notwithstanding our professed reverence for its Creator, have hitherto covered with opprobrium, the *promise and potency of all terrestrial life*'.[9]

The point is not that Tyndall is denying religion as an integral part of human life. (The exchange between the imaginary scientist and bishop in Tyndall's Belfast Address shows the oppposite). The point is rather that Tyndall actually argued for the compatibility of science and religion in his famous Address, whereas the Bishop of Limerick considered them as implacably opposed – at least when discussed within the frontiers of Ireland! Tyndall's Irish mind was clearly more ecumenical than Bishop Newman's; and more in keeping, curiously, with the radical doctrines of pantheism and immanentism for which his predecessors, Eriugena and Toland, were also condemned in their time. (The Belfast Address was explicitly denounced for these heresies by the Churches). When Tyndall proclaimed life and mind to be latent in the cosmos, he was echoing (no doubt unbeknownst to himself) the views of both Toland in his self-penned Latin epitaph apostrophizing mother earth and of Eriugena in the *Periphyseon* (vol. 3): 'We ought not to understand God and the creature as two things distinct from one another, but as one and the same'.[10]

A TRANSGRESSOR OF BOUNDARIES

It is important, for the purposes of the arguments in this volume, to locate Tyndall within the British–Irish cultural debate. But it is equally important to trace the salient features of Tyndall's life and work at international as well as national level. Most of what follows is a critical summary of the research conducted by Norman McMillan who established the first International Tyndall School in 1993 in Carlow, the place of Tyndall's birth.[11]

John Tyndall was born circa 1820 in Leighlinbridge, Co. Carlow, not far from the birthplace of George Berkeley. His father was a Quaker, while his mother is believed to have been of well-to-do Catholic farmer stock. Tyndall was educated in four Irish schools of different denominations; but it was his apprenticeship (1836–39) with the Catholic hedge schoolteacher, John Conwill, in Ballynockan and Ballinabranna that left the most lasting mark. This included training in mathematics, surveying, English and book-keeping. With these qualifications, Tyndall was first employed by the Ordnance Survey in Carlow and Youghal, before transferring to the English Survey in 1842.

In his early 20s, Tyndall read avidly in philosophy and was particularly impressed by the radical ideas of the Chartist Movement and the arguments of Thomas Carlyle (later to become a friend). From the outset, therefore, it seems that Tyndall was simultaneously drawn towards both a scientific materialism and a spiritual account of nature. Dismissed by the English Survey for his vigorous protest against the exploitation of Irish workers, Tyndall pursued studies at the local Mechanics Institute in Preston and eventually became Superintendent to the Engineering Laboratory in Queenwood College in 1847 (a Quaker college associated with Robert Owens's experiments in utopian socialism). It was here that Tyndall conducted the first experiments on these islands in practical engineering and science teaching and developed the famous 'heuristical method'.[12] In 1848 Tyndall travelled to Marburg University where he secured a professional scientific training in physics, chemistry and mathematics (then unavailable in England) under the distinguished Professor Robert Bunsen; he completed his PhD in 1851. During his time in Marburg, Tyndall began his career as a popularizer of science, publishing his first scientific pieces in the *Carlow Sentinel* back home. After graduation, Tyndall moved to Berlin where he became acquainted with such leading scientists as Helmholz and Kirchhoff and established the modern theory of diamagnetism with Knoblauch in the the 1850s. It was also during his stay on the Continent

that Tyndall was deeply influenced by the revolutionary ferment sweep-
ing Europe, becoming an enthusiastic reader of the *Naturphilosophie* of
Goethe and Fichte, and an intrepid Alpine adventurer (effecting the
first traverse of the Matterhorn).

On his return to Britain and Ireland, Tyndall maintained his vocation
as propagandist of German science and philosophy, translating several
papers by leading German physicists for the *Philosophical Magazine*. In
particular, Tyndall wished to enrich philosophical thinking by the extension of the boundaries of natural science. Opposing obscurantism in
every guise, he resolved to promote the view that science was not hostile
to literature, thought and humanity. His campaign for evolutionary
thinking was always done in the face of the reductionist materialism of
the positivists.

In 1853, Tyndall was appointed to the Chair of Natural Philosophy
at the Royal Institution of Great Britain, conducting path-breaking
experiments in glaceological research, speculative method, meteorology
and radiation (which led directly to Planck's quantum theory). It was
during his tenure here that Tyndall published his famous studies founding the sciences of nephelometry, infra-red analysis and fluorescence
analysis. His studies on monitoring atmosphere and water established
him as the 'first environmental scientist'. He was also responsible for a
number of influential lecture tours in the USA, taking him to the universities of Yale, Harvard and Columbia and making him the 'most
celebrated public lecturer of his day'.[13] But while he effectively defined
and professionalized the discipline of Physics in Britain, drafting the
first syllabus in the subject for the new school curriculum, Tyndall was,
from beginning to end, an Irish cosmopolitan: an internationalist who
took as much from French physics and German organic science as he
did from his experiments on heat, light, sound and electromagnetism at
the Royal Institution[14] – never losing sight, the while, of his early
training in mathematics, surveying and practical knowledge with John
Conwill of Carlow. It is with this eclectic education in mind, that
McMillan can insist that Tyndall was less an 'English materialist' than
an 'Irish evolutionist'.[15]

Tyndall's stalwart advocacy of evolutionary scientific method and its
philosophical principles was to involve him (along with Huxley and
Spencer) in a spate of acrimonious controversies with the British establishment. One of his most famous lectures was undoubtedly his 1870
address to the British Association 'On the Scientific Use of
Imagination'. Here he argued that the role of imagination in science is
that of an 'active force of matter', citing as example the famous discovery in Ireland of conical refraction. By affirming thus the crucial use

of imagination in scientific breakthroughs, Tyndall was in fact reiterating the conviction of his compatriot, George Berkeley, that imagination is by no means inimical to truth.

Tyndall's greatest, and most controversial, philosophical contribution came in the form of his famous Belfast Address in 1873. Conducted in the form of a fictional dialogue between a Bishop and a Lucretian, Tyndall explored the agnostic argument of the impossibility of comprehending the rapport between psychic and physical occurrences. Once again, his cosmopolitan range of learning and reference was evident, from his raising of the fundamental question of spontaneous generation (inspired by his 1871 meeting with Pasteur in Paris) to his championing of the German Mayer's principle of the conservation of energy. But the real disputes centred on three main propositions: (i) the unconditional freedom to investigate cosmological questions untrammelled by authority; (ii) the uncompromising promotion of evolutionary theory; and (iii) the argument, on the basis of the continuity of nature, that we must proceed with 'vision of mind' to consider both life and mind as latent in the cosmos.

The resulting uproar was to put the evolution debate onto the front pages of the world's newspapers, provoking a concerted protest from the churches, the scientific establishment and the public at large. Of special vehemence was the response of the Irish Catholic Church: the Bishop's pastoral of 1875 declared that 'under the name of Science, [Tyndall] obtruded blasphemy upon the Catholic nation'. This Pastoral effectively made Tyndall *persona non grata* in his native country. But despite rejection by many of his compatriots, Tyndall's pioneering contribution to science earned him great fame throughout Europe and America. In the nineteenth century his textbooks on physics were even translated into Japanese and used in schools in that country (unlike his own).

Like most great Irish scientists between the seventeenth and nineteenth centuries, John Tyndall transgressed the rigid ideological criteria of both colonial and cultural nationalism. And while the question of 'Irishness' may appear, at first blush, an irrelevant one, it serves the useful therapeutic purpose of reminding us that the Irish mind is at its best when it resists ideological uniformity of any kind, celebrating an openness to experimental curiosity and questioning. The greatest Irish thinkers were almost invariably migrant minds, who flouted the confines of geographical and mental maps, choosing instead to criss-cross national frontiers, creeds and cultures in order to make their mark on the intellectual map of the world. Tyndall – like most other intellectuals of the Irish Enlightenment – was first and last a cosmopolitan. *Cos-*

mopoli sum: I am of the world, was the motto of every great Irish scientist and philosopher.

Tyndall was committed to free and creative inquiry of mind. While he held natural science to be a crucial discipline in this inquiry, he was equally adamant that it must sustain constant dialogue with philosophical questions of value, religious questions of spirit and poetical questions of sentiment. All of these questions, he insisted, have their part to play in the development of the 'whole man'. Opposed to closed-minded fanaticism, Tyndall's credo is summed up in the wonderful passage in the Belfast Address where he exhorts his listeners to prefer 'commotion before stagnation' and not to 'purchase intellectual peace at the price of intellectual death'. This remains a fitting credo for all contemporary thinkers, Irish and non-Irish alike.

Postscript
Towards a postnationalist Ireland

We cannot live very much longer under the confusions of the existing 'international' economy and the existing 'nation-state'. If we cannot find and communicate social forms of more substance than these, we shall be condemned to endure the accelerating pace of false and frenetic nationalisms and of reckless and uncontrollable global transnationalism. Moreover, even endurance is then an optimistic estimate. These are political forms that now limit, subordinate and destroy people. We have to begin again with people and build new political forms.

(Raymond Williams, 'The Culture of Nations', 1983)[1]

TOWARDS A COUNCIL OF ISLANDS OF BRITAIN AND IRELAND

The preceding chapters have indicated the need to transcend the chronic sovereignty neurosis that has bedevilled relations between these islands for too long.[2] There are multiple signals of change in this regard. The diminution of national sovereignties in the context of increased EU integration, the correlative move towards regional development and the ongoing constitutional debates in both Britain and the Republic, all gesture toward new possibilities of co-existence. The notion of national 'self-determination', as expounded by Woodrow Wilson after the First World War and legitimately invoked by many developing post-colonial countries, no longer has the same relevance in the context of these islands.[3] 'No surrender' and 'Ourselves alone' are catch-cries of the past.

Within the outer periphery of the evolving European community, it is probable, and certainly desirable, that the residents of these islands may rediscover themselves as a new inner circle, both geographically and culturally. The argument for a pooling of sovereignty has come from both nationalist and unionist quarters. The advocacy of people like

John Hume for a 'Europe of regions' and of Garrett Fitzgerald for shared-sovereignty are now well rehearsed in the nationalist community. The latter's reasoning on this hitherto taboo subject today commands, I believe, a considerable degree of support: 'Even after the achievement of Republican status in 1949 had finally exorcised the pre-occupation with sovereignty issues and symbols, a further decade was to elapse before the limited effectiveness of the political sovereignty of a small country as a means of promoting its economic interests in relation to the rest of the world was realised. . . . By the late 1950s there was a belated realisation that a diminution of the sovereign power of neighbouring larger countries to exploit us would be far more important for Ireland than the retention of an ineffective Irish sovereign power to exploit them'.[4] In strict trade terms, the greatest net benefits of diminishing sovereignty have accrued to smaller countries like Ireland, which in the domain of international economic relations – especially after entry to the European Community and the Single European Act – never had much effective sovereignty to give up. Negotiations on GATT and the internal market, for instance, are clearly matters of collective determination. (This remains distinct from Ireland's right to run domestic affairs which is rightly retained at 'regional' level.) But the advantages of sharing sovereignty with Britain and other EU member-states extend beyond purely economic considerations to include a wide range of issues from justice and human rights provisions, to protection of minorities and the environment, a social charter and, not least, a recognition of our status as 'mongrel islanders'.

This last point is crucial. Several British commentators, alert to a more amplified European perspective, are proposing a new social geography and history of these islands according to which the 'Irish' and 'British' nations may be reconceived as binary constructs of a larger whole. Viewed from this more inclusive perspective – variously called the 'Britannic melting pot', the 'British–Irish archipelago' or 'Islands of the North Atlantic'(IONA) – the different peoples of these islands are shown to be 'mixed-up' with each other at many levels, cultural, ethnic, linguistic.[5] This extension of identity reference allows an abandonment of the obsession with national self-sufficiency and conflict in favour of *both* a transinsular network of association *and* a radical subsidiarity within both states in response to the demand for greater local democracy. This open shutter also permits us to see how the established borders between Wales and England, England and Scotland, Scotland and Northern Ireland and (most obviously) Northern Ireland and southern Ireland, are actually modern constructs which do not correspond to the porous and interwoven character of the communities themselves. As one historian remarks: 'The concept of "nation" provided modern historians with a convenient framework around which to organise their materials but a price had to be paid. What later became national boundaries were extended backwards into a past where they had little or no relevance. . . . This point may be reinforced if it is borne in mind that episodes which are generally recognised as having been of decisive importance in the history of the various "nations" of the British Isles in fact transcended the national boundaries of a later date. The Roman Conquest, the Barbarian invasions, the Viking raids, the Norman conquest, the Reformation and the Industrial Revolution were all "events" which affected the British Isles as a whole and brought about crucial changes in the relations between the various Britannic societies of the period concerned. To deal with any of these episodes requires in every case something wider than a national framework'.[6] The radical implication of this analysis is that there are in fact no pristine nations around which definitive nation-state boundaries – demarcating exclusivist sovereignty status – can be constructed. As a result, the futility of both the UK's and the Republic's claims to construe 'Northern Ireland' as a natural and necessary part of their respective 'national territories' becomes apparent.

What is true of the past is even more true of the future. The European configuration calls for postnationalist ways of thinking. It is emphatically not a question of abandoning self-determination for some European super-state. On the contrary, it is a question of finding modes of self-determination – political and cultural – that are more effective and accommodating than the purely 'national'.

As Eric Hobsbawm observes in *Nations and Nationalism since 1780*, '"nation" and "nationalism" are no longer adequate terms to analyse the political entities . . . once described by these words. It is not impossible that nationalism will decline with the decline of the nation-state, without which being English or Irish or Jewish, or a combination of all these, is only one way in which people describe their identity among the many others which they use for this purpose as occasion demands. It would be absurd to claim that this day is already near. However, I hope it can at least be envisaged'.[7]

As I have argued in several of the above chapters, the EU principles of subsidiarity and regionalism, as outlined in the European *Charter of Local Self-Government* and Maastricht Treaty, offer the prospect of a real postnationalist alternative to the clash of Irish–British nationalisms that has paralysed Northern Ireland for decades. A Council of Islands of Britain and Ireland – analogous to the Nordic Council of transnational cooperation – would ultimately foster a network of interconnecting regions guaranteeing parity of esteem for cultural and political diversity. The challenge, in Simon Partridge's words, is 'to abandon our mutually reinforcing myths of superiority (largely British) and ethnic purity (largely Irish) and face this more mundane post-imperial, postnationalist mixed reality. Could it even be an inspiration to other parts of Europe and the globe so hopelessly enmired in the devastations of exclusive ethnic "self-determining" nationalism?'[8]

The relevance of the Irish–British paradigm to the wider international community is crucial. We are not talking here about an exclusively Irish–British solution to an Irish–British problem. The whole question of federal and regional alternatives to the modern crisis of the nation-state is currently one of global significance. Foremost amongst those who have cast their minds upon such scenarios is the Czech author and President, Vaclav Havel. In his Address to Harvard University in June 1995, Havel spoke of the pressing need to reconcile the twin demands of contemporary society – the trend towards transnational integration and the longing of 'every valley for independence'. He does not specifically cite the Irish–British paradigm, but the implications are evident. Transnational networking, counterbalanced by processes of real subsidiarity, must 'be one of the instruments enabling countries and peoples who are close to each other geographically, ethnically, culturally and economically and who have common security interests, to form associations and better communicate with each other and the rest of the world'.[9]

FEDERAL REGIONALISM IN EUROPE

This brings us to the controversial issue of federal regionalism as alternative to the nation-state. If a federal–regional model offers the most feasible solution to the British–Irish problem, it is most likely to succeed, as my first five chapters have argued, in a European context. But what, in summary, would a federal–regional Europe entail?

It would not, first of all, be a *Europe des états unies* along the lines of the one-nation USA. Nor would it be a return to the *Europe des empires* which fostered hegemonic dreams of a supranational state obliterating the cultural and political diversity of each constituent region (e.g. the 'Third Empire' ideologies of Napoleon, Hitler or Mussolini). Nor would it be a glorified *Europe des patries* as proposed by the Gaullists, using the European umbrella as no more than a convenient security guard to consolidate the nation-state. Nor, finally, would it be a *Europe des éthnies*, where exclusivist notions of racial homogeneity work to divide the continent into ancient tribalisms. The European federation I am speaking of is a *Europe des régions*, where a proper balance is reached between federal association (at transnational level) and regional self-government (at subnational level).

What precise form of federation would be required then, in such a Europe of Regions? Let me rehearse some basic features:

1 A multi-state federation rather than a single-state monolith ruled by 'Brussels bureaucracy'. Though membership is bound by obvious geographical and political requirements, any state may, in principle, be included which is willing to accept the rules of association (and the meta-rule that such rules are ones they all agree on). Federal association cannot be imposed. The very term 'federal' derives from *foedus*, Latin for covenant, implying a *voluntary* convocation or contract between different consenting units. Where such consent is lacking, the federation, quite logically, collapses.[10]

2 A 'league of peace', in Kant's famous phrase, built upon international federalism but not constituting one international nation (which for Kant is contradictory). On this principle, the cosmopolitan character of federalism would be predicated on guarantees of universal freedom for all and not simply on the perceived benefit of multinational over single-nation economic opportunities.[11]

3 A bottom–up model of power based on the subsidiarity principle that only those decisions – legislative, executive and judicial – are transferred to federal level which cannot be better fulfilled at regional level. The implementation of direct forms of genuine local government is crucial here. Failing that, the infamous 'democratic deficit' grows.[12]

4 An association allowing every one of its members to express *multiple identities* expanding outward in concentric circles – individual (as person), regional (as resident), national (as heritor), constitutional (as citizen), federal (as member). The circles would move from the concrete and specific to the more abstact and cerebral, implying a complementarity of inward and outward directions.[13]

5 A form of *dual democracy* – participatory and representative – permitting each member: (a) to decide electorally on the composition of their own quasi-autonomous regional government; and (b) to choose parliamentary representatives in an enlarged European Chamber of Regions in addition to having direct access to federal power as individuals who may use European courts to seek their rights or take action against their own governments (in contradistinction to confederal institutions where relations between power and member are indirect). If *internal democracy* is not operative as decentralized local government with a separation of powers, or as individual access to

judicial redress, then the federal association will lack legitimacy. Likewise, local democracy unanswerable to federal democracy runs its own risks. 'If regional autonomy is based on developing your own authentic culture and individuality and working towards federal arrangements with the guy across the river, that would be very healthy. . . . [But] if it is based on hatred of the guy across the river, it is ugly and unpleasant'.[14]

6 An association of law (*état de droit*) based on political–juridical references of democratic rule and universal human rights – making for that form of 'constitutional patriotism' which Habermas identifies with postnational societies.[15]

7 A form of integration whose requirements of shared authority – at the level of guiding constitutional principles – in no way diminishes the development of diversity at regional level. On the contrary, the non-exclusionary, universalist and cosmopolitan character of federal membership needs to be complemented by strong regional identities of cultural heritage, local memory and linguistic specificity. In other words, the regional goal of *identity* and the federal goal of *peace* need each other. 'There is no territorial homeland that is the site of the federal offer', as Attracta Ingram puts it. 'Everyone stays home, so to speak. But they all participate in a practice of common decision-making and subscription to law on matters they all agree belong to the federal rather than domestic political level'.[16] Indeed the multi-cultural and multi-ethnic composition of European society today includes many minorities of *non-European* origin whose legimate needs for identity and esteem also need to be safeguarded under a comprehensive subsidiarity principle.[17]

If the proper balance between federal and regional democracy – outlined in these seven conditions – is not struck, there is no real answer to the sovereignty neurosis which underlies many forms of contemporary nationalism. Several of these forms are quite understandable, both in the EU context (Scots, Welsh, Irish, Basque) and in the wake of crumbling, because largely involuntary, erstwhile federations (Soviet Union, Yugoslavia). The nationalist cause is not dead and gone. The point is not to deny it, but to comprehend why it exists and how it might, eventually, be superseded in favour of alternative regional–federal projects.

It is my view that identity-needs which still seek expression in the formation of nation-states might be better accommodated in some form of cultural and/or political regionalism. The nationalist aspiration is entirely legitimate as an aspect of a people's desire for self-expression and self-legislation. The difficulty arises when 'emergent' nationalism congeals into 'dominant' nationalism and begins to assume exclusivist proportions. This shift often sees notions of absolute sovereignty being invoked to define the 'people' according to a single homogeneous grid which casts others as adversaries and eliminates, or absorbs, minorities.[18] (Was there ever a nation without its minorities?) We witness this, for instance, in the formation of centralized nation-states in Europe, from the eighteenth century onward, which imposed a single set of cultural, political or linguistic norms on a multiplicity of constituent citizens.

This exclusivist–centralist paradigm has led not only to the phenomenon of ethnic intolerance but also, ironically, to the emergence of a new phenomenon of *nationalism against nationalism*. The return of the repressed: dormant inner nations rise up against the hegemonic nation-state which has disenfranchised them. We witness the resurgent claims of minority nations to their place in the sun: the Welsh, Scots and Irish (within the British nation-state), the Basques, Bretons and Corsicans (within the French nation-state), or the Slovenes, Croats and Serbs (within the former Yugoslav nation-state). What is sometimes denounced as 'nationalism' in today's Europe is often this form of resistance to larger (state–state) nationalisms. And the same might be said in the context of the break-up of the Soviet bloc.

If we grant, therefore, that legitimate nationalism is the expression of a normal need for *identification* (by others as much as by ourselves), regressive nationalism would cover the efforts of those who refuse to accept, or to mourn, the inevitable passing of the nation-state – real or imaginary.[19] Thus defined, regressive nationalism is often 'depressive' nationalism. It is the expression of an originally valid need for identity-acknowledgement which – because humiliated or forbidden by some imperial hegemony (British, Soviet . . .) – assumes the deferred and deviant form of narrow, xenophobic exclusivism. Such nationalism represents a collective variation on Nietzsche's *ressentiment*. It arises when the normal stage of cultural–political growth is blocked, forcing identitarian energies inwards to a separatist–narcissistic extreme which often results in terrorism, war, scapegoating or 'ethnic cleansing'. Whence arises the obsessional sovereignty neurosis of several post-imperial nations. As Julia Kristeva observes in respect of the collapse of the communist empire, Baltic, Serbian, Slovak or Croatian nationalisms are separatist expressions of peoples whose regional–national identity was suppressed under communism and so now takes on the 'anti-depressive' forms of manic exaltation of archaic origins, folk values and even hatred of the 'old enemy' (since communism is gone). The enemy becomes 'the other ethnic group, the other nation, the scapegoat and so on. This pathology can last for a long time and such settling of accounts can hamper the cultural and economic development which those countries need'.[20]

The difficulty facing the postnationalist paradigm is how to surmount – or, to use Hegel's term, sublate – the arrested dynamics of nationalism while still commanding the allegiance of citizens. This is, fundamentally, a question of motivation and affectivity – or what David Hume, with a deeper understanding than Kant of such matters, referred to as the 'passions' that underlie political and moral transformation. It is clear that the lawyers' concept of European citizenship and constitutionality, while indispensable, is not enough. It is a necessary but not a sufficient condition for a new Europe – and certainly seems a pale and unpersuasive substitute for the robust attraction of traditional identity based on language, religion, ethnicity and nationhood. We may reasonably ask, therefore, if it is possible for the collective loyalty of a society to be galvanized and sustained by a set of universal laws and norms, as Habermas and other advocates of 'constitutional patriotism' argue. We may ask if it is feasible to dismiss nationalism as no more than a reactionary anti-modernist ideology, replacing it with an 'abstract idea of the universalisation of democracy and the rights of the person'. In other words, can the rational–liberal values of citizenship ever fully substitute for the concrete need to *belong* to a particular community of memories, heritages, myths? Can we dispense with the need for *recognition*? Can citizens live by law alone?[21]

The answer, I submit, is in the negative. The challenge facing us is not to abrogate the desire for regional–national identity – repeating the errors of Enlightenment rationalism or totalitarian imperialism – but to find more appropriate forms for its expression – a regional model of cultural and political democracy within an overall federal framework. The refusal to cater for such identity-needs will, in my view, result in either (a) a revived sense of frustrated nationalism, expressed as ethnic separatism; or (b) a displaced nationalism at supranational level. The danger for a federal Europe, in the latter instance, would be the upsurge of a new Eurocentrism which refuses to see Europe as one society amongst others, assuming a hostile attitude toward non-European cultures both within its borders (emigrants) and beyond (geo-politics).[22] Arguably, the best antidote to such a prospect is the reminder that Europe is composed of mutiple languages, dialects and identities which can never be homogenized into a single pan-European nation. Europe is, and always has been, polylingual and polycentric in its very make-up. It has the wherewithal to resist the straitjacket of one-nation federalism.[23]

In the case of Irish nationalism, independence was something of a saving grace. Because most Irish people enjoyed the status of a 'Free State' for over seventy years (and of a Republic for more than half that), they have had the opportunity to express their need for an autonomous 'sovereign' identity, permitting them not only to cease military operations against Britain but even to pool sovereignty, at least partially, with the UK and other European countries in the Single European Act and Maastricht Treaty. A minority of nationalists in the North chose to continue the 'armed struggle' because, they argued, they did not have the possibility of adequately expressing their national identity. But while many Irish people today would be prepared to countenance some form of postnationalist identity there are deep nationalist claims still inscribed in the opening articles of the Irish Constitution, and especially Article 3 which describes the division of the island as a temporary matter 'pending the re-integration of the national territory'. In this respect, Irish nationalism could be said to be sustained, both north and south of the border, by a constitutional claim to exclusivist nation-state sovereignty mirroring the parallel British claim to the same territory.

Indeed, if Irish nationalism could be described as still 'not come of age' – and therefore 'arrested' in some respects – the charge of immaturity is just as pertinent to British nationalism, albeit for different reasons. As Tom Nairn deftly remarks: 'Unlike the true *anciens régimes* with which it was allied ... the early-modern [British] State proved quite capable of concocting a viable popular patriotism from which the dangerous acids of populism and egalitarianism were bleached out. And from the start a vital feature of that surrogate national identity was a new emphasis on Monarchy. The Crown alone could provide a compensatory symbolic focus and give a phoney yet concrete and imaginable sense of equality – of belonging within a traditional State-family, of a community putting both gender and class "in their place". Another way of describing this is to say that "maturity" (by what became the standard canons of nationalist development) was avoided. Far from being complete by the 17th century, it was deliberately and permanently eschewed in the 19th. The United Kingdom's contribution to the spectrum of nationalism was to be a unique familial patriotism intended to suppress all the awkward and plebian aspects of national awakening – its capacity for a democratic assertiveness "from below"'. He concludes: 'Instead a kind of permanent *immaturity* was chosen: the cautious arm's length from modernity that suited a national patriciate defending an earlier economy and form of State – a social order now overtaken by the second wave of bourgeois revolution but still capable of defending its historical corner for a very long time'.[24] The prolonged resistance by the British state to the twin processes of European federalism and regionalism shows just how long.

NATIONAL IDENTITY AND THE AVOIDANCE OF WAR

A final and perhaps most important reason why a federal Europe of Regions is desirable is the avoidance of war. Hannah Arendt's classic argument is that the obsessional equation of national independence with state sovereignty is a recurring impediment to peace. In other words, as long as the unlimited pursuit of national objectives is allied with the readiness of nation-states to wage war in those interests, it is impossible to guarantee long-term international cooperation under a law of nations that recognizes the right to war.[25] This is why Kant famously endorsed the creation of an international federal union as a *moral duty* to transcend the Hobbesian rivalry between nation-states. Indeed, it is curious how relevant his *Perpetual Peace* proposal of the late eighteenth century still is in the late twentieth: 'Peoples who have grouped themselves into nation states may be judged in the same way as individual men living in the state of nature, independent of external laws; for they are a standing offence to one another by the very fact that they are neighbours. Each nation, for the sake of its own security, can and ought to demand of the others that they should enter along with it into a constitution similar to the civil one, within which the rights of each could be secured. This would mean establishing . . . a particular kind of league, which we might call a pacific federation'.[26]

The federalist vision of Monnet and Spinelli, founders of the post-war European movement, sought to retrieve this motive of international peace. Beneath the economic interests of European cooperation lay a moral interest in securing long-term peace (even when it goes against the ostensible interests of consituent states – which is when it really counts). This moral interest takes the form of both a communitarian responsibility to live together as neighbours (*socii*) and a libertarian–Kantian right of individual freedom (that each citizen be treated as an end and not merely as a means). Both moral imperatives – other-regarding and prudential – combine to secure the existence of a federal civil society regulated by just law. A federalist regionalism might thus be regarded as a moral goal where each citizen, and each region of citizens, acts under the ideal of all as members of a universal kingdom of ends. But if this federalist imperative is secured on human rights grounds – where each citizen or region agrees to observe reciprocal guarantees of freedom in the interests of all (not just itself) – it is ultimately sustained, I believe, on communitarian grounds of social solidarity and interdependence.[27] It might be said, therefore, that a Europe of Regions can find support in the main philosophies of contemporary European politics: (a) *liberal democratic*, inspired by the Enlightenment vision of a humanist state of law (*état de droit*); (b) *social democratic*, inspired by the socialist vision of equal opportunity and exchange; and (c) *Christian democratic*, inspired by the Catholic social philosophy of subsidiarity and solidarism. Indeed, it is precisely because the federal project can rely upon such deeply based value traditions – in addition to the purely rationalist allegiance to the rule of law and constitution – that it is likely to continue not just when the conflicting interests of constituent members converge but, more importantly, when they diverge. In other words, taking account of such value-based motivations for federalism enables us to promote a Europe of Regions which is no utopian fantasy but a viable project for long-term stability and justice.[28]

What is to be done, then, with the enduring quest for national identity? My proposal is that such a quest be gradually channelled away from the nation-state, where history has shown its tenure to be frequently insecure and belligerent, to more appropriate levels of expression: the regional level of local democracy and the federal level of international democracy. In the Irish–British context, this would mean that the citizens of these islands come to express their identity less in terms of impervious nation-states than in terms of locally empowered provinces (Ulster, Scotland, Wales, etc.) and larger transnational associations (e.g. the British–Irish archipelago and European Union). This is why I fully endorse Charles Taylor's belief that the emerging Europe must allow for multiple layers of compatible identification – regional, national and federal – fostering, in turn, a fuller way of being: 'People do not have simple identities any more, they are not just a member of their own nation. They have a complex identity where they relate to their nation, and their region, and they also have a sense of being European'.[29]

Citizens of these islands do best to think of themselves as 'mongrel islanders' rather than as dwellers in two pure, god-given and rival nation-states.[30] There is no such thing as primordial nationality. Every nation is a hybrid construct, an 'imagined' community which can be reimagined again in alternative versions. The ultimate challenge is to acknowledge this process of ongoing hybridization from which we derive and to which we are constantly subject. In the face of resurgent nationalisms fired by rhetorics of purity and purification, we must cling to the recognition that we are all happily mongrelized, interdependent, impure, mixed up.

Notes

INTRODUCTION

1 One of the guiding hypotheses of this volume is the formative role of narratives in the development of communal or 'national' identity. Narratives are understood here in the generic sense of stories, myths or other forms of dramatic collective representation – what I call the 'political imaginary'. These formative narratives generally cover the functions of (1) positing goals and origins, (2) establishing and resolving crises, and, perhaps most importantly, (3) creating a distinctive sense of cultural self-identification and self-imagining in the guise of a narrative 'voice' or 'viewpoint'. Combining these various functions, the particular stories of a community serve to legitimize or delegitimize the political, social and cultural tenure of that community, both in its own eyes and in the eyes of the world. I am particularly indebted for my understanding of the socio-political role of narrative to the recent work of thinkers such as Fredric Jameson, Paul Ricoeur, Howard Gardner, Benedict Anderson and Homi Bhabha. For a more detailed philosophical analysis of the role of narrative in the formation of identity, see 'The Narrative Imagination: Between Poetics and Ethics' in my *The Poetics of Modernity* (Humanities Press, New Jersey, 1995), pp. 92–106.
2 Michael Ignatieff, *Blood and Belonging: Journeys into the New Nationalism* (Farrar, Strauss and Giroux, New York, 1993), pp. 6–7.
3 On this tension between civic universalism and state nationalism see Attracta Ingram, 'Constitutional Patriotism', Paper delivered at seventeenth IVR World Congress, Bologna, June 1995; Tom Garvin, 'Ethnic Markers, Modern Nationalisms, and the Nightmare of History' in *Ethnicity and Nationalism* (ed. Peter Kruger, Hitzeroth, Marburg, 1993), pp. 73–74; and Paul Ricoeur, 'Universality and the Power of Difference' in *States of Mind: Dialogues with Contemporary Thinkers on the European Mind* (ed. R. Kearney, Manchester University Press, Manchester and New York University Press, New York, 1995), pp. 33–39. One of the main dangers of the equation of nation with state, as Ricoeur observes, is the eclipse of society behind the state. Thus we see, for example, how the French Revolution apportioned political sovereignty to all levels of the community, from the government at the top to the individuals at the bottom, but allowed the state to become omnipresent in the process, reducing the citizen to a mere fragment of the state. On the relation between state and nation see also Quentin Skinner's

classic essay, 'The State', in *Political Innovation and Conceptual Change* (ed. T. Ball, J. Farr and R. Hanson, Cambridge University Press, Cambridge, 1988).

4 Desmond Fennell, *The Revision of Irish Nationalism* (Open Air, Dublin, 1989), p. 13. Fennell develops his analysis of territorial nationalism as follows: 'The definition of the nation as a community determined by a territory – the so-called national territory – was typical of much European nationalism. . . . As a matter of history, most European nation-states were constructed by using force, administrative pressures, and schooling to convert this theory into fact. . . . The primary aim of Irish nationalism, a united, self-governing Ireland, was also typically nationalist: the nation inhabiting the national territory, so the theory ran, had the right to political autonomy under a single government' (pp. 20–21). Fennell outlines his own position on a new nationalism thus: 'I believe that the revised nationalism, unlike its rivals, offers a cast of mind and a direction of effort which are of real use to Irish people today. Anti-nationalist revisionism abandons, and cuts us off from, the only intellectual tradition and thread of continuous meaning that runs through our modern history. It promotes collective discouragement, national disintegration and provincial decline. Traditional nationalism, by failing to learn from experience and to think again, imposes a battering of heads against stone walls in a vacuum of reality. By contrast, revised Irish nationalism – this far from finished readjustment of our inherited nationalism to facts, changing circumstances and our real goals and needs – makes our present, to quote Hyde, a "rational continuation of our past" which can face us confidently into the future' (p. 11). See also Fennell's other attempts to rethink Irish nationalism beyond the alternatives of anti-nationalist 'revisionism' and die-hard traditionalism, *Beyond Nationalism* (Ward River, Dublin, 1985) and *The State of the Nation* (Ward River, Dublin, 1983). While granting the validity of many of Fennell's critical aguments and distinctions, I will be attempting in these studies to articulate a *postnationalist* position.

5 Tom Garvin, 'Nationalism and Separatism in Ireland, 1760–1993: A Comparative Perspective' in *Nationalism in Europe Past and Future* (eds J. Bermanendi, R. Maiz and X. Nunez, Universidade de Santiago de Compostela, 1994), p. 84: 'The image of the Emerald Isle alone and inviolate in the ocean has itself become a cultural symbol, a mute argument for the unity of Ireland and its necessary separation from Britain. This argument from geography has commonly impressed not only Irish separatists themselves, but also many British observers and, perhaps most third-country observers of the tortured and tortuous relationship, one of mutual love and mutual hatred, between the two islands. Anti-partitionists in parictular commonly justify the Republic's constitutional claim to Northern Ireland by claiming that what God and History have united, no man, and certainly no Englishman, can sunder'. This debate has direct relevance to current discussions of a revised Irish Constitution. De Valera's constitution of 1937 described the 'Nation' in terms of three articles. The Irish nation is asserted (axiomatically) rather than defined in Article 1. It is described in terms of national territory encompassing the entire island in Article 2; and refers to the divided condition of the island as a temporary matter, 'pending the re-integration of the national territory' in Article 3. The subsequent descriptions of the

'State' which follow – Articles 4 to 9 – are equally nebulous and ambiguous. Hence the need for a revised Constitution setting out a clear definition of citizenship and nationality, and taking into consideration the new status of Northern Ireland as a region relating concentrically to the island of Ireland, the British archipelago, the European Union and the UN. I am indebted to Philip McGuinness for several of the above comments. I am also indebted to Michael Gallagher's insightful analysis, 'How Many Nations Are There in Ireland?' in *Ethnic and Racial Studies* (Vol. 18 No. 4), pp. 715–740. His thesis is that there are three nations in Northern Ireland – an Irish nation, an Ulster Protestant nation and part of the British nation.

6 See Hans Sluga on the romantic philosophy of Germany as an ethnic nation in *Heidegger's Crisis: Philosophy and Politics in Nazi Germany* (Harvard University Press, Cambridge, Mass., 1993), pp. 60, 91, 103–108. In his *Addresses to the German Nation* (1807), Fichte called on the spirit of the German people to remember 'its own true nature' and to realize that the battle against other nations cannot be 'fought without one's household gods, one's mythic roots, without a true "recovery" of all things German' (sec. 23). It was not a huge leap from these musings of the German romantics to the argument of a Nazi ideologue like Rosenberg who, in his speech on 'The Crisis and Construction of Europe' (1934), called for a rejection of the Enlightenment universalism that had dominated European thought and politics, concluding: 'The point, the idea, the fact from which we must start today is the fact of the nation' (cited Sluga, *Heidegger's Crisis*, p. 60). The antisemitism, racism, social Darwinism and antipathy to all forms of internationalism that typified National Socialism were not, it is fair to say, qualities shared by Irish or British nationalists in any general sense. For further discussion of German nationalism, particularly in the contemporary context where the traditional equation of 'people', 'nation' and 'state' is becoming more and more confused and questioned, see Eric Hobsbawm, *Nations and Nationalism since 1780* (Cambridge University Press, Cambridge, 1990), pp. 180–181. It is worth noting here that while British and French nationalisms are in principle civic rather than ethnic, some recent responses to the 'emigration problem' have revived some concept of the latter, albeit frequently at a cultural level – e.g. the British heritage industry or the French neo-conservative revivalism.

7 Fennell, *The Revision of Irish Nationalism*, p. 13.

8 Ignatieff, *Blood and Belonging*, p. 7. On this vexed distinction between civic and ethnic nationalism see Ricoeur's pertinent remarks in 'Universality and the Power of Difference', pp. 35–36: 'The notion of "people" according to the French Constitution is not ethnic. Its citizenship is defined by the fact that somebody is born on the territory of France. For example, the son or daughter of an immigrant is French because he or she was born on this territory. So the rule of membership has nothing to do with ethnic origin. This is why it was impossible to define Corsican people, because we had to rely on criteria other than citizenship, on ethnic criteria. . . . The Corsican people are also members of the French people. Here we have two meanings of the term "people". On the one hand, people means to be a citizen in a state, so it's not an ethnic concept. But on the other hand, Corsica *is* a people in an ethnic sense – within the French people which is not an ethnic concept. I think it's an example of what is happening throughout

Europe now'. A further conflict of interpretations with regard to French nationality / *Francophone* identity / 'Frenchness' applies to De Gaulle's famous Cabinet Statement of July 1967, where he spoke of the Quebec people as a 'population descended from her own [French] people and admirably faithful to their country of origin'. This effectively contravened the traditional civic, and non-linguistic, non-ethnic, definition of Frenchness as defined by the French revolutionary constitution (see Eric Hobsbawm, *Nations and Nationalism since 1780*, Cambridge University Press, Cambridge, 1990, p. 181). Hobsbawm notes the emergence of similar tensions in the British definition of citizenship and national identity: 'Until the 1960s "Britishness", in terms of law and administration, was a simple matter of being born to British parents or on British soil, marrying a British citizen, or being naturalized. It is a far from simple matter today' (p. 181). For a more detailed discussion of the tension between ethnic and civic nationalism, see Liah Greenfeld, *Nationalism – Five Roads to Modernity* (Harvard University Press, Cambridge, Mass., 1992), pp. 6–13, cited in Note 20 of this Introduction and Note 19 of Chapter I.

9 Tom Garvin, 'Nationalism and Separatism in Ireland', p. 84. Garvin acknowledges that the use of race theory has been rare and untypical 'on the part of both separatists and anti-separatists in the British/Irish relationship' (p. 83).

10 See report by Andy Pollack, *Irish Times*, 15 April 1995 based on research by Professor Dermot Keogh into Government Papers of the pre-war and war period.

11 On this question of the 'migrant nation' see contributions by Liam Ryan, Maurice Hayes, Graeme Kirkham, Kirby Miller, J.J. Lee, George Quigley, Seamus Heaney *et al.* in *Migrations: The Irish at Home and Abroad* (ed. R. Kearney, Wolfhound Press, Dublin, 1990). See also Benedict Anderson's Lectures on 'Exodus, Exile and the Nation-State' in Dublin City University and Trinity College Dublin, 1 December 1995. Anderson argues that the notion of a 'national people' or population is becoming increasingly porous, if not outdated, in many countries today where three-generation families are now a rarity and multiculturalism, pluralism and mass migration are eroding the old connection between people and land (see Bossuet's seventeenth-century phrase about those who 'live and die in the land of their birth'). Increasingly, nationality is becoming something you carry with you rather than a fixed attachment to a specific place of birth (see Leopold Bloom's definition of the nation as 'the same people in the same place'). When one considers, moreover, that some 17 million people crossed the Atlantic to North America between the seventeenth and nineteenth centuries, and that over 125 million 'non-resident aliens' lived and worked temporarily in the USA in the 1980s – with no allegiances as 'national citizens' regarding defence, elections or taxation – one begins to grasp how attenuated the notions of national population and original homeland are becoming. Understanding nationalism to be one of the greatest means of commanding the loyalty and allegiance of people, the USA has deployed various means to 'renationalize' the landscape (e.g. the frontier myth of the 'western') and the emigrant 'melting pot' population (e.g.through a them/us strategy of war, from the old Independence and Mexican wars to the two World Wars this century and subsequent campaigns in Korea, Vietnam, the

Middle East and Latin America). Remarking on the British need to *nationalize* its own pluralist and ethnically mixed populations – accentuated by secessionist demands by the Scots and Irish as well as post-colonial demands for multicultural diversity – Anderson cites how a Thatcherite exploitation of an adversarial alliance of General Galtieri / Bobby Sands / Arthur Scargill / General Gadafy / Sadam Hussein and (to a modified extent) Jacques Delors, managed to galvanize the various peoples making up Britain into a single and sovereign nation – for a time. Combined with the gradual erosion of inherited notions of 'national economy' (because of the globalization of money-markets), 'national culture' (because of the internationalization of media and communications, in spite of the rearguard efforts of the British heritage industry) and 'national politics' (because of co-decision-making, joint-defence in NATO / WEU / UN and shared sovereignty within the European Union), the hybridization of the so-called 'national population' together with mass circulation across frontiers is now, it would seem, an irreversible process in Britain as elsewhere. So also Jean Franco, 'The Nation as Imagined Community' in *The New Historicism* (ed. H. A. Vesser, Routledge, London, 1989) and Homi Bhabha, 'Dissemi-Nation: Time, Narrative and the Margins of the Modern Nation' in *Nation and Narration* (Routledge, London, 1990), pp. 291–322. Bhabha's basic argument, derived largely from the postmodern theory of deconstruction, is that the 'nation' is 'the measure of the liminality of cultural modernity' (p. 292). He suggests that the nation is a metaphor, or imaginary subject, invented to fill the void opened by the uprooting of communities and seeking to compensate for that loss.

12 An additional variation on the post-nation-state model is what Benedict Anderson calls 'long-distance nationalism'. His basic hypothesis here is that several forms of contemporary nationalism are the products of exile and exodus – expatriate populations looking back nostalgically on the lost homeland – rather than expressions of atavistic / nativist tradition, as is commonly supposed. The cliché of the 'sea-divided Gael' has more significance than one might think. In this respect, one might cite how it is often expatriate Irish-Americans (frequently second-generation or more) who cling to the most 'traditionalist' forms of nationalism, as witnessed in Noraid support for the IRA and the controversies over the participation of Irish Gay and Lesbian Groups in the New York and Boston St Patrick's Day parades (or, one might add, expatriate funding for the 1995 Anti-Divorce Campaign). But the nostalgia neurosis that 'invents' outdated models of nationality/nationalism *retrospectively* can equally be a feature of a modern nation's *internal* sense of exile. Nationalism thus also reveals itself as a response to an internal experience of loss – e.g. a lost language (Gaelic) or ancient homeland (the four green fields). Indeed, the cultural critic Luke Gibbons goes so far as to argue that the ideal of authentic territorially based nationality is often a fiction of advanced, secular, urban centres. Or to put it another way, metropolitan modernity reacts to its sense of inner displacement by producing purist/fundamentalist/nativist forms of nationalism in compensation. Thus, for example, the famous St Patrick's Day Speech by De Valera in 1943 was, Gibbons suggests, a traditionalist portrait of the old, pristine nation delivered from the threshold of modernity. In this sense, notions of national tradition frequently turn out to be an

invention of modernity, as in the American fantasy of the Wild West or the Irish fiction of the West of Ireland (see Luke Gibbons and Fintan O'Toole). Or to put this paradox in another way, it is precisely when the old securities of the classic nation-state – fixed territorial boundaries, contractual citizenship, economic–political autonomy, civic allegiance and cultural identity – are threatened, that we find the need to retrieve and revive so-called 'primordial' nationalism, namely, the need to combine a sense of homeland with a sense of accountability. This phenomenon of 'late nationalism', or what we might call retro-nationalism, is a phenomenon which Anderson links with the dislocationary processes of late capitalism. The more people feel surrounded by a *disenchanted* universe – an alienated, simulated, mass-produced world – the greater their need for a return to a *re-enchanted* universe. Neo-nationalism seems a response to such a need (as witnessed in the doubling of newly formed nation-states since the First World War, accelerated by the break-up of the 'Communist Bloc'). And yet another feature of 'long-distance nationalism' is the internationalization of national politics as evidenced in the growing number of expatriate or foreign citizens – usually American or Canadian – entering the presidential compaigns of post-communist nation-states (e.g. Croatia, Poland, Estonia). Nor should we underestimate the influential role played by American-Irish politicians, especially the Kennedys and President Clinton, in the Northern Ireland Peace Process (1994–96).

Our own hypothesis in this book is, *pace* Anderson, that an appropriate combination of the need for identity-recognition (home) and accountability (allegiance–loyalty) can be achieved by a regional–federal model of government, rather than by late/neo/retro-nationalism. It is surely telling, for example, that, in accordance with Anderson's index of willingness to pay taxes as a token of belonging to a community, emerging quasi-autonomous regions like Catalonia and the Basque country claim as primary the right to levy and regulate taxes.

13 Garvin, 'Nationalism and Separatism in Ireland', p. 86. for a contrasting view, see Brendán Ó Buachalla, 'Irish Jacobitism and Irish Nationalism: The Literary Evidence' in *Nations and Nationalisms* (eds M. O'Dea and K. Whelan), Voltaire Foundation, Oxford, 1996.

14 *Ibid.*, p. 88. It was through the use of the English language, Garvin claims, that 'the idea of an Irish Republic, free of aristocratic privilege, monarchical trappings and religious distinctions was transmitted to a popular culture . . .' (p. 86). In this respect language proved to be a far more malleable badge of national identity than say race or religion. 'Language has the great advantage from the point of view of nation-builders, of being learnable; unlike one's religion, there is no spiritual price to pay for "changing sides"' (T. Garvin, 'Ethnic Markers, Modern Nationalisms, and the Nightmare of History', p. 72). See also here John McNamara's more psychological–philosophical–linguistic approach to this subject in 'The Irish Language and Nationalism' in *The Crane Bag*, vol. 1, no. 2. 1977, reprinted in *The Crane Bag Book of Irish Studies*, vol. I (1977–81) (eds M.-P. Hederman and R. Kearney, Blackwater Press, Dublin), pp. 124–129. The complex relationship between language and nation extends beyond the Irish case and has many repercussions in the emerging European context. As Paul Ricoeur puts it: 'There is no political distribution of borders which is

adequate to the distributions of languages and cultures, so there is no political solution at the level of the nation-state. This is the real irritator of the nineteenth century (legacy), the dream of a perfect equation between state and nation. That has failed so we have to look for something else. But there is a political problem here. Is the project of European federalism to be a confederation of regions, or of nations? This is something without a precedent. Modern history has been made by nation-states. But there are problems of size. We have five or six nation-states in Europe of major size, but we also have micro-nations which cannot become micro-states in the same way as national states have done' ('Universality and the Power of Difference', *States of Mind,* pp. 34–35). This problem of size relates as much to regions as to nations, of course, as N. Ascherson points out in 'Nations and Regions' (*States of Mind,* pp. 20 f.). Regions in the European context, for example, range from a German *Land* like Bavaria to the smaller regions of Italy or Spain where, in some instances like Catalonia or the Basque region, considerable cultural–linguistic–educational autonomy and even fiscal-economic devolution is allowed. We will return to this variable definition of regions below; suffice it to say here that we understand a region, for the purposes of our ideal argument, as a quasi-autonomous, often subnational, unit operating on principles of radical subsidiarity and local democracy within an overall transnational federal framework. In some respects, Catalonia could be taken as something of a model 'region' in that it manages to combine a sense of local self-government and cultural autonomy with a vivid sense of cosmopolitanism. A case study of a region like Catalonia would enable us to spell out some of the more desirable, and practicable, features of cosmopolitan regionalism in a post-nation-state context (see note 30 below). The emphasis on a cosmopolitan dimension here expresses our determination to distinguish between 'region' and 'ethnic nation', *pace* Yann Fouere *Towards a Federal Europe – Nations or States?* (Christopher Davies, Swansea, 1980). As we intend the term, a region would not be an *ethnie* but rather a *localité*, in line, for example, with the Council of Europe's *Charter for Local Self-Government* and the postnationalist idea of 'subsidiarity' outlined in the Maastricht Treaty, where democratic power proceeds from the smallest political unit.

15 See Marianne Elliott on this complex but intimate relation between nationalism and religion in the Irish context, 'Religion and Identity in Northern Ireland' in *Race, Ethnicity and Nationalism at the End of the Twentieth Century* (Proceedings of University of Wisconsin Conference, 1993, ed. Winston A. Van Horn, SUNY Press, 1996). Elliott claims that the Ulster Protestants' rejection of Irish nationalism is dominated by their rejection of Catholicism. See also Conor Cruise O'Brien's trenchant critique of what he calls 'sacral nationalism' in *Ancestral Voices: Religion and Nationalism in Ireland* (Poolbeg Press, Dublin, 1994); my own 'Faith and Fatherland' in *The Crane Bag,* vol. 8, no. 1 (1984), pp. 55–68; John A. Murphy, 'Religion and Irish Identity' and Dermot Keogh, 'Catholicism and the Formation of the Modern Irish Society', both in *Irishness in a Changing Society* (Princess Grace Irish Library 2, Barnes and Noble, New Jersey, 1988), pp. 132–152 and pp. 152–178. Nor should one forget, in this connection, the significant support given to the Irish nationalist cause by the emigré Catholic communities in the armies, trades and Roman Catholic 'Irish colleges' of

continental Europe during several centuries. The relationship between nationalism and Catholicism resurfaced, in a very different context, during the heated debates on abortion information and divorce in the 1990s, particularly as they affected the Irish Constitution. The narrow passing of the controversial Divorce Referendum in November 1995 was a particularly significant moment in this ongoing process of Irish 'self-identification'. The reverse side of the Catholic–nationalist equation is the Protestant–unionist; on the relationship between Protestantism and Orangeism, see for example, Ed Moloney, 'Paisley' in *The Crane Bag*, vol. 4, no. 2, 1980, pp. 23–28; and Jim Smyth, 'The Men of No Popery: The Origins of the Orange Order', *History Ireland*, Autumn 1995, pp. 48–53.

16   Garvin, 'Nationalism and Separatism in Ireland', p. 89. See also Garvin, 'The Return of History: Collective Myths and Modern Nationalism' in *Irish Review*, no. 9 (Autumn 1990), pp. 16–20. For further discussion of this issue, see Declan Kiberd, *Inventing Ireland* (Jonathan Cape, London, 1995). An additional reason for the reversion of Irish nationalism to confessional allegiance may have something to do with the more general issue of new nation-states experiencing a foundational crisis of legitimation. As Paul Ricoeur points out: 'A la racine du politique, à son fondement, il y a l'énigme de l'origine de l'autorité. D'où vient-elle? C'est une chose qui est toujours non reglée, et qui fait que l'ombre ou le fantôme du théologique continue de rôder autour du politique' (*La Critique et la Conviction*, Calmann-Lévy, Paris, 1995, p. 201). We will return to this crucial question of the crisis of authority, arising from the problematic question of the 'origin' of sovereignty, in several of the chapters of this volume; see, in particular Chapter 1, Note 3.

17   Fennell, *The Revision of Irish Nationalism*, p. 87. See also Peter Neary, 'The Failure of Economic Nationalism' in *Ireland: Dependence and Independence, The Crane Bag*, vol. 8, no. 1 (1984); and Mary Daly, 'The Impact of Economic Development on National Identity' in *Irishness in a Changing Society*, pp. 95–109.

18   This question of the line dividing national, international and regional models of wealth has been the subject of much recent debate between political and economic theorists. Among the most cogent analysts of the economic factors behind the erosion of the nation-state is Benedict Anderson, who emphases the 'material infrastructure' conditioning the shift from nationalism to postnationalism. Anderson's basic point is that the ideology of a 'national economy' is in effect nullified by the unification of the global economy under late (print) capitalism with its attendant processes of mass communications and mobilization of populations. The model of the classical nineteenth-century nation-state with its combination of a sense of home (the desire for identity) and accountability (the willingness to pay taxes) is now being superseded. The fact that in the 1990s over 125 million wage earners in the USA are classified as 'non-resident aliens' (as opposed to 2.5 million in the 1940s) means that their economic allegiance is virtually 'extra-territorial', allowing for large tax exemption in the land of employment and limited tax liabilities on the sums 'repatriated' to their land of origin/residence/nationality. Anderson argues that *taxation* becomes, in the postnationalist era, a telling material index of one's sense of *belonging*. Anderson also counts recent developments in satellite and digital com-

munications, cybernetics and media technology as integral parts of the late capitalist 'material infrastructure' which dissolves the boundaries of the sovereign nation-state – along with international banking and security, arms trade, drug traffic, cheap aviation transport, the AIDS virus, monetary exchange and mass migration. See also here Al Lingis, 'Political Economy and Ethics in the New World Order' (unpublished): 'The traditional organization of human societies into nation-states with independent administrative bodies and national industries and local markets is rapidly being displaced by the new archipelago of technopoles. The capital, the researchers, the investments, the labor force, the markets of the high-tech industries, banking and commerce are not Japanese, American, or German any more, but transnational. Today the advanced industrial nations have accepted the New World Order of NAFTA, the European Union, GATT, the Pacific Rim and the Southeast Asia Free-Trade zone, and the WTO. The Parliamentary committees of governments, which up to recently were representatives of powerful industries and businesses in their districts, now find that protectionist measures for local industries only reduces their competitiveness before the multinational corporations. . . . It is not the parliamentary committees of nation-states but the experts in the technopoles that will regulate investments, salaries, the distribution of profits'. It is also a sobering thought to bear in mind that one of the antidotes to this postmodern anonymity of control is the rise of the entertainment industry's Star system: 'Sylvester Stallone, Arnold Schwarzenegger, Michael Jackson, and Madonna have annual incomes superior to the governments of half of the nations represented in the UN'. For a more benign model of inter-regional cooperation in the new postnationalist Europe, see Neal Ascherson's positive analysis of the successful 'Four Motors' network – Catalonia, Rhône-Alpes, Lombardy, Baden-Würtemberg – in *Games with Shadows* (Radius, London, 1993). For further discussion of the economic infrastructure of the new 'transnationalism', see *New Times: The Changing Face of Politics in the 1990s* (eds Stuart Hall and Martin Jacques, Lawrence and Wishart, London, 1989), in particular David Held, 'The Decline of the Nation State', pp. 191–205.

19 Garvin, 'Ethnic Markers, Modern Nationalisms, and the Nightmare of History', p. 63. Amongst the contradictions and complexities of Irish cultural nationalism, Garvin points to the tension between the Anglo-Irish and Gaelic traditions which Yeats sought to combine in a *single* narrative. 'Yeats, himself a Protestant, wished to devise an Irish national myth that provided room for people of his own "Anglo-Irish" tradition. The trouble was that the materials he wished to use were mutually incompatible, being derived from Anglo-Irish and Celtic Irish traditions, which had historically always been at loggerheads and, worse, were still known to have been so' (p. 64). (On this point see also our own Chapters 7 and 8.) Another more general contradiction involves the conflict between modern–secularist and tribal–traditionalist aspects of Irish nationalism. 'The modern self-contradictory, attempted derivations of Irish nationality from Gaelic, Catholic, or even Anglo-Irish aristocratic identities would have horrified and bewildered Wolfe Tone and the other France-inspired Irish Jacobins of the 1790s. The Enlightenment concept of "citizenship" independent of one's traditional identification has survived in Ireland, but it has faced very severe

competition from, in particular, religion-based identities' (p. 65). While conceding that modern *political* nationalism is a child of Enlightenment universalism, in principle, Garvin argues that nationalism as a *cultural* phenomenon (with political consequences) is far more ancient, and more atavistic, than the modern universalized version. 'In Ireland, land hunger, a quasi-racist sense of common "stock", memories of confiscation and a strong Catholicism . . . lie behind the theoretically secular modern national identity of English-speaking Ireland. The inheritance is ambivalent, and has several ideological repertoires that may be drawn upon' (p. 66).

20 Liah Greenfeld, *Nationalism – Five Roads to Modernity* (Harvard University Press, Cambridge, Mass., 1992), p. 7. Greenfeld thus sees nationalism as an 'emergent phenomenon' whose nature is determined not by the specific criteria of its particularist elements – race, religion, language, land, etc. – which vary greatly between and even within developing nationalisms, but in the function of *self-interpretation* which enables any nation to legitimate its own process of selection, election and identification. In contradistinction, therefore, to an exclusively class-based, religious or even ethnic identity, national identity cannot be predicated on any 'objective' characteristics (however intimately associated) but only on the view which the members of the 'nation' in question have of themselves. 'Identity is perception', as Greenfeld puts it. 'If a particular identity does not mean anything to the population in question, this population does not have this particular identity' (pp. 12–13). Greenfeld concludes accordingly that 'no clear line separates selection from artificial construction. A language of a part may be imposed on the entire population and declared native to the latter. . . . An "ancestral" territory may be acquired in conquest, "common" history fabricated, traditions imagined and projected into the past. One should add to this that the unique identity of a community is not necessarily ethnic, because the community may not see any of the (allegedly) inherent attributes of the population as the source of its uniqueness, but may concentrate, for example, as was the case in France, on the personal attributes of the king or on high, academic, culture. Some populations have no "ethnic" characteristics at all, though this is very unusual. The population of the USA, the identity of which is unmistakably national and which undoubtedly possesses a well-developed sense of uniqueness, is a case in point: it has no "ethnic" characteristics because its population is not an "ethnic community"' (p. 13). This understanding of nationalism as a *hermeneutic construct* is central to our understanding of nationalism in the chapters of this volume.

21 Any critical development of this mirror-imaging of Irish and British nationalism should take account of the recent work of Linda Colley, *Britons: Forging the Nation, 1797–1837* (Yale University Press, New Haven, 1992) and 'Britishness and otherness: an argument', *Journal of British Studies*, No. 31 (1992). Colley's basic thesis is that the various peoples that made up the British nation were brought together as a national identity by confrontation with the 'other'. In parallel with this, several advocates of a 'new British history' – ranging from Hugh Kearney and R. R. Davies to J. G. A. Pocock and Tom Nairn – are suggesting that British national identity is contingent and relational (like most others) and is best understood as an *interaction* between several different histories and peoples. Without endorsing the Four

Nations model of British history, Colley contends that most inhabitants of the 'British isles' lay claim to a double, triple or multiple identity – even subsequent to the invitation of a British national identity after 1700. Thus it was quite frequent, up to the late nineteenth century, for so-called British subjects to mentally identify themselves in terms of a town, landscape, region or country as well as nationally. Or to take one of Colley's own examples, an individual might see himself as being, at one and the same time, a citizen of Edinburgh, a Lowlander, a Scot and a Briton. The decisive factor in forging the artificial nation of Great Britain was, according to Colley, not so much the union of England and Wales in the early sixteenth century, but 'a series of massive wars between 1689 and 1815 which allowed its diverse inhabitants to focus on what they had in common rather than on what divided them, and which forged an overseas empire from which all parts of Britain could secure real as well as psychic profits' ('Britishness and Otherness', p. 66). The three main 'others' which served this role of *alternative* to the emerging British *native/national* were, for Colley: (1) France, (2) the global empire, and (3) the Catholicism of continental Europe (and of most of Ireland) *in contrast* to which they defined themselves in terms of a 'common Protestantism'. Britons defined themselves, thus, 'not just through an internal and domestic dialogue, but in conscious opposition to the *Other* beyond their shores' (p. 67). Colley glosses her thesis with the following graphic image: 'The powerful sense that the British had of themselves as a Protestant sanctury under siege persisted long after the majority of them had ceased to attend church on a regular basis: one has only to call to mind the famous photograph of London during the Blitz, showing St Paul's Cathedral – the parish church of the empire as it was then styled – emerging defiantly and unscathed from the fire and devastation surrounding it. There can be few more striking images of a Protestant citadel, encircled by enemies, but safe under the watchful eye of a strictly English-speaking deity' (p. 72). Borrowing this dialectic of national identity and otherness from Edward Said's famous thesis in *Orientalism* (New York, 1978) that the Orient helped to define the European empire as its contrasting image, Colley demonstrates how different Britons agreed to act in unison, sharing the same cult of empire, when confronted with the same hostile enemy. Interpreting Britain, accordingly, as an 'invented nation' sustained by a sense of otherness, helps one to understand why Ireland was to serve as the 'poor relation' of the United Kingdom: '[Ireland's] population was more Catholic than Protestant. It was the ideal jumping-off point for a French invasion, and both its Protestant and its Catholic dissidents traditionally looked to France for aid. And although Irishmen were always an important component of the British armed forces, and individual Scots–Irishmen like Macartney and Anglo-Irishmen like the Wellesley clan played leading imperial roles as diplomats, generals and pro-consuls, Ireland's relationship with the empire was always a deeply ambiguous one. How could it not be, when London so persistently treated the country, in a way that it never treated Scotland and Wales, as a colony rather than as an integral part of a truly united kingdom? Ireland was in many respects the laboratory of the British empire. Much of the legal and land reform which the British sought to implement in India, for example, was based on experiments first implemented in Ireland' (p. 76). Colley concludes that current talk of the break-up of Britain should be understood in the context of the following: (1) the weakening of Protestantism as a mainstay of British identity, (2) the end of its war-making, empire-building era, and (3) the uncomfortable fact that it can neither control Europe nor avoid it. Because it has become part of Europe it can no longer define itself over and against it. The current dissolution of British national identity – attendant upon the concomitant dissolving of the Other (be it Catholicism, exotic empire or a militant France or Germany) – has led naturally to a renewed sensitivity to internal regional differences (Welsh, Scots, Northern Irish). Unless the British come to appreciate the crucial role played by their own identity, they will, in Colley's words, 'scarcely be able adequately to understand themselves' (p. 77). On this mirror-image relationship between Irish and British national-ism, see also Terry Eagleton, *Heathcliff and the Great Hunger* (Verso, London, 1994), as well as the post-colonial critiques of a new generation of Irish commentators such as David Lloyd, Kevin Whelan, Luke Gibbons, Seamus Deane, Belinda Loftus, Emer Nolan and Declan Kiberd whose respective works are cited in several of the studies below.

22 Greenfeld, *Nationalism*, p. 6. She continues her analysis of this extraordin-ary change in attitude thus: 'The stark significance of this conceptual revo-lution was highlighted by the fact that, while the general referent of the word "people" prior to its nationalisation was the population of a region, specifically it applied to the lower classes and was most frequently used in the sense of "rabble" or "plebs". The equation of the two concepts implied the elevation of the populace to the position of an (at first specifically political) elite. As a synonym of the "nation" – an elite – the "people" lost its derogatory connotation and, now denoting an eminently positive entity, acquired the meaning of the bearer of sovereignty, the basis of political solidarity, and the supreme object of loyalty' (pp. 6–7). In this pioneering book, Greenfeld traces the development of the term 'natio/nation' from (i) 'a group of foreigners' to (ii) a 'community of opinion' to (iii) an 'elite' to (iv) its modern sense of a 'unique sovereign people'. The author reminds us, however, that the original emergence of nationalism in the modern era was also synonymous with the development of *democracy* (pp. 10–11). Declan Kiberd offers a 'post-colonial' reading of the symbiotic relationship be-tween British and Irish nationalism in *Inventing Ireland: The Literature of a Modern Nation* (Jonathan Cape, London, 1995). See, for example, his claim that 'insurgent nationalism is perpetually doomed to define itself in the loaded language and hegemonic terms set by the coloniser'. He cites the work of Wilde and Shaw in particular to show how Ireland served as England's unconscious. For a somewhat contrasting view of the symbiotic relationship between Irish and British nationalism see *Culture in Ireland: Division or Diversity* (ed. Edna Longley, Proceedings of the Cultures of Ireland Group Conference, IIS, Belfast, 1991).

23 The historian R.R. Davies offers a revealing analysis of how England – as early as the fourteenth century – was defining itself as a distinct people or nation (*gens* or *nacio*) over and against the neighbouring Irish: 'Fourteenth-century English government officials, especially in their comments on and policy towards Ireland, had a revealing label for it. It was degeneracy, literally defecting from and compromising one's own identity as a people or *gens*' ('The Peoples of Britain and Ireland 1100–1400 I. Identities' in

Transactions of the Royal Historical Society, Royal Historical Society, London, 1994, p. 7). To halt this process of degeneracy, and to bolster the differences between the English and the Irish, English legislators in Ireland issued the infamous Statutes of Kilkenny, seeking to distinguish the English by such traits as language, law, name-forms and apparel. But what the English – a *gens* largely invented by Bede – and later the British, could never fully accept was that after the invasion of the Normans, both Wales and Ireland were now countries of *multiple* peoples and identities which included, in part at least, the culture of the colonizer who was so desperately struggling to retain (even if it meant reinventing) his own sense of pure, uncontaminated identity. Ethnic characteristics were thus often exploited as the most basic means of re-establishing criteria of 'otherness' for reasons of colonial convenience and division. In short, in order to protect themselves against their Irish double, the English constructed laws and institutions to separate themselves from the Irish along racial lines. It was indeed because the English settlers in Ireland were so insecure and unsure of their own porous and ambiguous status as a 'middle nation' that they insisted, often in strident and exaggerated fashion, on their own ethnic purity *vis-à-vis* the native Irish. Thus the match between people and polity which was achieved in England (and to a lesser extent Scotland) was not replicated in Ireland (or Wales). As early as 1317, the Irish, in the name of Donald O'Neill, King of Ulster and self-proclaimed heir of the 'whole of Ireland', responded to the English divisionary tactics by appealing to the Pope in a Remonstrance which was, in Davies's words: 'an affirmation of the unbroken historical continuity of the Irish, especially through their kings, and of the individuality of their laws, way of life and speech, and a catalogue of the tribulations they had suffered at the hands of the English settlers in Ireland' (p. 19). But while the peoples of England (including the Normans) were, by the fifteenth century, welded into an integrative unit by such strategies of colonial division and 'apartheid' against their colonized 'others', Ireland remained a victim of such divisions. What would continue, however, to haunt the contrived national unity of Englishness, and later Britishness, was the ghost of their ethnic alien – Ireland – whose very *difference* was part and parcel of their own English/British *identity*. Their other was uncannily part of themselves, the familiar spectre hidden in strangeness, the original double they had forgotten to remember, the threatened *revenant* of their own repressed political unconcious.

24 Neal Ascherson, 'Nations and Regions' in *States of Mind*, pp. 19–20. See also Desmond Fennell, *The Revision of Irish Nationalism*, p. 10: 'The nationalism which "revisionists" reject is also, it is important to note, specifically *Irish* nationalism; not, apart from fringe instances, nationalism *per se* nor, in particular, English/British nationalism. Indeed, the "revisionist" view of the Irish past and present which is substituted for the Irish nationalist view is often, to a greater or lesser degree, that of English or British nationalism as applied to Ireland'. To the extent that British nationalists do admit to their nationalism it is usually by claiming theirs to be positive (civic, secular, pluralist, rational and multicultural) and the Irish to be negative (irridentist, ethnic, primitive, reactionary).

25 Ascherson, 'Nations and Regions', p. 21. See also Stephen Mennell who argues that in Britain the recent emergence of doubt about its 'place in

Europe' is a symptom of its traumatic forfeiture of Great Power status ('Civilization and Decivilization, Civil Society and Violence', Inaugural Lecture at University College Dublin, 6 April 1995, p. 16).

26 *Ibid.*

27 Tom Nairn, *The Enchanted Glass: Britain and its Monarchy* (Radius, London, 1988), p. 137. See also the passage in the same section of that book, entitled 'English Nationality', where Nairn argues that British nationalism in the post-1776 and post-1789 era was decidedly anti-revolutionary, absolutist and top–down, 'This had to be a national-popular identity composed decisively "from above": an ideological sense of belonging dispensed by quasi-parental law, securing its unwritten authority-structure and proposing a kind of compensated deference' (pp. 136–137). Nairn develops this point in a related section entitled 'Monarchy and Nationalism', p. 131: 'Contrary to much British thinking on the subject, nationalism is in itself neither foreign, narrow, neurotic, merely accidental nor *dépassé*. All that such odd ideas reflect is the heteronomy of British and UKanian nationalism itself: a national identity isolated from the main-stream of nation-building by its own history, and which now (like Humpty-Dumpty on top of his wall) habitually judges the passing parade only in its own preconceived terms'. See also our discussion of English republicanism and nationalism in Chapters 2 and 3.

28 I am indebted to Simon Partridge here for bringing to my attention the analysis of Liah Greenfeld, *Nationalism – Five Roads to Modernity* (Harvard University Press, Cambridge, Mass., 1992). Partridge's own view is that a full resolution of the British–Irish conflict requires a coming together of the best aspects of the British–American democratic tradition and French–Irish republican tradition which would transcend both. If this were achieved, Partridge argues, then a fully reconnected Irish–British archipelago and a working Irish–British democracy might provide a model for Europe and ultimately the world. For a discussion of the differing models of American, French, English and Irish 'republicanism' see Chapters 2 and 3.

29 Benedict Anderson, *Imagined Communities: Reflections on the Origins and Spread of Nationalism* (Verso, London, 1983). Anderson demonstrates how nations become the heroes of their own national stories by inventing narra-tives – mainly through the print and other media – which justify their par-ticular identity and history. Nationalist elites have been especially effective in creating such 'imagined communities' through the propagation of collect-ively shared national myths (pp. 37–42). What this means, in effect, is that no nation is *primordial*, because every nation is culturally and socially con-structed. For further remarks by Anderson on nationalism and postnation-alism see Notes 11, 12 and 18 above.

30 See Eric Hobsbawm, *Nations and Nationalism since 1780* (Cambridge Uni-versity Press, Cambridge, 1990) where he suggests how the 'nation', when extracted from the hard shell of the 'state' – with its functions of defence, money, taxation, borders, etc. – can take on the 'wobbly shape' of a more flexible *cultural* process. This opens the possibility of nations assuming 'cul-tural' forms independent of 'political' institutions or constitutions. In this sense, cultural nations or nationalisms, detached from the procrustean mould of a state, may well emerge as more enabling agencies of both differ-ential *identity* and *democracy*. But Hobsbawm's basic prognosis is of a

postnationalist order. He concludes that as we approach the twenty-first century, nationalism is becoming historically less important than in the nineteenth-century world of 'nation-building'. A history of the emerging epoch will, he suggests, be one 'which can no longer be contained within the limits of "nations" and "nation-states" as these used to be defined, either politically, or economically, or culturally, or even linguistically. It will see "nation-states" and "nations" or ethnic/linguistic groups primarily as retreating before, resisting, adapting to, being absorbed or dislocated by, the new supranational restructuring of the globe. Nations and nationalism will be present in this history, but in subordinate, and often rather minor roles' (p. 182). Taking the example of Catalonia, Hobsbawm concedes that new channels – such as education and culture – may be found for the expression of regional identity in more complex and cosmopolitan forms: 'This does not mean that national history and culture will not bulk large – perhaps larger than before – in the educational systems of particular countries, especially the smaller ones, or that they may not flourish locally within a much broader supranational framework, as, say, Catalan culture today flourishes, but on the tacit assumption that it is Catalans who will communicate with the rest of the world through Spanish and English, since few non-residents in Catalonia will be able to communicate in the local language' (p. 182).

For further analysis of the specifically *cultural* dimensions of a post-nationalist Europe (past and future) see *Imaginer L'Europe*: *Le marché européen comme tâche culturelle et économique* (ed. Peter Koslowski, Cerf, Paris, 1992); Jacques Darras and Daniel Snowman, *Beyond the Tunnel of History* (Macmillan, London, 1990); *L'Europe sans rivages* (Cerf, Paris, 1990); Claudio Magris, *Danube* (Collins Harvill, London, 1990); and the contributors to *States of Mind: Dialogues with Contemporary Thinkers on the European Mind* (Manchester University Press / Manchester, NYU Press, New York, 1995).

31 This is precisely where the largely conceptual/representational/paradigmatic character of our own analysis needs to be supplemented and earthed by the more empirical/material/socio-economic analyses of research scholars like Kevin Whelen, Tom Barrington, Liam O'Dowd, Arnold Horner, Anne Buttimore and Brigid Laffan, whose works on Irish and European regionalism are cited below. See, in particular, K. Whelan's excellent article, 'The Region and the Intellectuals', in *Ireland and its Intellectuals* (ed. Liam O'Dowd, Institute of Irish Studies, Belfast, forthcoming); and the pioneering work conducted by Anne Buttimore's multi-disciplinary forum on Irish and European regionalism, *LLASS Working Paper*, No. 18, University College Dublin, 1995.

32 See Elie Kedourie, *Nationalism* (Blackwell, Oxford, 1993); Ernest Gellner, *Nations and Nationalism* (Cornell University Press, Ithaca, New York, 1962); Benedict Anderson, *Imagined Communities* (Verso, London, 1983); Liah Greenfeld, *Nationalism – Five Roads to Modernity* (Harvard University Press, Cambridge, Mass., 1992); Homi Bhabha (ed.) *Nation and Narration* (Routledge, London, 1990); Eric Hobsbawm, *Nations and Nationalism since 1780* (Cambridge University Press, Cambridge, 1990); John Breuilly, *Nationalism and the State* (Manchester University Press, Manchester, 1993). Hobsbawm and Breuilly, for example, criticize both Anderson and

Gellner for assuming that the self-evident success of nationalism, at a certain period in modern political history, means that it is fundamentally and progressively rooted in the minds and actions of people. Hobsbawm goes so far as to suggest that the very self-reflective nature of current debates on nationalism is itself a token of a postnationalist consciousness: 'The very fact that historians are at least beginning to make some progress in the study and analysis of nations and nationalism suggests that, as so often, the phenomenon is past its peak. The owl of Minerva which brings wisdom, said Hegel, flies out at dusk. It is a good sign that it is now circling round nations and nationalism' (*Nations and Nationalism since 1780*, pp. 182–183). For a more specific debate on the three readings of nationalism in the modern Irish context, see the following commentators – Tom Garvin, *The Evolution of Irish Nationalist Politics* (Gill and Macmillan, Dublin, 1981); Desmond Fennell, *The Revision of Irish Nationalism* (Open Air, Dublin, 1989); Marianne Elliott, *Wolfe Tone: Prophet of Irish Independence* (Yale University Press, New Haven and London, 1989); Liam de Paor, *Unfinished Business: Ireland Today and Tomorrow* (Hutchinson, London, 1990); Roy Foster, *Modern Ireland 1600–1972* (Penguin, London, 1988) especially the Prologue and Chapters 2, 16, 18 and 23; J. J. Lee, *Ireland 1912–1985: Politics and Society* (Cambridge University Press, Cambridge, 1989) especially section 8; John Ardagh, *Ireland and the Irish: Portrait of a Changing Society* (Hamish Hamilton, London, 1994); John A. Murphy, *Ireland in the Twentieth Century* (Gill and Macmillan, Dublin, 1975); Padraig O'Malley, *The Uncivil Wars: Ireland Today* (Blackstaff, Belfast, 1983); Kevin Whelan, *Tree of Liberty* (Cork University Press, Cork, 1996); K. Whelan, D. Dickson, D. Keogh, *The United Irishmen: Republicanism, Radicalism and Rebellion* (Lilliput Press, Dublin, 1993); Tim Pat Coogan, *The Troubles* (Hutchinson, London, 1995); Seamus Deane, *Nation or State?: The Clarendon Lectures 1995* (Oxford University Press, Oxford, 1996); Conor Cruise O'Brien, *States of Ireland* (Hutchinson, London, 1972) and *Ancestral Voices* (Poolbeg, Dublin, 1995); Luke Gibbons, *Transformations in Irish Culture* (Cork University Press, Cork, 1996); Joseph Lee, David Harkness, John A. Murphy, Terence Brown, R.V. Comerford, Maurice Goldring, Garrett Fitzgerald, Mary Daly, John Hume *et al.*, in *Irishness in a Changing Society* (Barnes and Noble, New Jersey, 1988); Declan Kiberd, *Inventing Ireland* (Jonathan Cape, London, 1995); David Lloyd, 'Nationalism Against the State: Towards a Critique of the Anti-nationalist Prejudice', in *Gender and Colonialism* (ed. T. Foley *et al.*, Galway University Press, 1995). Finally, I should mention here the various debates on the 'Varieties of Irishness' and 'Britishness' published by the Cultural Traditions Group Conference in Belfast (ed. Maurna Crozier, Institute of Irish Studies, 1988–1990) and the debates on Irish nationalism published by *The Crane Bag* journal (1977–1985), in particular 'A Sense of Nation' (C.C. O'Brien, Seamus Deane, Liam de Paor, *et al.*), vol. 1, no. 2, 1977 and 'Ireland: Dependence and Independence' (Ronan Fanning, Michael Laffan, Peter Neary *et al.*), vol. 8, no.1, 1984.

33 When I speak of going-beyond/sublating/transforming nationalism I am thinking of the Hegelian concept of *Aufhebung* which designates a dialectical process of preservation-through-negation, supersession-through-retrieval. Some of the current arguments for postnationalism are informed by an Enlightenment cosmopolitanism, often inspired by Kant's 'Idea of a

Universal History from the Point of View of a Citizen of the World' (1784), while others espouse a more postmodern perspective, as expounded in Chapter 4. We return to this debate in several of our chapters. Suffice it here to outline some of the most recent arguments. See, for example, Noam Chomsky's delineation of two possible directions for Europe in a post-nationalist era: 'What's happening in Europe seems to me to be an evolution beyond the nation-state, but in two different and opposed directions – which one wins will be of great consequence. One is towards centralisation of power in a transnational executive authority which is essentially immune from popular influence, because nobody knows what's going on there. These quasi-governmental institutions, like the World Bank, the IMF, the G-7 executive, GATT, and so on, reflect the interests of transnational capital. If they have executive authority, free from the influence of parliamentary institutions, that is extremely dangerous in my opinion. On the other hand, you have the opposite development towards some kind of devolution, and regional autonomy' ('The Politics of Language' in *States of Mind*, pp. 48–49). Our view here would be that a postnationalist scenario could only succeed in the European context if it secures a proper balance between a democratically empowered federal parliament and an effective form of regional–local self-government. See here Kristeva's 'postmodern' reading of a postnationalist cosmopolitan Europe in *Strangers to Ourselves* (Columbia University Press, New York, 1994) and *Nations without Nationalism* (Columbia University Press, New York, 1993). The main argument against a postnationalist paradigm seems to be that it does not convincingly explain how the collective loyalty of a community or society can be galvanized and sustained by a constitution or related set of universal laws and norms. See T. Garvin, 'Ethnic Markers, Modern Nationalisms, and the Nightmare of History', p. 74: 'The lawyer's concept of *citizen*. . . offers only a secularized and emotionally unappealing substitute for the linguistic, racist, historicist and socialist dreams of the past'. See also Wayne Norman's critique of the Habermasian substitution of 'constitutional patriotism' for nationalism. In contrast to the argument by Habermas and his supporters (Jean-Marc Ferry, André Berten and Attracta Ingram), that the rational–liberal values of citizenship, predicated upon the 'abstract idea of the universalisation of democracy and the rights of the person' (Habermas, 'Citizenship and National Identity', *Praxis International*, 12 (1), 1992), must defeat the 'pathological' and 'anti-modernist' ideology of nationalism, Norman (citing Charles Taylor, 1992) replies: 'Il faut considérer qu'il ne s'agit pas d'une forme d'unité définie *a priori* par le philosophe comme étant théoriquement légitime ou admissible, mais qu'il s'agit d'une unité qui paraisse significative pour les gens eux-mêmes. Autrement, ça ne marchera pas; il nous est donc impossible de dicter à partir des seules positions philosophiques que le principe d'unité ou d'identité devrait être celui du patriotisme constitutionnel'('Unité, Identité et Nationalisme Libéral', *Lekton*, 3(2), 1993, p. 59). Other defences of nationalism against the universalist/cosmopolitan position include David Miller, 'In Defence of Nationality', *Journal of Applied Philosophy* 10(1), pp. 3–16; Ernest Renan, 'Qu'est-ce qu'une nation?' in *The Dynamics of Nationalism* (ed. L. Snyder, Van Nostrand, New York, 1964); and R. Scruton, 'In Defence of the Nation' in *Ideas and Politics in Modern Britain* (ed. J. Clark, Macmillan, London,

1990). Our response to both anti- and pro-positions would be that no federal constitution can prove effective without a basic recognition of the fundamental need for more local forms of belonging and identity at regional or
national level; though we would argue that such forms do not – at least in
the emerging European context – need to be equated with nation-state
sovereignty or 'national self-determination'.

1 BEYOND SOVEREIGNTY

1 Paul Ricoeur, 'Universality and the Power of Difference' in *States of Mind:*
Dialogue with Contemporary Thinkers on the European Mind (ed. R. Kearney, Manchester University Press and New York University Press, 1995), p.
36.

2 The question as to when, or indeed whether, these *needs* are actually *realized*
is another matter. In Ireland it is often said that things have to get worse
before they get better. The present chapter, like those following, hopes to
surmount such an apocalyptic mind-frame.

3 See John Whyte, *Interpreting Northern Ireland* (Clarendon Press, Oxford,
1991); John McGarry and Brendan O'Leary, *Explaining Northern Ireland:*
Broken Images (Blackwell, Oxford, 1995); and Stephen Mennell, 'Civilization and Decivilization, Civil Society and Violence', University College
Dublin Inaugural Lecture, 1995, p. 16: 'The debate is conducted in the
emotive mythical language of "sovereignty", that being understood as a
nation's ability to do absolutely as it pleases. Sovereignty, in the real world,
was never absolute, but Great Powers precisely because of their power – feel
as if they are absolutely independent. The illusion is increasingly inadequate
to the reality of the world today'.

4 'Sovereignty' in *Encyclopaedia Britannica*, vol. 11, pp. 56–57. See also here
David Rasmussen, 'Ethics and Democracy under the Deliberative Paradigm' (a paper delivered to the Staff–Student Philosophy Seminar at University College Dublin, November, 1995). Here Rasmussen identifies the
origin of the modern state with Hobbes's notion of the people as a unitary
sovereign. Anticipating Rousseau's concept of a united 'General Will',
Hobbes argues in *Leviathan* (1651) that the multitude of many wills be
reduced to 'one will', adding that 'this done, the Multitude so united in one
Person is called a COMMON-WEALTH, in latin *Civitas*' (*Leviathan*, p.
227). Hobbes reckoned accordingly that power, interpreted in terms of this
unitary principle of sovereignty, would be sufficient to account for the validity of the state/*civitas*: 'One person . . . may (thus) use the strength and
means of all, as he shall think expedient, for their Peace and Common
Defence' (p. 228). But while thus legitimating the notion of coercive state
power, sovereignty still left open the question of the 'authorship', and therefore 'authority', of the covenant of state. By conceiving the notion of sovereignty *instrumentally* and *strategically*, Hobbes was unable to include an
ethical dimension into his theory of politics, opening it instead to a somewhat vicious *circle of interpretation*. Hobbes's equation of power/
sovereignty/law-of-state/reason-of-state ultimately lacked any kind of normative justification or legitimacy. From the outset then, the concept of
unitary sovereignty was linked with a 'crisis of authority' which expressed
itself in a circular spiral of legitimation. The circle went something like this:

sovereignty requires validity in 'law' to exercise its instrumental control, but the law itself is subject to sovereign power. Law, as Hobbes put it, is not 'counsel' but 'command'. It no longer derives from the authority of tradition or custom, as in the Aristotelian/classical dispensation, nor from some theological authority, as in the medieval dispensation. 'It is not the Length of Time that maketh the Authority, but the Will of the Sovereign' (p. 313). In short, the modern concept of sovereignty seeks to express itself in law but the legitimacy of law is subject to the sole authority of the sovereign. In a move to resolve this circle, Hobbes invoked the argument of Sir Edward Coke to the effect that 'Law can never be against Reason'. But here again the crisis of legitimation recurs for we are left with the question '*Whose* Reason?' The answer is as predictable for Hobbes as it is circular: it is the reason of 'our Artificiall Man the Common-wealth' which is none other than the single Person of the Sovereign. 'The Commonwealth being in their Representative but *one Person*, there cannot easily arise any contradiction in the Lawes' (p. 317). In other words, the standard of 'consistency' demanded by Reason, in order to legitimate Law, is only guaranteed by the singularity of the principle of sovereignty. By concluding, finally, that social cohesion can only be generated through the instrumental activity of the sovereign (rather than from the ethical commitments of a plurality of political subjects), Hobbes prefigured the unitarian – some would say 'totalizing' – character of sovereignty embodied in many modern nation-states. In brief, when tradition no longer provides the necessary cohesion and consent to sustain the socio-political order, the coercive power of law, predicated upon sovereignty, steps in to close the gap.

Two important responses to this 'legitimation crisis' of the modern nation-state are liberalism and republicanism. While the liberal position, running from Kant and Locke to Rawls, tends to stress the priority of individual rights and autonomy, the 'republican' (epitomized by such thinkers as Arendt and, to a modified extent, the post-Hegelian Habermas and Taylor) has given primacy to the process of 'public will-formation'. In the latter view, politics is seen as a 'normative' activity – based on a communitarian model of mutual agreement, intersubjective recognition and reciprocal communication – which deals with 'questions of value' and the 'good life' in addition to 'questions of preference'. But even here we are compelled to ask: *whose* view of the good life? Rawls seeks to overcome the so-called democratic deficit at the heart of liberalism – i.e. the emphasis on private interest at the expense of public solidarity; the attempt to base public authority on private autonomy and necessary coercion – by promoting an idea of 'overlapping consensus' based on an understanding of deliberative justice as 'fairness'. But again the recurring question: *whose* view of fairness? Even Rawls's attempt to resolve the dilemma of liberal versus republican priorities, in terms of a 'co-originality of private and public', runs up against the old Hobbesian questions – who legitimates the legitimating power of reason? who justifies justice? (On this, see the Habermas–Rawls debate, *Journal of Philosophy*, XCII(3), March 1995, pp. 109–180. I am indebted to David Rasmussen for bringing this debate to my attention.) In the heel of the hunt, there would seem to be no way out of this circle of interpretation. Perhaps we need to apply here Heidegger's famous advice about the 'hermeneutic circle': that it is less a matter of how to get out of this circle than of how to get into it in the right way. In any event, the key issue remains the need to pluralize sovereignty, or transcend it altogether. On this hermeneutic circularity of value criteria – issuing from the crisis of legitimation/origination/representation – see the Postscript 'Whose Poetics? Which Ethics?' to my *Poetics of Modernity: Towards a Hermeneutic Imagination* (Humanities Press, New Jersey, 1995), pp. 203–211.

5 *Ibid.*, p. 57. See also Benedict Anderson's powerful analysis of how the notion of sovereignty, associated with the classic nation-state characteristics of fixed territorial boundaries, contractual citizenship, politico-economic autonomy and national allegiance, is being steadily eroded in the late capitalist era of mass communication, mobilization and migration (see Notes 11, 12, 18, 27 to our Introduction).

6 See my joint-submission with Robin Wilson to the Forum for Peace and Reconciliation, Dublin Castle, 1995 in Chapter 5. See also Simon Partridge's pioneering article, 'Re-imagining these Islands: The Need for a Britannic Framework', European Regionalist Association Discussion Paper, 1995, p. 5: 'The Nordic Council was first established in 1953 as a body of parliamentarians and now brings together five nation-states and three autonomous regions: Denmark, Finland, Iceland, Norway, Sweden, and the Faeroe Islands, Greenland and the Aland Islands. The latter may be of particular relevance since it is a Swedish-speaking area, completely demilitarized, but within the Finnish state (where there is also a substantial Swedish-speaking minority with full parity of treatment with the Finnish-speaking majority) – the parallels with Northern Ireland are obvious. The Council advises the Nordic parliaments on questions needing their co-operation and co-decision-making within the objectives laid down in the Helsinki Treaty of 1962. In 1971 a Council of Ministers was added which has certain decision-making powers within the Treaty. All decisions are made unanimously, although a country or autonomous region can abstain from voting'. Such a transnational council can only prove democratic, however, when allied with a network of regenerated local government at sub-national level. In this regard, as Partridge observes, 'it is a disgrace that neither Dublin nor London have signed the *European Charter of Local Self-Government* which has been drawn up by the Council of Europe and which entrenches the inalienable rights of local government to political and fiscal autonomy'.

7 This passage is analysed in Chapter 2, 'Ideas of a Republic'.

8 Keith M. Baker, 'Sovereignty' in *A Critical Dictionary of the French Revolution* (ed. François Furet and Mona Ozouf, trans. A. Goldhammer, The Belknap Press of Harvard University Press, Cambridge, Mass., 1989), pp. 844–845. See also K.M. Baker's treatment of this concept in *The French Revolution and the Creation of Modern Political Culture*, vol. 1 (Pergamon, Oxford, 1987); and Julian H. Franklin, *Jean Bodin and the Rise of Absolutist Theory* (Columbia University Press, New York, 1963).

9 Baker, *A Critical Dictionary of the French Revolution*, p. 846.

10 *Ibid.*, p. 847.

11 *Ibid.*, p. 847.

12 *Ibid.*, p. 848. See J.-J. Rousseau, *The Social Contract* (Penguin, London, 1968), in particular, Book II, Chapters 1–3 on the inalienability of sovereignty.

13 Baker, *A Critical Dictionary of the French Revolution*, p. 850.
14 *Ibid.*, p. 851.
15 *Ibid.*, p. 856.
16 *Ibid.*, p. 858.
17 For extended critiques of the modern notion of absolute sovereignty as it relates to nation-states see in particular, Claude Lefort, *L'Invention Démocratique* (Fayard, Paris, 1981) and *Essais sur le Politique* (Editions du Seuil, 1986); Michael Ignatieff, *Blood and Belonging: Journeys into the New Nationalism* (Farrar, Strauss and Giroux, New York, 1993), notably his definitions of political, cultural and moral nationalism and his distinction between civic and ethnic nationalism; Hannah Arendt, *Crises of the Republic* (Harvest, New York, 1972) and *On Revolution* (Penguin, New York, 1987), in particular her critique of national sovereignty as a single 'general will' which carries on the principle of absolutism embodied by the monarch or God-King; Charles Taylor, *Reconciling the Solitudes: Essays on Canadian Federalism and Nationalism* (McGill–Queen's University Press, Montreal, 1993), especially his argument for a multinational federation based on citizen participation, liberal democracy and national pluralism; Michel Foucault, 'Governmentality' in *The Foucault Effect* (eds G. Burchell, C. Gordon and P. Miller, The University of Chicago Press, Chicago, 1991), pp. 87–105 for a typically 'postmodern' critique of nation-state centralization and its relation to the 'end of sovereignty' as a self-referring circle; also on this postmodern critique see our own chapter on 'Postmodernity and Postnationalism', as well as Drucilla Cornell, 'The Postmodern Challenge to the Ideal of Community' in *The Philosophy of the Limit* (Routledge, New York and London, 1992), pp. 39–62. For challenges to nation-state sovereignty in a European context see Richard Body's *Europe of Many Circles: Constructing a Wider Europe* (New European Publications, London, 1990) and Yann Fouere, *Towards a Federal Europe: Nations or States* (Christopher Davies, Swansea, 1968).
18 Liah Greenfeld, *Nationalism – Five Roads to Modernity* (Harvard University Press, Cambridge, Mass. 1992), pp. 10–11.
19 *Ibid.* Greenfeld adds the following gloss to her distinction: 'The two dissimilar interpretations of popular sovereignty underlie the basic types of nationalism, which one may classify as individualistic-libertarian and collectivistic-authoritarian. In addition, nationalism may be distinguished according to criteria of membership in the national collectivity, which may be either 'civic', that is, identical with citizenship, or 'ethnic'. In the former case, nationality is at least in principle open and voluntaristic; it can and sometimes must be acquired. In the latter, it is believed to be inherent – one can neither acquire it if one does not have it, nor change it if one does; it has nothing to do with individual will, but constitutes a genetic characteristic. Individualistic nationalism cannot be but civic, but civic nationalism can also be collectivistic. More often, though, collectivistic nationalism takes on the form of ethnic particularism, while ethnic nationalism is necessarily collectivistic' (p. 11).
20 For critiques of nation-state sovereignty in the specifically Irish and British contexts, see the studies by John Whyte and John McGarry cited in Note 2 above; *Cultural Traditions in Northern Ireland* (ed. M. Crozier, Institute of Irish Studies, Belfast, 1990); Desmond Fennell, *The Revision of Irish*

Nationalism (Open Air, Dublin, 1989) and *Beyond Nationalism* (Ward River Press, Dublin, 1985); Tom Nairn, *The Enchanted Glass: Britain and its Monarchy* (Radius, London, 1988), in particular his chapters on 'Monarchy and Nationalism', 'English Nationality' and 'Parliamentary Sovereignty' and *The Break-up of Britain?* (London, 1977); Neal Ascherson, *Games with Shadows* (Radius, London, 1988); Linda Colley, *Britons: Forging the Nation, 1707–1837* (Yale University Press, New Haven, 1992); Hugh Kearney, *The British Isles: A History of Four Nations* (Cambridge University Press, Cambridge, 1989); R.R. Davies, 'The Peoples of Britain and Ireland 1100–1400 I. Identities' in *Transactions of the Royal Historical Society* (RHS, London, 1994), pp. 1–20. and John Hume, Desmond Fennell, Ivor Browne, T.J. Barrington, Luke Gibbons, Michael D. Higgins, J.-F. Lyotard, A. Moravia, J. Kristeva *et al.* in R. Kearney ed. *Across the Frontiers: Ireland in the 1990s* (Wolfhound, Dublin, 1988). For a scholarly genealogy of sovereignty as it first emerged in a 'Celtic' context see Proinsias MacCana, 'Notes on the Early Irish Concept of Unity' in *The Crane Bag Book of Irish Studies(1977–1981)* (Blackwater Press, Dublin, 1982), pp. 205–219. I am indebted to Michael Dillon of Lancaster University and Kevin Whelan at Boston College for several insightful discussions on the origins and ends of British and Irish nationalism.

21 See Paul Ricoeur, 'Fragility and Responsibility' in *Ricoeur at 80: The Hermeneutics of Action* (Sage, London, 1995) where he advocates the formation of new forms of civil society in a postnationalist world: 'We must consider a new entity, in need of creation rather than recognition, namely the post-national state which is sought in Europe and perhaps in other continents. The problem is serious if the well-known structures of the nation-state are not to be repeated at the superior level of supranationality. The properly political question is certainly without precedent. Hence it calls for a reflection on the ethical and spiritual behaviour of individuals, intellectuals and cultured people, as well as societies of thought and religious communities, capable of contributing to the required political imagination'. This exploration of a *new political imaginary* is developed in several of the chapters herein. Such work has already been initiated by pioneering scholars like Homi Bhabha (ed.) *Nation and Narration* (Routledge, London, 1990), and in the specifically Irish context by Luke Gibbons, *Transformations in Irish Culture* (Cork University Press, Cork, 1996) and David Lloyd, *Anomalous States: Irish Writing and the Post-colonial Moment* (Lilliput, Dublin, 1993).

2 IDEAS OF A REPUBLIC

1 Conor Cruise O'Brien, *New York Review of Books*, April 1989 and J. L. Talmon, *The Myth of the Nation and the Vision of Revolution* (Secker and Warburg, London, 1981).

2 See Michel Vovelle, 'Les Droits de L'Homme au Present – Les Enjeux du Bicentenaire' in *L'Homme et la Société*, nos 85–86, Paris, 1988, pp. 146–154. He writes: 'The French revolution is neither a sure value nor a refuge-value. It is not turned toward some appeasing past . . . it is rather a dynamic solicitation. The French Revolution is to be best celebrated and conceived, in my view, as a promise of the future and as a renewable reality because in the last analysis it is the simple and basic idea that it is possible to change

the world' (p. 146). Vovelle sees the inherent dynamism of this legacy as inextricably related to its 'universalist' appeal. He concludes accordingly: 'The [French] Declaration of the Rights of Man was the first to claim to legislate for men of all times and in all societies. . . . On this basis, I think that this Declaration should not just be taken in its old sense of 'intemporality' which dates it historically in a certain context but should be taken also in the sense of a flux, of a dynamic. It is because the French Revolution inaugurated this dynamic, which led to the Declaration of the Rights of Man from 1789 to 1793, from the first certitudes to what Ernest Lebrousse defined as the 'time of anticipations', that the Declaration of the Rights of Man appears, still today and essentially, not as a *point d'aboutissement*, but as a *point de départ* of a dynamic still at work' (p. 148).

3 For this and several other citations and arguments in this section of our study, see Marianne Elliott's *Watchmen in Sion: The Protestant Idea of Liberty* (Field Day Publications, Derry, 1985) and *Wolfe Tone: Prophet of Irish Independence* (Yale University Press, New Haven and London, 1989). For a fuller discussion of the complex relations between Protestant nationalism, Presbyterian nationalism and Catholic nationalism, see Thomas Bartlett, 'Protestant Nationalism in Eighteenth-century Ireland' in *Nations and Nationalisms* (ed. K. Whelan and M. O'Dea, Voltaire Foundation, Oxford, 1996, pp. 79–88); Ian McBride, 'Presbyterians in the Penal Era', *Bullán*, no. 2, Oxford, 1994, pp. 73–86; Dáire Keogh, 'Maynooth: A Catholic Seminary in a Protestant State' in *History Ireland*, Autumn 1995, pp. 43–48.

4 M. Elliott, *ibid.*

5 I am deeply indebted to Liam de Paor's arguments in 'The Rebel Mind: Republican and Loyalist' in *The Irish Mind* (ed. R. Kearney, Wolfhound Press, Dublin, 1984 / Humanities Press, New Jersey, 1984). For a contrasting view of the active role played by Catholics in the 1798 rebellion, see Dáire Keogh, *The French Disease* (Four Courts Press, Dublin, 1993) and Jim Smyth, *The Men of No Popery* (Macmillan, London, 1992).

6 M. Elliott, *Watchmen in Sion*. For a critical development of the relationship between Catholicism and nationalism, see Emmet Larkin, *The Historical Development of Irish Catholicism* (Washington, Catholic University of America Press, 1984) and David Miller, 'Irish Catholicism and the Great Famine', *Journal of Social History*, IX, no. 1 (1975), pp. 81–98.

7 Faced, time and again, with the material differences of class, the republican idealists in the United Irishmen found themselves trapped in compromise. In order to make their revolutionary movement a popular one, enlisting the support of the Catholic majority, the leaders of the United Irishmen had to appeal to what basically amounted to 'sectarian' demands. The grievance against tithes was a case in point – for while this could be given a republican cast, it was already set in a sectarian mould. Divisions were already apparent in the '98 uprising itself, as de Paor and Elliott point out. Contrary to the mythological history of republicanism, which sees 1798 as the golden year of Protestant–Catholic unity, the facts tell a different story. For the Rising to be a success it was necessary for the United Irishmen's cosmopolitan republicanism to join forces with local populist movements like Defenderism. Most Catholics joined the movement in the expectation of a radical reversal of their material condition – an expectation scarcely separable from the old idea that Protestants must be ousted before Catholics

could come back into their own. As one Defender confessed to Counsellor Curran during the Louth Trials in 1794: 'I expected I would get what livings the likes of *you* have, for *myself . . .*'.

8 M. Elliott, *Watchmen in Sion.* See the contrasting argument by Kevin Whelan that it was the colonial state that disseminated sectarianism among the population by encouraging the establishment of the Orange order and Maynooth in the 1790s with a counter-revolutionary intent, *Tree of Liberty* (Cork University Press, 1996). See also Jim Smyth, 'The Men of No Popery: The Origins of the Orange Order', *History Ireland*, Autumn 1995, pp. 48–54.

9 L. de Paor, 'The Rebel Mind', p. 174.

10 John Hume, 'Europe of the Regions' in *Across the Frontiers* (ed. R. Kearney, Wolfhound Press, Dublin, 1988), p. 40. On the prospects, and possible perils, of transcending the nation-state towards a new republicanism allied with a new regionalism, see J.-F. Lyotard, 'What is Just?' in *States of Mind*, p. 300: 'It is essential for the Republic to become universal. In its name, the "market" is permitted to assume world proportions. That is why, today, the privilege of sovereignty which nation-states enjoyed for centuries (at most), appears an obstacle to the furtherance of development in every domain: multinational transactions, immigrant populations, international security. . . . It may even be the case, despite appearances, that the unification of Europe is more easily achievable through the federation of "natural communities" (regions like Bavaria, Scotland, Flanders, Catalonia, etc.) than through sovereign states – with all the risks attendant upon the dominance of the *demos* in each of these communities'. One might also mention here the recent critiques of the British nation-state carried out by Welsh regionalists, see Stephen Evans, 'Exiles in Whose Country?' in the *TLS*, March 1996, p. 30.

3 GENEALOGY OF THE REPUBLIC

1 Quoted by Hannah Arendt, *On Revolution* (Penguin, New York, 1963), p. 119.

2 Cicero, *The Republic*, I, 26. On the ancient Greek roots of classical republicanism see Ellen M. Wood, *Peasant-Citizen and Slave: The Foundations of Athenian Democracy* (Verso, London, 1988).

3 *Ibid.* Augustine criticized Cicero's notion of the 'originary bond' (*vinculum*) in *The City of God* when he argues that, since there is no common sense of justice or right given in nature or society, there can be no republic. Identifying the circular nature of Cicero's argument – without justice there can be no common sense of right and without a common sense of right there can be no justice – he concludes accordingly: 'Therefore, where there is no true justice there can be no "association of men united by a common sense of right" and therefore no people answering to the definition of Scipio, of Cicero. And if there is no people then there is no "weal of the people", but only a mob, not deserving the name of a people. If, therefore a commonwealth is the "weal of the people", and if a people does not exist where there is no justice, the irresistible conclusion is that where there is no justice there is no commonwealth' (p. 882). Since for Augustine there was no valid process of 'will-formation' anchored in a concept of justice the classical

republican model of government foundered and needed to be supplemented by a theological model of authority – the City of God – which would provide the basis of divinely elected Sovereigns in Medieval Christendom and the Holy Roman Empire. (I am indebted to my colleague at Boston College, David Rasmussen, for the above citation.) This Augustinian critique of the 'originary bond' (*vinculum*) touches on one of the recurring conundrums in the entire genealogy of republicanism. While for classical republicanism the founding act of society was generally attributed to a lone founder, in more modern and liberal forms of republicanism this founding or originary act is identified with the social contract. (Although Hobbes identifies the legitimation of the modern state with 'One Person', the Sovereign, see Note 4 of Chapter 1.) From the contractarian position evolves the recent position of 'constitutional' republicanism (Habermas/ Ferry/Berten/Ingram) which claims that the state itself is the source of its own unity and identity. A key problem here is, of course, whether a self-founding state, appealing solely to law, can mobilize and sustain the sense of loyalty and identification necessary for citizens to feel they actually *belong* to a given society. On this issue of belonging and identity – which raises the question of the relationship between a republic and a nation, constitutionalism and nationalism – Ingram supports the Habermasian rejection of nationalism, while thinkers like Taylor and Norman argue for a more dialectical accommodation between the two. For more detailed references to this specific debate on the implications of 'postnationalism', see Note 33 to our Introduction and our Postscript to this volume.

4 Cicero is here recalling the three forms of government – monarchy, aristocracy, democracy – first outlined by the Greeks, by Plato in the *Statesman*, by Aristotle in the *Politics*, III, vii, and by Polybius in the *Histories*. Whereas Plato had a deep distrust of democracy and urged hierarchical rule by the one (the Philosopher-King of the Republic), Aristotle had tended towards a more genuinely republican mixture of joint rule by the many and the few together, his chosen examples of the best practical states being Sparta and Carthage. But it was certainly the Greek historian, Polybius, who gave most common currency to the triadic classification of rule, with his ideas of divided power, balance and permanence in government. Writing just before the century of civil strife which occasioned the fall of the Roman republic, Polybius hailed Rome for its gradual readjustment of power between the one, the few and the many, and praised Sparta where the legal wisdom of Lycurgus had founded a constitution ensuring a judicious balance between monarchy, aristocracy and democracy. Although Polybius (like Plato and unlike Aristotle) retains the possibility of monarchy, he takes the original step of qualifying this to include rule by consuls, as in Rome, instead of Kings. This modification was to exert a deep influence on subsequent theories of mixed government, facilitating the identification of this *executive* branch of government with an elected consul, council, doge (as in Venice) or – in modern republics – Presidents. By extension, the second branch of government, the aristocracy, was later reinterpreted as the *legislative* power of senate or council. The third branch of government, democracy or rule by the people, would, in republican theory at least, be consequently identified with the *judiciary*. Cicero cites the examples of King Cyrus, the Marseillese

aristocracy and Athenian popular rule as empirical examples of his three forms of government. Writing of Cyrus, however, he notes that even though he was a just and wise king, the business of the people was not well administered when responsibility resided in one person only.

5 Cicero's praise of Lucius Brutus was to ensure a venerable place for him, alongside Cato, as a hero of classical republicanism. While Cicero tends, at times, to follow Aristotle and Polybius in preferring rule by wise aristocracy with the people's consent, the principle of republican balance compels him to admit that the one defect remaining in even the Roman republic is that the rights of the people are insufficiently provided for due to the existence of enslavement for debt. See Zera Fink, *The Classical Republicans* (Northwestern University, Evanston, 1945), p. 7.

6 Cicero goes so far as to declare corrupt aristocracy to be even worse in certain respects than corrupt monarchy. 'One cannot imagine a species of government in which the wealthiest is supposed to be the best. For what can be more truly glorious than a commonwealth (*res publica*) guided by virtue?' (I, 34).

7 J.G.A. Pocock, *The Machiavellian Moment: Florentine Political Thought and the Atlantic Republican Tradition* (Princeton University Press, Princeton, NJ, 1875), p. vii.

8 *Ibid.*, pp. 4–6. For an interesting selection of original texts by the Italian humanists on government and society, see *The Earthly Republic* (ed. B.G. Kohl and R.G. Witt, Manchester University Press, 1978). See also Franco Venturi, *Italy and the Enlightenment* (Longman, London, 1972).

9 Pocock, *The Machiavellian Moment*, pp. 30–32.

10 *Ibid.* p. 61. See also p. 62: 'The conversation with the ancients which results in knowledge is affiliated with the conversation among citizens which results in decisions and law. Both take place between particular men, located at particular moments in time'.

11 Cited Fink, *The Classical Republicans*, pp. 12–13. Machiavelli's attribution of the origination of the state to 'one man only' is echoed in Hobbes's identification of the Commonwealth with 'one Person', 'one Will', 'the Sovereign'. Moreover, Hobbes will recognize that this unitary Sovereign of the Common-wealth is an 'Artificiall Man' to the extent that the state derives its authority–power–sovereignty from a 'fictional' contract which was said to exist at the time of the beginning of the political order. Indeed this notion of a fictional contract is repeated in later 'social contract' theories running from Rousseau to Rawls (in particular the latter's 'veil of ignorance' fiction). See Note 4 of Chapter 1 and our various comments in later chapters concerning the crisis of legitimation/representatation/identification which is inextricably linked to the 'imaginary' constitution of government and authority.

12 *Ibid.*, p. 21. See also pp. 24–25: 'All that men read of mixed government in the classical masters and their Renaissance exponents, told them that in mixed politics the monarchial element was subject to greater limitations than royalists could admit. The champions of mixed politics had debated over whether predominant power should be placed in the democractic or aristocratic elements; it had not even occurred to most of them to think of putting it in the regal element; the constitutions they had drawn up had all been characterised by weak, strictly limited monarchial elements. In the second place, the theory afforded a plausible justification of resistance, even

of armed resistance to the royal will'. On the circular connundrums of absolute sovereignty, particularly in Hobbes, see Note 4 of Chapter 1 above.

13 Pocock, *The Machiavellian Moment*, pp. 334–380. See also Fink, *The Classical Republicans*, pp. 23–26 *et seq.* While republicanism of the 'classical' variety, which prevailed in seventeenth-century Europe, invoked the city rather than the empire of Rome as its model of 'virtue' (e.g. frugality, martial arts and devotion of citizens to the public good), English republicanism retrieved the 'imperial' dimension. English republicanism also revised the classical model by introducing the demands of commercial expansion. Henceforth the virtue of frugality associated with republican Rome, and Sparta, was abandoned as England (and Britain) became leaders of world commerce conjoining colonial–financial success with national pride: a conjunction also copied by the American republic which celebrated its 'frontier' Roman virtues while also becoming oriented towards commercial and imperial interests. Part of this conjunction entailed the enmeshing of republicanism not only with imperialism but with forms of nationalism associated with emergent nation-states. Republicanism thus altered between the seventeenth and nineteenth centuries as large nation-states like Britain, France and Spain shifted the focus of sovereignty from the local community, city or *polis* (advocated by classical republicanism) to more collective forms of identity. This search for a secure basis of identity was particularly acute in Britain, which hid its status as a multi-national state under a veneer of triumphalist English nationalism and opposed both the Enlightenment model of a 'Republic of Letters', transcending nation-states, and the French Revolution's declaration of the universal Rights of Man. See Linda Colley, *Britons: Forging the Nation 1707–1837* (Yale University Press, New Haven, 1992) and John Barrell, *Poetry, Language and Politics* (Manchester University Press, Manchester, 1988). I am indebted to Seamus Deane for the above references. Another aspect of English republicanism, not to be ignored, is the radical, if unsuccessful, role played by the Levellers and Diggers, see E. P. Thompson, *Witness Against the Beast: William Blake and the Moral Law* (New Press, New York, 1993).

14 Harrington, *Oceana* (ed. S.B. Liljegren, Heidelberg, 1924), pp. 19, 185–186. See also Fink, *The Classical Rebublicans*, pp. 53–55.

15 Harrington, *Oceana*, pp. 117–119, 123, 146, 108, 142. See also Fink, *The Classical Republicans*, pp. 56–59.

16 Harrington, *Oceana*, p. 32; quoted Fink, *The Classical Republicans*, p. 65.

17 Harrington, *Oceana*, p. 123.

18 *Ibid.*, p.119. Despite Harrington's openness to certain forms of wise (non-hereditary) nobility and even the possibility of recourse to a constitutional dictatorship in times of crisis, Harrington ultimately stood with Machiavelli, and against several other advocates of mixed government, in holding that in mixed states the preponderance of power should reside in the people (Fink, *The Classical Republicans* p. 60).

19 Fink, *The Classical Republicans*, p. 71

20 Quoted Fink, *The Classical Republicans*, p. 85. The publication caused a great stir in the English-speaking world. 'No sooner did this treatise appear', remarked the Irish philosopher John Toland, who published an edition of Harrington's *Oceana and other Works* in 1700, but 'it was greedily bought up, and became the subject of all men's discourse' (p. 85). See

Toland's promotion of the English republican-commonwealth movement in his writings on Harrington, Cromwell, Milton and Ludlow (see Chapter 10 below), in particular his statement: 'I have always been, now am, and ever shall be persuaded that all sorts of magistrates are made for and by the people and not the people for or by the magistrates . . . I am therefore and avowedly a Commonwealthman'. See also Sean Kearney on Toland and the English republican tradition, 'John Toland: An Ulster Freethinker' in *The Humanist*, 3(6), 1995, pp. 10–14. Note also the important 'republican' influence exerted by Irish figures like Charles Lucas and Napper Tandy in the 1740s and 1750s.

21 Harrington, *Oceana*, p. 187; quoted Fink, *The Classical Republicans*, p. 82.

22 See Pocock, *The Machiavellian Moment*, pp. 336–380 on the clash between the radical and conservative aspects of the Puritan revolution, especially as it related to the apocalyptic-nationalist notion of England as the 'Elect Nation'. See also Fink, *The Classical Republicans*, p. 104 on Milton's mixed republicanism. Milton's support of the Aristotelian–Machiavellian view that a republic was superior to a monarchy was reinforced by his witness of the behaviour of Charles I which turned him against not only kingship but all forms of single-person magistracy in favour of a more balanced and mixed form of government weighted in favour of popular sovereignty.

23 Fink, *The Classical Republicans*, pp. 125, 139.

24 See Hannah Arendt, *On Revolution* (Penguin, New York, 1963) and *Crises of the Republic* (HBJ Books, New York, 1969); and Arne Johan Vetlesen on 'Hannah Arendt, Habermas and the Republican Tradition' in *Philosophy and Social Criticism*, 21(1), 1995, pp. 1–17. See also Daniel Boorstin, *The Genius of American Politics*, (University of Chicago Press, Chicago, 1953). For alternative views on the American Revolution's understanding of republicanism, see Bernard Bailyn, *The Ideological Origins of the American Revolution* (Harvard University Press, Cambridge, Mass., 1967) and Caroline Robbins, *The Eighteenth-Century Commonwealth Man* (Harvard University Press, Cambridge, Mass., 1959).

25 Boorstin, *The Genius of American Politics*.

26 *Critical Dictionary of the French Revolution*. (ed. F. Furet and M. Ozouf, Belknap Press of Harvard University Press, Cambridge, Mass., 1989), p. 797.

27 *Ibid.*, p.799. See also Dale Van Kleg (ed.), *The French Idea of Freedom. The Old Regime and the Declaration of Rights of 1789* (Stanford University Press, San Francisco, 1994).

28 *Critical Dictionary of the French Revolution*, p. 801.

29 Irish republicanism suffered stress from its inception because of an inherent tension between conflicting demands: (i) the demand for the old republican virtues of frugality, simplicity and self-sufficiency; (ii) the demand for the new Enlightenment virtues of cosmopolitan liberty and universal rights (transcending sectarianism); (iii) the demand for prosperity and material amelioration; and (iv) the demand for a national identity specific to Ireland's status as a small, economically peripheral, nation. The difficulty for the United Irishmen was to introduce enlightenment and prosperity to a nation that appeared resistant in its customs and religion to these things. But the turn away from Enlightenment republicanism towards a more nationalist republicanism was necessitated in Ireland not only because of the

failure of the 1798 rebellion and British sectarianizing of it, but because Irish republicanism needed something specific to its national identity to explain its difference from the British system against which it was rebelling (and Enlightenment universalism pointed to common qualities). That is, arguably, why we find several Irish 'republicans' from Davitt to Connolly and the Ryans seeking forms of national rebellion, and even of socialism, predicated upon specifically Irish origins. In short, Irish republicanism was always bifocal, at once nativist and enlightened; but it was encased in a British system which would not allow it either enlightenment or nativism but, instead, deployed economic and often sectarian pressures to subdue it late into the nineteenth century. Sectarianism may be seen, accordingly, as not so much a product of republican nationalism in Ireland as a product of British hostility to it. I am indebted to Seamus Deane for the above observations.

30 Letter from Simon Partridge, founder of the European Regionalist Movement, 6 November 1995: 'In the final analysis, the idea of nation/republic/democracy is not time- nor place-bound – it belongs to nobody and everyone; it embraces our common humanity, but it must also find room for our diversity. A full resolution of the British–Irish conflict requires a coming together of the best aspects of the British–American and French–Irish democratic traditions that would transcend both. A fully reconnected Irish–British archipelago, a working Irish–British democracy, would indeed provide a model for Europe and perhaps, ultimately, the world'. I agree. Moreover, bearing in mind the close association between 'republic' and 'commonwealth' in the British–American tradition, might it not be conceivable for such an 'Irish–British' democracy to develop a new association with the Commonwealth itself? In this connection, see the discussion of the influence of the English–Scottish Enlightenment (Locke, Hutheson, etc.) and American revolutionary thinking on the United Irishmen republicanism in Kevin Whelan, *The Tree of Liberty* (Cork University Press, Cork, 1996) and Nancy Curtis, *The United Irishmen* (Clarendon Press, Oxford, 1994).

4 POSTNATIONALISM AND POSTMODERNITY

1 A number of political theorists and philosophers have made impressive attempts to provide criteria for such discriminations. Julia Kristeva, for example, distinguishes between (a) nationalism as a genuine 'choice' of self-identification and (b) nationalism as pathological regression to a lost origin (see 'Strangers to Ourselves: The Hope of the Singular' in *States of Mind: Dialogues with Contemporary Thinkers on the European Mind* (ed. R. Kearney, Manchester University Press and New York University Press, 1995) pp. 6–13. This piece is quoted in some detail in Chapter 7, Note 14). David Llyod contrasts state and anti-state in 'Nationalism against the State', *Gender and Colonialism* (ed. T.P. Foley *et al.*, Galway University Press, Galway, 1995, pp. 256–281). Desmond Fennell distinguishes between 'revised nationalism', in tune with the complexities of contemporary reality, and 'die-hard nationalism' which imposes its preconceived ideology on people (see *The Revision of Irish Nationalism* (Open Air, Dublin, 1989), pp. 30–61). Charles Taylor distinguishes between authentic nationalism, as a legitimate need for recognition, and regressive nationalism as a refusal to

accept, and to mourn, the passing of the nation-state (real or imagined). He writes: 'National identity is a very fascinating thing. In some ways, it's an inward-turning thing but in fact, deep down, it's an outward-turning thing. People want to be recognized by others. And when they feel not recognized, that creates the strains and tensions' (see 'Nations and Federations: Living among Others' in *States of Mind*, p. 25). Taylor envisages a solution to the historic problem of nationalist conflict, especially in the European context, with the emergence of multiple layers of compatible identification – regional, national, federal. Hence Taylor's relatively optimistic prognosis for an emerging Europe of regions: 'As Europe is formed, paradoxically, the national state becomes less important and the region can become more important. And the national hatreds between European states, because of the bloodbath that ended in 1945, are so discredited that Europe can enter a phase where it's willing to put some of that behind it. So, because of this constellation of circumstances – the memory of Hitler and the hope of more space for regional societies – I think Europe has a real chance . . .' (p. 26). The biggest danger here would be for Europe to replace the old nationalism with a new Eurocentrism where it refused to see itself as one society amongst others and assumed a hostile and exclusivist attitude to non-European cultures both within its borders (emigrants) and beyond (international politics) (p. 28). For perhaps the finest historical account of the variations of nationalism, particularly anti-colonial and separatist movements of the nineteenth and twentieth centuries (e.g. Indian, African, Arab and east-central European) see John Breuilly, *Nationalism and the State* (Manchester University Press, Manchester, 1993). For the purposes of our present enquiry see especially Part III on varieties of nationalism in a world of nation-states. Breuilly's central thesis, as both historian and theorist, is that nationalism is a form of politics that arises in opposition to modern states. See, finally, Joseph Ruane's cogent arguments on Irish nationalism and anti-nationalism as 'double dislocation' in *Etudes Irlandaises* (Lille University Press, Lille, 1992).

2 Michael Ignatieff, *Blood and Belonging* (Farrar, Strauss and Giroux, New York, 1993), p. 7.

3 Isaiah Berlin, 'European Unity and its Vicissitudes' in *The Crooked Timber of Humanity: Chapters in the History of Ideas* (Knopf, New York, 1991), pp. 176–177. Berlin contrasts the modern ideology of nationalism, based on the romantic ideas of heroism, martyrdom and self-affirmation (refusing the notion of a common humanity) with the old universalist philosophy of wisdom, reason, harmony and a belief in international law. See also Hannah Arendt's critique of nationalism in *On Revolution* (Penguin, New York, 1965), pp. 76–77, 161–168 and 248–249. Arendt identifies the birth of nation-state nationalism with Rousseau's reduction of the political principle of consent to that of the 'general will' (later invoked by Robespierre when he demanded: '*Il faut une volonté UNE . . .*'. Thus Rousseau and Robespierre contrived to equate the many (of democracy) with the one (the nation-state as a single body driven by one will). Hence the myth of nation-state sovereignty – *la nation une et indivisible* – comes to merely replace, rather than subvert, the centralizing role of monarchy (p. 76). The subsequent need to represent the changing, and conflicting, wills of the multitude in a *single unified body* soon led to the rise of revolutionary dictators.

Arendt makes much here of Robespierre's comparison of the nation to an ocean: 'it was indeed the ocean-like sentiments it aroused that drowned the foundations of freedom' (p. 96). 'What saved the nation-state from immediate collapse', claims Arendt, 'was the extraordinary ease with which the national will could be manipulated and imposed upon whenever someone was willing to take the burden or the glory of dictatorship upon himself. Napoleon Bonaparte was only the first in a long series of national statesmen who, to the applause of a whole nation, could declare: "I am the *pouvoir constituant*". However, while the dictate of one will achieved for short periods the nation-state's fictive ideal of unanimity, it was not will but interest, the solid structure of a class society, that bestowed upon the nation-state for the longer periods of its history its measure of stability' (p. 163).

4 See Vincent Geoghegan's useful discussion of this separation of national identity from nationalism in the context of a 'post-nationalist citizenship' in 'Socialism, National Identities and Postnationalist Citizenship', *Irish Political Studies*, 9, 1994, pp.76–77. See, in particular, his conclusion, p. 78: 'Amongst the rights of citizenship there must be recognition of a right to one or more identities of nationality, or to none at all. No one, therefore, can have a biological, cultural or historical veto on self-descriptions of nationality. . . . There are, of course, a whole range of sub- and supra-national identities that are of immense importance, and that must be addressed in a deeper and broader citizenship. In this way one can conceive of a possible plurality of national identities at the individual level, and certainly at the community level, coexisting with a multitude of other identities, guaranteed by a citizenship, located in a state, multi-state or conceivably non-state, political system'. On the complex relationship between national identity, nation-state and nationalism in more specifically Irish contexts see also Desmond Fennell, *The Revision of Irish Nationalism*, pp. 9–18; George Boyce, *Nationalism in Ireland* (Croom Helm, London, 1982); Joseph Lee 'State and Nation in Independent Ireland' and David Harkness 'Nation, State and National Identity in Ireland' in *Irishness in a Changing Society* (Princess Grace Irish Library 2, Barnes and Noble, 1988), pp. 95–132; and Michael O'Dea and Kevin Whelan (eds), *Nations and Nationalisms: France, Britain and Ireland and the Eighteenth-Century Context* (Voltaire Foundation, Oxford, 1996).

5 See Tom Nairn's critique of British nationalism in *The Enchanted Glass: Britain and its Monarchy* (Radius, London, 1988), pp. 101–213. See similar analyses by Bernard Crick, 'The Sense of Identity of the Indigenous British' in *New Community*, 21(21), April 1995, pp. 167–183; and Neal Ascherson in 'Nations and Regions', analysed in some detail in Notes 24–26 to our 'Introduction: Beyond the Nation-State'. By contrast see Prime Minister John Major's rabble-rousing call to the party faithful during the Conservative Party Conference (13 October 1995): 'Others may join a federalist Europe, but not Conservative Britain!'; see also Major's equally 'one-nationist' defence of the British Constitution (against the move towards devolved parliaments for Scotland and Wales) on 26 June 1996, the same day on which England faced Germany in the semi-finals of the European Football Cup to war-mongering press slogans such as 'Let's Blitz Fritz', 'Achtung, Surrender!', 'Watch out Krauts, England are going to bomb you to bits!' or

'Images of war [seem] appropriate . . . making an Englishman proud to be English' (*Daily Telegraph*). Ironically, the very one-nationism in evidence on this symbolic day was less British (in the four-nation-in-one constitutional principle) than *English*. This separatist slip of the mask was witnessed not only in the xenophobic riots that took place in Trafalgar Square following the Wembley defeat but also in the fact that most Scottish, Welsh and Irish viewers supported Germany! Little wonder that Mitterrand and Kohl should have agreed a year previously, looking askance at the upsurge of an English backlash against Europe, that 'Nationalism is war'. (Kohl would be even more explicit in his address to the University of Louvain, 1995: 'The Policy of European integration is in reality a question of war and peace in the 21st century'). The fact that British nationalism is being increasingly exposed as 'English' nationalism in disguise is evident from the most casual perusal of the London press on current cultural matters: the following extract from the *Mail on Sunday*, 4 April 1996, is a typical case in point: 'Contemporary popular culture is swamped with Scottish heroes, most of whom – like Mel Gibson playing William Wallace in *Braveheart* or the lead character in the cult movie *Trainspotting* – spend their time attacking the English. . . . Meanwhile, we English, who now enjoy the status of a persecuted minority, have lost touch with our own heritage . . . English history is being rewritten to suit the other three nations and our language, which has in any case been stolen and perverted by Australia and the US, remains the only thing in which we can have pride. . . . Two hundred and fifty years ago this week the Battle of Culloden secured the future of the United Kingdom. But now, England, my England, is nothing more than a Celtic colony'.

6 Agnes Heller, 'Europe: Modern, Pre-Modern, Postmodern' in *The Irish Review*, 10, 1990, pp. 86–89.

7 For a development of this argument in the Irish and European contexts see my Open Letter to Jacques Delors, 'The Implications of a Federal Europe on a Divided Belfast' in *The Irish Times*, 18 May 1990. See also here Kevin Boyle, 'The European Opportunity' in *National Identities* (ed. Bernard Crick, Blackwell, Oxford, 1991), p. 78. Citing a number of recent developments in the Irish–British relationship within the European Community in the 1990s, Boyle concludes that 'a new concept of the integration of the peoples and states on these offshore European islands on conditions of equality . . . augers well for a less destructive future for Northern Ireland and therefore for these islands as a whole. Separatism, as expressed in the Unionism and the Nationalism which partitioned Ireland and created a gulf between the state of Ireland and Britain, is obsolete. Dominance and the subordination of the cultures of these islands by England is equally obsolete. What can replace them is the concept of a European citizenship with allegiance distributed between region, country and Europe. Such developments, for example, could allow for the development of a more inclusive sense of Irishness to embrace the Northern Unionist. *The emancipation of the four nations and cultures of these islands from the strait jacket of national sovereignty and exclusive national identities,* expressed in exclusive and hostile territorial arrangements, should be the goal for the decade of the 1990s'.

8 See, for example, Jacques Delors, *Antenne 2*, 24 June 1990.

9 Hans-Magnus Enzensberger, *Europe, Europe* (Hutchinson, London, 1989), pp. 301, 307.

10 Quoted by Ralf Dahrendorf, *Reflections on the Revolution in Europe* (Chatto, London, 1990), pp. 123–125.

11 Neal Ascherson, 'Beyond the Endgame of Sovereignty', *Independent on Sunday*, London 19 May 1991; see also his more advanced version of this position in 'Europe of the Regions', *We are All Europeans Now* (ed. M. Crozier, Institute for Irish Studies, Belfast, 1991). Other useful contributions to this debate include David Martin, 'A European Charter of Regions' in *Scotland and the New Europe* (John Wheatley Centre Publications, Strathclyde, 1989); Yann Fouere, *Towards a Federal Europe: Nations or States* (Davies, Swansea, 1980); the essays by Mike Featherstone, J.-F. Lyotard, Michael Ryan and Gianni Vattimo in *Postmodernism: Theory, Culture and Society*, 5(2–3), 1988; the essays by John Hume, Edgar Faure, Ivor Browne, Frank Barry and T.J. Barrington in *Across the Frontiers* (ed. R. Kearney, Wolfhound Press, Dublin, 1988); and Edgar Morin's *Penser l'Europe* (Gallimard, Paris, 1987). Morin's advocacy of European multiplicity and creative democratic conflict stems from a savage indictment of the centralizing nation-states (p. 53): 'The notion of Europe which emerged in the 18th century corresponded to a common age of national sovereignties, wars, the Right of Peoples and the balance of powers. Europe harboured within her both conflict and the means of regulating conflict. Her wars prevented any attempt at hegemonic unification and upheld polycentrism. But when the national states transformed themselves into Nation-States, when the wars became massively and totally national and when advances in armament made carnage possible on a huge scale, then Europe had reached its peak and began to sink into the abyss'. On the specific discussions of regions in Ireland, see A. Horner, 'Dividing Ireland into Geographical Regions', in *Geographical Viewpoint*, vol. 21, 1993, pp. 5–24; P. O'Drisceóil (ed.), *Regions: Identity and Power* (Institute of Irish Studies, Belfast, 1992), pp. 5–62; T. Barrington, *Local Government Reorganization and Reform* (Dublin, 1991) and 'Ireland: The Interplay of Territory and Function', in *Tensions in the Territorial Politics of Western Europe* (eds R. Rhodes and V. Wright, London, 1987); and K. Whelan, *The Territorial Spiral* (LLASS working paper, no. 4, Dublin, 1993).

12 In the British context, see the regionalist readings of 'new British historians' such as Hugh Kearney, R.R. Davies, Simon Partridge and Tom Nairn, cited above. For the most adventurous version of postmodern regionalism in the Irish context, see, in addition to the references in Note 11 above, the article by Kevin Whelan, 'The Region and the Intellectuals' in *Ireland and its Intellectuals* (ed. Liam O'Dowd, Institute of Advanced Studies, Belfast, forthcoming). Here the author argues for a grounding of the 'Europe of Regions' project in a structurally rooted manner which can engage with the material local level at which people's lives are actually lived – in contrast to the centrally imposed divisions used by administrative bureaucrats as management tools. Whelan enlists here an emancipatory reading of postmodernism: 'Post-modernism's concern to disperse and decentralise power, its willingness to conjugate past and present, its emphasis on spatial as much as temporal analysis, have all revitalised the concept of regionalism. In a sense, post-modernism has made the region intellectually respectable once more.

Working within this framework, one might wish to emphasise that living regions are organic creations, not just inherited, passive or inert, but are proactive, created by specific people in specific circumstances'. Whelan draws from a variety of concrete examples in archaeology, environmental practice, music culture, local history and participatory political democracy, to support his case for a postmodernist model of the region which would contest the centralizing orthodoxy of both the old nationalist perspective and its newer revisionist counterpart – in favour of a more genuinely pluralist message. But Whelan is far from sanguine in his advocacy of a new regionalism. He acknowledges, quite rightly, that it requires a constant hermeneutic of critical suspicion lest the contemporary appeal to regions revert to traditionalist pieties: 'Does the traditional region, statically defined in local, fixed and essentially rural terms have any continuing purchase in this diversified, mobile and dynamic world? There are obvious problems in translating the regional concept to the urban context. Can we match town-land against street, parish against suburb, *pays* against city? And the very notions of place, territory and identity embedded in the regional construct may well disenfranchise those who have been displaced or alienated from it; it may also have in-built gender and generational biases. Stable regions with fixed boundaries may create an arbitrary, artificial sense of identity which ignores difference and individuality. The construction of regions must therefore constantly involve their deconstruction. . . . The living tissue of community must continuously shed its initially protective, eventually sclerotic protective carapaces, if it is to grow. That growth may initially be wobbly, amorphous, amoeboid; eventually, newer, broader, more comfortable territorial shells will form over it too, before they in turn will also be shed in a further cycle of growth'. Whelan concludes accordingly that regional cultures can prove a powerful vernacular force, harbouring salubrious democratic valencies and supporting a vibrant sense of multi-cultural diversity, once stripped of Herderian melodrama and conservative nostalgia for hearth and home. Such a vision of bottom–up regional culture is persuasively articulated by Seamus Heaney as follows: 'Empowered within its own horizons, it looks out but does not necessarily look up to the metropolitan centres. Its impulses and possibilities abound within its boundaries but are not limited by them. It is self-sufficient but not self-absorbed, capable of thought, undaunted . . . a corrective to the infections of nationalism and the cringe of provincialism' ('The Sense of the Past' in *History of Ireland*, 4, 1993, pp. 33–37, cited by Whelan).

13 To cite some of the most significant discussions of postmodern models of politics: see J.-F. Lyotard, *The Postmodern Condition* (Manchester University Press, Manchester, 1984); Gary Madison, *The Hermeneutics of Postmodernity* (Indiana University Press, Bloomington, 1988); Michel Foucault, 'Governmentality' in *The Foucault Effect: Studies in Governmentality* (ed. G. Burchell, C. Gordon and P. Miller, The University of Chicago Press, Chicago, 1991), pp. 87–104; Honi Fern Haber, *Beyond Postmodern Politics: Lyotard, Rorty, Foucault* (Routledge, New York, 1994); Richard Bernstein, *The New Constellation* (Polity Press, Cambridge, 1991); Bernard Flynn, *Political Philosophy at the Closure of Metaphysics* (Humanities Press, New Jersey, 1992); *Postmodernism and Politics* (ed. J. Arac, Manchester University Press, Manchester, 1986); *Postmodern Culture* (ed. H. Foster,

Pluto Press, London, 1985); Thomas Doherty, *After Theory: Postmodernism – Postmarxism* (Routledge, London, 1990); Tuija Pulkkinen, *The Postmodern and Political Agency*, Hakapaino Oy, Helsinki, 1996. Most of these theorists critique the modern concept of the nation-state which claims legitimacy in the appeal to some foundationalist essence or ethnocentrist origin.

14 Jacques Derrida, 'Structure, Sign and Play' in *Writing and Difference* (University of Chicago Press, Chicago, 1978). Derrida explores the 'deconstructive' consequences of certain political, institutional and ideological discourses in a number of publications, notably *The Gift of Death* (University of Chicago Press, Chicago, 1995); *Du Droit à la Philosophie* (Galilée, Paris, 1990); his essays on Mandela and apartheid in *Psyché* (Galilee, Paris, 1987); his critical re-reading of European identity in *The Other Heading: Reflections on Today's Europe* (Indiana University Press, Bloominton, 1992) and *Spectres of Marx* (Routledge, London, 1995).

15 M. Foucault, 'Governmentality', p. 88.

16 *Ibid.*, pp. 83–84.

17 *Ibid.*, pp. 100–101.

18 J.-F. Lyotard, *The Postmodern Condition*.

19 J.-F. Lyotard, *Peregrinations* (Columbia University Press, New York, 1988), p. 39.

20 *Ibid.*

21 *Ibid.*

22 *Ibid.* See here Homi Bhabha, 'DissemiNation: Time, Narrative and the Margins of the Modern Nation' in *Nation and Narration* (ed. Homi Bhabha, Routledge, London, 1990), pp. 291–322.

23 Kenneth Frampton, 'Critical Regionalism' in *The Postmodern Condition*, p. 21.

24 *Ibid.*, p. 17.

25 *Ibid.* See also Frampton's contribution to this debate in *Postmodernism*, ICA Documents, 4, 1986, p. 27.

26 Frampton, 'Critical Regionalism', p. 20.

27 *Ibid.* See also Charles Jencks, *Current Architecture* (Academy Editions, London, 1982).

28 J.-F. Lyotard and J.-L. Thébaud, *Just Gaming* (Manchester University Press, Manchester, 1985), pp. 26 and 47; see also Lyotard, *Political Writings* (UCL Press, London, 1993), pp. 3–33 and 'What is Just?' in *States of Mind* (ed. R. Kearney, Manchester University Press, Manchester, 1995), pp. 293–307; and Bill Readings, *Introducing Lyotard* (Routledge, London, 1991), pp. 125–128.

29 Hannah Arendt, *Crises of the Republic* (HBJ Books, New York, 1972), p. 229.

30 See Arendt, *On Revolution*, pp. 240–254; also Jeffrey Isaac, *Arendt, Camus and Modern Rebellion* (Yale University Press, New Haven, 1992), pp. 149–150, 182–188, 217–226. Internationalism, as Arendt understands it, is not a supranationalism, which would be merely to replace the centralized nation-state with a centralized global state. Nor should it be confused with multinationalism, in the purely commercial sense of global capitalism. If the solution to the crises of modern nationalism does not lie in the revivalist dream of a unified 'nation-once-again', nor a blanket dismissal of all that nationalism has achieved, neither does it lie in the gold rush of

multinational consumerism. Selling oneself to the highest financial bidder or compromising one's singular freedoms and opinions in some geopolitical power block offers no answer. For a more detailed treatment of this argument, as it relates to the specifically Irish context, see my 'Postmodern Ireland' in *The Clash of Ideas* (ed. Miriam Hederman, Gill and Macmillan, Dublin, 1987).

31 J. Isaac, *Arendt, Camus and Rebellion*, pp. 146–150.

32 *Ibid*. See, in particular, Isaac's critique of nation-states in favour of a postmodern global government, pp. 219,‑ 224–225 forward. See also here our own critique of 'revivalist nationalism' in 'Myth and the Critique of Tradition' in *Transitions* (Wolfhound Press, Dublin, 1987).

33 For a development of this universality-in-diversity argument see my 'Across the Frontiers: Ireland and Europe' in *Ireland and Europe* (ed. D. Keogh, University College Cork Press, Cork, 1989); my 'Pour une Intelligentsia Européenne' in *L'Europe sans Rivages: De L'Identité Culturelle Européenne* (Proceedings of International Symposium, Paris, January 1988, Albin Michel), pp.114–119; and E. Morin, *Penser l'Europe* (Gallimard, Paris, 1987). Morin argues here that European culture remains properly elusive for the reason that it is not reducible to some common 'essence' but is a 'cauldron of diversities' – the very absence of homogeneity being, in his view, its greatest strength. 'Europe is a community of multiple faces which cannot be superimposed on each other without creating a blur', Morin writes. 'Europe's only unity lies in its multiplicity. Its unity is itself plural and contradictory, stitched together from the interactions between peoples, cultures, states and classes. The difficulty of "thinking Europe" is first of all the difficulty of thinking about this unity in multiplicity – this *unitas mutiplex*' (p. 27). Morin goes on to argue, accordingly, that European history can no more be defined by geographical frontiers than geographical Europe can be defined by historical ones. In fact, Europe cannot really be understood in terms of frontiers at all (which are always shifting), but only in terms of the particular originality which produces and organizes it – namely, its very *absence* of unity (p. 36). This appreciation of Europe as essentially polycentric and polylinguistic is the best safeguard against the opposing view of Europe as a hegemonic empire in its own right – a view not only evident in the chauvinistic Euro-centrism of colonial policies in the nineteenth and twentieth centuries but also in the barbaric dreams of a 'New Europe' championed by Hitler and Mussolini. For Morin, European identity resists cultural and political hegemony by promoting its own truly pluralist character – made up of (a) transnational cultures (Slav, Germanic, Latin, Celtic, etc.), (b) national cultures and (c) regional 'micro-cultures' irreducible to the boundaries of nation-states and expressing themselves as 'little cultural departments at local, regional and provincial' level (p. 67). Whence the curious fact that California and New England have more in common (despite the huge distance between them) than such proximate European regions as Brittany and the Basque country, Portugal and Denmark, Germany and Italy, etc. Morin concludes accordingly: 'The organizing principle of Europe can only be found in that historical principle which links its identity with perpetual becoming and metamorphosis. It is the vital urgency to save its identity which today calls Europe towards a new metamorphosis' (p. 67).

Vaclav Havel sees the future of Europe's political identity as dependent upon a choice between this process of metamorphosis and tribal stagnation and regression: 'On one side is the modern concept of an open civil society, in which people of different nationalities, ethnic roots, religions, traditions and convictions can live together and creatively cooperate. On the other side is the archaic concept of a tribal state as a community of people of the same blood. That is, on the one side stands a concept that has been one of the cornerstones of the current European integration process, one that represents the only hope for today's global interconnected civilisation to survive. On the other side is a concept which for millennia has stained human history with blood and brought forth lethal fruits, the most horrifying of them to date being the Second World War. On the one side, a concept with its emphasis on equality for all human beings, on the other a conviction about the exclusive status of some group who through only a chance of birth were made to belong to a certain tribe. On the one side an emphasis on what brings all people together, and their respect for the otherness of others and their solidarity; on the other, a cult of collectivism under which an affiliation to the pack is more important than a person's own qualities' ('A Conflict between Blood and Civilisation', *Irish Times*, 3 January 1996).

34 I am indebted here to Kevin Whelan's argument for a postmodern meshing of Kantian universalism with Burkean regionalism: 'In Burke's formulation, the region represents the integrity of traditional society and its local loyalties, and it can be set against abstract universalising claims, which violate the customary affections and rooted relations which make society adhesive and stable. Any political system which placed abstract principles or claims above those of family, community or region would inevitably lack the crucial binding force that gives political systems their endurance – the affection and, hence, acquiescence of the people who live under them. In Burkean terms, therefore, one must weigh the primacy and potency of a particularist past against the rational, progressive and utopian claims of the enlightenment modernisation project, with its (Kantian) appeal to the cosmopolitan future'. Whelan concludes his argument by calling for a reconciling of universal and local narratives: 'Only if the meta-narratives by which intellectuals structure their thoughts are in dialogue with the micro-narratives by which people understand their lives will there be fruitful co-operation. Thus, the intellectual engaged with the region has to be equipped with a bifocal vision – the eye of the mammoth and the eye of the microbe' ('The Region and the Intellectuals' in *Ireland and its Intellectuals*, ed. Liam O'Dowd, Institute of Irish Studies, Belfast, forthcoming).

35 Cornelius Castoriadis, 'Psychoanalysis and Politics' in *Speculations after Freud: Psychoanalysis, Philosophy and Culture* (ed. S. Shamdasani and M. Munchow, Routledge, London, 1994), pp. 6–7. See also on this question of a society's 'social imaginary', Paul Ricoeur 'Myth as the Bearer of Possible Worlds' in *States of Mind*, p. 239–240: 'Beyond or beneath the self-understanding of a society there is an opaque kernel which cannot be reduced to empirical norms or laws. This kernel cannot be explained in terms of some transparent model because it is constitutive of a culture *before* it can be expressed and reflected in specific representations or ideas. It is only if we try to grasp this kernel that we may discover the *foundational mytho-poetic* nucleus of a society. By analysing itself in terms of such a foundational nucleus (or social imaginary) a society comes to a truer

understanding of itself; it begins to critically acknowledge its own symbolising identity'. For futher discussion of Ricoeur's analysis of this crucial role of identification/recognition/representation in both the construction and legitimation of a society see the concluding note to our Postscript.

36 *Ibid.*, pp. 7–8.

5 RETHINKING IRELAND

1 John Whyte, *Interpreting Northern Ireland* (Clarendon Press, Oxford, 1990).
2 Cited in J. Darby and A.M. Gallagher (eds), Centre for the Study of Conflict, University of Ulster, *Occasional Paper 4*, 1991.
3 Edward Mortimer, 'European Security after the Cold War' (International Institute of Strategic Studies, London, 1992).
4 Misha Glenny, *The Fall of Yugoslavia* (Penguin, New York, 1992).
5 Neal Ascherson, *Fortnight*, no. 296.
6 Neal Ascherson, *Independent on Sunday*, 9 February 1992.
7 Hugh Miall, *New Conflicts in Europe: Prevention and Resolution* (Oxford Research Group, no. 10, 1992).
8 F. Willeit, *Independent on Sunday*, 29 September 1991.
9 Mark Thompson, *Guardian Europe*, 8 January 1993.
10 Elizabeth Meehan, *Citizenship and the European Community*, Queens University Belfast Inaugural Lecture, 14 May 1992.
11 *European Community Structural Funds in Northern Ireland*, no. 94, April 1992.
12 Kevin Morgan, *Innovating-by-Networking*, Dept of City and Regional Planning, University of Wales, December 1991.
13 *TSB Business Outlook and Economic Review*, 7(1), March 1992.
14 Dennis Kennedy, *The Irish Times*, 7 January 1993.
15 Joe Lee, *Ireland 1912–85* (Cambridge University Press, Cambridge, 1989).
16 Note the important critical research on Irish and European regionalism being conducted by sociologist Liam O'Dowd of Queen's University, Belfast, and by James Anderson of the Open University, Milton Keynes, England. See also the remarkable studies of regions and sub-regions in Ireland published by Kevin Whelan, 'The Territorial Spiral' in *Landscape and Life: Appropriate Scales for Sustainable Development*, LLASS Paper No. 4, University College Dublin, November 1993; and Arnold Horner, 'Dividing Ireland into Geographical Regions' in *Geographical Viewpoint* vol. 21, 1993, pp. 5–24. For an adequate appraisal of the kinds of regions that might prove practicable in Ireland, north and south, it is important to compare indigenous regional, and subregional, models with those in the UK and other European countries. See, for example, the growing argument for city-regions in Scotland, Wales and England (*The Scotsman*, 1 April 1996; *Financial Times*, 19 February 1996; *Planning Week*, 30 November 1995) and the equally grass-roots project for a British–Irish Federation of Provinces advanced by the Campaign for Political ecology in Autumn 1996; see also the discussion of the four categories of region in the EU – ranging from those with extensive powers like the German and Austrian *Länder* and Belgian communities to those with little or none like the Greek *Nomoi* and Irish/British counties – in *Newsletter of the Regions in the European Union* (EIPASCOPE, No. 1995, 3); and the inspirational Bordeaux Declaration of

the Council of Europe on the 'Regional Authorities of Europe' (Bordeaux, February 1978), in particular paragraphs 1 to 6. A fascinating instance of how European regionalism can succeed in overcoming historic conflict between national allagiences is analysed by Anthony Alcock, Professor of European Studies at the University of Ulster and European Spokesman for the Official Unionist Party, in his pioneering essay, 'Trentino and Tyrol – From Austrian Crowland to European Region' in *Europe and Ethnicity* (Routledge, London, 1996). The fact that both nationalists like Hume and unionists like Alcock can agree on the positive contribution of a Europe of Regions to the Northern Ireland conflict offers hope for future developments along these lines.

6 THE FIFTH PROVINCE: BETWEEN THE LOCAL AND THE GLOBAL

1 R. Kearney and M. P. Hederman, Editorial, *The Crane Bag Book of Irish Studies (1977–81)* (Blackwater Press, Dublin, 1982), pp. 10–11. See also John Water's excellent chapter on 'The Fifth Province' in *Race of Angels: Ireland and the Genesis of U2* (The Blackstaff Press, Belfast, 1995), pp. 189–214.
2 This international/cosmopolitan/universalist dimension of Irish culture dates back to the Celtic and pre-Celtic civilizations of ancient Ireland where nation-state boundaries were non-existent and the inhabitants of this island were intermixed with those of the neighbouring islands and the continent. This sense of belonging to a pre-national culture continued, in somewhat modified form, in the evolution of early and medieval Ireland as a Christian region of a larger Christian civilization. Hence the 'universalizing spirit' of Irish scholars and monks between the seventh and ninth centuries, from Columbanus to Eriugena, who made major contributions to the emergence of a transnational European culture. It is arguable that Columbanus was the first to actually invoke the 'idea of Europe' as a distinct unity freed from the tribalism of local chieftains and clergy; he addressed Gregory the Great, for example, as the 'august flower of all Europe' (*augustissimo flori totius Europae*). Similarly, the Armagh Annalists in Ireland referred to Charlemagne not as *rex francorum* but as *Imperator totius Europae*. The Irish were also the first to celebrate the feast of 'All saints of Europe' and to establish, in the seventh century, celebrated scriptoria and centres of learning (Latin and Greek) throughout the European continent in such places as Luxueil, Fontaines, Annegray and St. Gallen. I have attempted to explore this cosmopolitan heritage of the early Irish monks, Columbanus and Gallus, in my philosophical fiction, *Sam's Fall* (Hodder and Stoughton, London, 1995). Interestingly, Robert Schumann, one of the founders of the European Community, was to refer to Columbanus as the 'Patron Saint of Europe'. The roots of such a cosmopolitan/internationalist spirit in early Ireland were made much of by the seventeenth-century Irish philosopher, John Toland, analysed in Chapter 10.
3 Neil Jordan, 'Migrant Minds' in *Across the Frontiers* (ed. R. Kearney, Wolfhound Press, Dublin, 1988), pp. 105–204.
4 R. Kearney, 'Introduction' to 'Migrant Minds', p. 185.
5 Roy Foster, 'Varieties of Irishness' in *Cultural Traditions in Northern Ireland* (ed. M. Crozier, Institute for Irish Studies, Belfast, 1989), p. 20.

6 Proinsias MacCana, 'Notes on the Early Irish Concept of Unity' in *The Crane Bag Book of Irish Studies (1977–81)*, p. 206.

7 D. A. Binchy in *The Impact of the Scandinavian Invasions on the Celtic-speaking Peoples c. 800–1100 A.D.* (ed. Brian Ó Cuiv, Dublin 1975), p. 128.

8 P. MacCana, 'Notes on the Early Irish Concept of Unity', p. 216. Luke Gibbons offers a fascinating, if at times contrasting, analysis on this unity/ diversity dialectic in Irish culture and politics in 'Identity without a Centre: Allegory, History and Irish Nationalism', *Cultural Studies*, 6 (3), 1992, pp. 362–363. Taking up Tom Dunne's argument that native Irish culture in the early modern period failed to develop a coherent nationalist ideology because it lacked the centralizing mechanisms of the absolute monarchies that provided the infrastructure of the first European nation-states, Gibbons writes: 'It is hardly surprising that "outside pressures" (e.g. from England) did not succeed in producing a clone of the centralized state, for it was precisely such a concentration of power in the centre that native culture was resisting. The strategem of "divide and rule" is one of the bogies of the imagined community of nationalism, but in certain cases it was the amorphousness of native cultures . . . which offered the most effective long-term defence against conquest' (p. 362). Remarking on the telling fact that it took almost four centuries to subjugate the sprawling indigenous tribes of North America, while the powerfully centralized societies of the Aztecs and Incas fell almost immediately, Gibbons suggests that a similar strategy of decentralized resistance was proposed by several leftist commentators in Ireland. These commentators sought links between the pre-invasion Gaelic culture, devoid of central authority, and James Connolly's syndicalist version of socialism averse to centralized state power. The absence of political centralization – which most historians see as a weakness impeding the development of a national state – may thus be construed as a strength. The many-headed hydra of Ireland confused the invader who did not know which head to strike at.

9 *Ibid.*

10 *Ibid.*, p. 218. See also MacCana's discussion of cultural sovereignty in relation to Celtic goddesses in *Celtic Mythology* (Hamlyn, London, 1970), pp. 94–95, 117–120.

11 Address delivered at the launch of 'The Northern Issue' of *The Crane Bag*, Abbey Theatre, Dublin, 9 December 1980.

12 See the work of such cultural commentators as Simon Partridge, Neal Ascherson, Robin Wilson, Tom Nairn, Kevin Whelan and Liam O'Dowd mentioned in previous studies, as well as the various contributors to the Europe of Regions debate in *Visions of Europe* (ed. R. Kearney, Wolfhound Press, Dublin, 1992) and *Across the Frontiers* (ed. R. Kearney, Wolfhound Press, Dublin, 1988).

13 Seamus Heaney, *Preoccupations* (Faber, London, 1980), p. 148. See also Heaney's fascinating article on regional divides in *Bullán*, no. 1, Spring 1994, Oxford; and his description of an enabling regional culture, 'The Sense of the Past' in *History Ireland*, 4, 1993, pp. 33–37, cited in note 12 of Chapter 4.

14 Jacques Darras, *Beyond the Tunnel of History* (Macmillan, London, 1990), pp. 92–93.

7 MYTHS OF MOTHERLAND

1 Mircea Eliade, *Myths, Dreams and Mysteries* (Fontana, London, 1968). See also Jean-François Lyotard's analysis of the a-temporalizing and synchronizing power of mythic narrative, which he contrasts to Enlightenment scientific rationality, in *The Postmodern Condition* (Manchester University Press, Manchester, 1984); and Homi Bhabha's analysis of the symbolic 'time of the nation' as a form of *double* time wherein the homogenizing–centralizing time of the 'motherland' (with its claim to autonomous sovereignty) is undercut by the disjunctive time of the nation's modernity (exposed by the experience of ambivalence, repetition, liminality, migration), in 'DissemiNation: Time, Narrative and the Margins of the Modern Nation', in *Nation and Narration* (ed. H. Bhabha, Routledge, London, 1990). This notion of doubled and ambivalent temporality, as a symptom of post-colonial nationalism, is applied to a specifically Irish context by David Lloyd in 'Nationalism Against the State' and *Anomalous States: Irish Writing and the Post-Colonial Moment* (Lilliput, Dublin, 1992).

2 Sigmund Freud, *On the Interpretation of Dreams* (Penguin, New York, 1976).

3 Claude Lévi-Strauss, *Structural Anthropology* (Penguin, New York, 1968).

4 See, for example, George Orwell's portrayal of the propagandist power of ideological myth as collective enslavement in *1984:* 'The Brotherhood cannot be wiped out because it is not an organization in the ordinary sense. Nothing holds it together except an idea which is indestructible. You will never have anything to sustain you except an idea which is indestructible. . . . We are dead. . . . We can only spread our knowledge outwards . . . from generation to generation'.

5 See Rudolph Bultmann's argument in *Theology of the New Testament* (SCM Press, London, 1952): 'To understand Jesus' fate as the basis for a mythic cult and to understand such a cult as the celebration which sacramentally brings the celebrant into such fellowship with the cult-divinity that the latter's fate avail for the former as if it were his own – that is the Hellenic idea'. See also Jurgen Moltmann's extension of this demythologizing programme into a critique of the sacrificial cult of martyrdom: 'The influence of cultic piety shows itself not only as a formal event in the self-preservation of Christianity on Hellenistic soil, but quite certainly extends also to the understanding of the event of Christ. The Christ event is here understood as an epiphany of the eternal (past) in the form of a dying and rising *Kyrios* of the *cultus.* . . . Initiation into the death and resurrection of Christ then means that the goal of redemption is already determined, for in this baptism eternity is sacramentally present. . . . The Cross becomes a timeless sacrament of martyrdom which perfects the martyr and unites him with the heavenly Christ' (*The Theology of Hope*, SCM Press, London, 1967). Moltmann rejects this mythology of sacrifice as a perversion of true Christianity. One might also mention here René Girard's critique of myth as a mechanism of collective scapegoating. The blood sacrifice of the scapegoat, upon whom the evils of a divided society have been projected, is mythically experienced as a means of restoring a new purity, harmony and unity – in short, a pristine imago of sovereignty. Ironically, a recurring feature of such sacrificial myths is that the reviled scapegoat is often deified,

through the purgatory sacrifice, into a mythological saviour. See R. Girard, *Le Bouc émissaire* (Grasset, Paris, 1982).

6 Statement by the IRA Army Council to Ed Moloney in *Magill* (Dublin, September 1978).

7 Statement by Provisional Sinn Féin in *Where Sinn Féin Stands* (Dublin, January 1970).

8 I am indebted for this quotation and several that follow to Tim Pat Coogan, *On the Blanket* (Ward River, Dublin, 1980).

9 For a more detailed treatment of this mythology of sacrificial martyrdom see 'Myth and Martyrdom I and II' in my *Transitions: Narratives in Modern Irish Culture* (Wolfhound Press, Dublin, 1987).

10 Quoted by Tim Pat Coogan, *On the Blanket.*

11 See also Thomas McDonagh, another 1916 leader and poet, who perhaps best summed up the sacrificial motif when, in his *Literature and Ireland*, he described the recurring aspiration for national renewal as the 'supreme song of victory on the dying lips of martyrs'.

12 For a more comprehensive treatment of the relationship between Catholicism and Irish nationalism see my 'Faith and Fatherland' in *Transitions* and the various references cited in Notes 3 to 8 in Chapter 2 of this volume.

13 The *Aisling* poems, as Daniel Corkery remarked, are more racial than personal in character. They are typical of mythic forms of expression in that they subordinate individual utterance to the archetypes of national experience. Ancestral heroines and heroes are more important than actual privacies of feeling. Thus, for example, we find Owen O'Rathaille revering Ireland as a 'fair daughter of celestial powers (*do geineadh ar gheineamhain di sé an tír uachtaraigh*) and declaring that he will suffer 'amid a ruffian horde' until the ancient heroes return from over the sea of death (*go bhfuillid na leoghain tar tinn*). This poetic cult of the *spéirbhean* was not confined to the Gaelic poets; it also became a common feature of such nineteenth-century poets as Mangan, Ferguson or Darcy Magee who cultivated the *aisling* motif as a means of translating colonial history back into pre-colonial myth – to that Great Time of the Holy Beginning when, as Magee wrote in *The Celts*, 'beyond the misty space of twice a thousand years in Erin old there dwelt a mighty race'.

14 On this phenomenon of the 'feminization' of the nation and the 'gendering' of land and homeland, see the recent work of Lynn Innes, *Woman and Nation in Ireland – Literature and Society, 1880–1935* (University of Georgia Press, 1994) (which pursues a post-colonial critique); Belinda Loftus, *Mirrors – William the Third and Mother Ireland*, Picture House, New York, 1990 (which compares loyalist and republican images of the feminized nation and contrasts the hapless image of Hibernia with the battle-hardy Britannia); T.P. Foley *et al.* (eds), *Gender and Colonialism* (Galway University Press, 1995); Emer Nolan, *James Joyce and Nationalism* (Routledge, London, 1995); and Luke Gibbons, *Transformations in Irish Culture* (Cork University Press, 1996) and 'Identity Without a Centre: Allegory, History and Irish Nationalism', *Cultural Studies,* 6(3), 1992, pp. 358–75. Gibbons brilliantly analyses the Whiteboys' use of female personification, and even impersonation, as part of a continuum with the 'allegorical figures of "Dark Rosaleen", "Kathleen ni Houlihan" in the visionary poetry and ballads of the period, who promised apocalyptic deliverance from the Williamite

confiscations in Ireland' (p. 366). In contrast to the standard reading of recourse to female figuration as a mere strategy of disguise, Gibbons suggests that such allegorical ploys derive from a profound disjunction between expression and experience, outward sign and recondite meaning – a disjunction which must be understood as part of consciousness itself under specific conditions of colonial persecution. Identifying the subversive power of ballads and popular oral culture, in which such female figuration first emerged, Gibbons offers this post-colonial reading: 'The peasantry may have been subject to the law but they did not owe their allegiance to it: their lives were regulated by an alternative public sphere which was not allowed material expression but which was none the less capable of negating what overlaid it. The mollusc in this case could not be contained within its outer shell. As with law, so with linguistic shifts in a colonised culture' (p. 367).

15 Julia Kristeva, 'Woman's Time' in *The Kristeva Reader* (ed. Toril Moi, Blackwell, Oxford, 1986), p. 205. Kristeva offers the following psycho-analytic critique of the excesses of nationalism in 'Strangers to Ourselves: the Hope of the Singular' in *States of Mind*: ' . . . nationalism is, in my eyes, a regressive and a depressive attitude. If you'll allow me this little psycho-analytic excursion, these separatist nationalists (Baltic, Serbian, Croatian, Slovak) are people who have long been humiliated in their identity. Soviet Marxism did not recognise this identity, so that they have now an anti-depressive reaction which takes manic forms, if I may put it like that. The exaltation of origins and of archaic folk values can take violent forms be-cause one wants an enemy; and as the enemy is not Communism any more – because it does not exist – the enemy will be the *other*: the other ethnic group, the other nation, the scapegoat and so on. . . . One can try to acceler-ate the process, one can try to avoid sinking into stagnation, to help it go a bit faster; and on that level, there is a huge amount of work that can be done, on one side, by the churches, and on the other, by the intellectuals. . . . [These have] a great role to play today in helping to transcend nationalism and to give to those people ideals which would not be strictly ethnic or archaically national. . . . Even economic problems cannot be solved without this moral renewal' (p. 10). She concludes: 'The great moral work which grapples with the problem of identity also grapples with the contemporary experience of death, violence and hate. Nationalisms, like fundamentalisms, are screens in front of this violence, fragile screens, see-through screens, because they only displace that hatred, sending it to the other, to the neigh-bour, to the rival ethnic group. The big work of our civilisation is to try to fight this hatred – without God' (p. 14). Elsewhere in the same dialogue, Kristeva is somewhat more modified and selective in her critique of nation-alism: 'I do recognize that we are going to live for a very long time in the frame of nations and nationalities. I am against that tendency of the Left to dismiss the idea of nation out of hand. I believe the idea of nation is going to have a long life. But it should be a *choice*, and not a reflex or return to the origin. When one lives it as a choice – that is to say, with clarity of vision, knowing the political, ideological, cultural reasons that make us adhere to France, Ireland, Great Britain, etc., and not because we are genetically linked to it – it can be a good choice' (p. 8). See Kristeva's argument for a cosmopolitan alternative to nationalism in *Strangers to Ourselves* (Colum-bia University Press, New York, 1994) and *Nations without Nationalism*

(Columbia University Press, New York, 1993). In the latter, Kristeva offers further illuminating observations on how nationalism often takes the form of displaced (and misplaced) libidinal attachments to the 'lost object', idealizing the nation accordingly as some sort of phallic mother. The fact that the nation is personified ideologically/mythically/symbolically as a mother, more often than as a sexualized woman, is particularly significant (as noted also by Benedict Anderson and Liam O'Dowd) in that mothers are *unavailable* and so ready metonyms for the displacement/projection/identification processes of repressed unconscious desires. The fact that mothers must be shared between 'sons' – unlike most other categories of women – is another cogent reason for their becoming likely candidates of national solidarity, consensus and identity. Indeed the additional fact that many emergent nationalist movements construe themselves as sons or adolescents (e.g. the 'Young Irelanders') confirms this filial/maternal symbolism.

8 MYTH AND NATION IN IRISH POETRY

1 See my comments on the 1916 Proclamation in the fourth section of Chapter 7 and in 'Myth and Martyrdom: Some Foundational Symbols in Irish Republicanism', Richard Kearney, *Transitions: Narratives in Modern Irish Culture* (Manchester University Press, Manchester, 1988), pp. 209 ff.

2 See Karl Mannheim, *Ideology and Utopia* (Routledge and Kegan Paul, London, 1979).

3 Tom Moylan, *Demand the Impossible: Science Fiction and Utopian Imagination* (Methuen, London, 1986), p. 28. For further analysis of this distinction between utopian and ideological myths, see my 'Myth and the Critique of Ideology', in *Transitions*; and also my 'Myth as the Bearer of Possible Worlds', in *Dialogues with Contemporary Continental Thinkers* (Manchester University Press, Manchester, 1984) reprinted in *States of Mind: Dialogues with Contemporary Thinkers on the Eurpoean Mind* (Manchester University Press, Manchester / New York University Press, New York, 1995).

4 Fredric Jameson, 'Of Islands and Trenches', *Diacritics*, 7(2), 1977, p. 11.

5 Samuel Beckett, 'Recent Irish Poetry', *The Bookman*, no. 86, August 1934.

6 Patrick Kavanagh, *Self-Portrait* (Dolmen Press, Dublin, 1964); reprinted in *Collected Prose* (Martin Brian and O'Keeffe, London, 1973), p. 13.

7 *Ibid.*, p. 16.

8 *Ibid.*, p. 13.

9 *Ibid.*, p. 22.

10 Seamus Deane, *A Short History of Irish Literature* (Hutchinson, London, 1986), p. 233.

11 John Montague, quoted by Deane, *ibid.*, p. 233.

12 Thomas Kinsella, 'Nursed out of Wreckage', in Seamus Deane, *Celtic Revivals* (Faber and Faber, London, 1985) p. 137.

13 Thomas Kinsella, 'The Divided Mind', in *Irish Poetry in English* (ed. Sean Lucy, Mercier Press, Cork, 1973), p. 209.

14 *Ibid.*

15 For a critical discussion of these postmodernist practices, see my *The Wake of Imagination* (Hutchinson, London, 1988; reprinted by Routledge, London, 1994); and, as applied to certain Irish writers, *Transitions*, pp. 14, 112, 278–280.

16 I am indebted for this and several other comments below to Seamus Deane, *Celtic Revivals*, p. 148. I am also indebted to Declan Kiberd, *Inventing Ireland – The Literature of the Modern Nation* (Jonathan Cape, London, 1995) and to David Lloyd, *Anomalous States: Irish Writing and the Post-Colonial Moment* (Lilliput, Dublin, 1993), particularly their respective discussions of the post-colonial dimension of much modern Irish poetry.

17 Seamus Heaney, *Preoccupations: Selected Prose 1968–1978* (Faber and Faber, London, 1980), p. 57; see also my analysis of 'Heaney and Homecoming' as it relates to this point in *Transitions*, p. 108.

18 Seamus Heaney, 'Unhappy and at Home', interview with Seamus Deane in *The Crane Bag*, 1(1), 1977, p. 62.

19 Derek Mahon, 'Lettre ouverte à Serge Fauchereau', *Digraphe*, no. 27, June 1983, p. 70. See also Seamus Deane, 'Derek Mahon: Freedom from History', *Celtic Revivals*, p. 161.

20 Peter McDonald, 'Home and Away' (review of Durcan's *Going Home to Russia*), *Irish Review*, no. 4, Spring 1988, p. 107.

21 *Ibid.*

22 Derek Mahon, 'Orpheus Ascending: The Poetry of Paul Durcan', *Irish Review*, no. 1, Autumn 1986, p. 16.

23 I am greatly indebted, in what follows, to Claire Wills's excellent analysis of McGuckian's work in *Improprieties* (Clarendon Press, Oxford, 1993).

24 Medbh McGuckian, 'Dovecoat' in *Venus in the Rain* (Oxford University Press, Oxford, 1984). See Wills, *Improprieties*, in particular the Introduction.

25 Wills, *Improprieties*, Introduction.

26 *Ibid.* See McGuckian, *The Flower Master* (Oxford University Press, Oxford, 1982). See also Luce Irigaray, *Speculum of the Other Woman* (Cornell University Press, Ithaca, 1984) and Julia Kristeva, 'Stabat Mater' in *Tales of Love* (Blackwell, Oxford, 1988).

27 C. Wills, *Improprieties*, Introduction.

28 Paul Muldoon, quoted in Edna Longley, *Poetry in the Wars* (Bloodaxe Books, Newcastle upon Tyne, 1987), p. 234. I am indebted to Edna Longley for several insightful comments on Muldoon's treatment of the *immram* motif.

29 Paul Muldoon, quoted in Longley, *ibid.*, p. 239.

30 Edna Longley, *ibid.*, pp. 207–209, offers this pertinent assessment of Muldoon's postmodern contribution to Irish poetry: 'Muldoon subverts martyrs and goddesses, fixed ideas and "concrete" categories, by means of language that undermines its own solidity. [His] sensibility reaches the parts where the hidden Ireland is usually kept hidden, where it involves suppressions as well as oppressions. Muldoon blows the whistle on the conspiracy between myth and cliche'. Muldoon's book, *Maddock*, develops several of these themes (Farrar, Strauss and Giroux, New York, 1991).

9 GEORGE BERKELEY: WE IRISH THINK OTHERWISE

1 J.-L. Borges in conversation with Seamus Heaney and Richard Kearney in *The Crane Bag*, 6(2), 1982, p. 75. Reprinted in R. Kearney, *States of Mind* (Manchester University Press, Manchester, 1995).

2 See in particular Harry Bracken, 'George Berkeley: The Irish Cartesian'

and David Berman, 'The Irish Counter-Enlightenment', both in *The Irish Mind: Exploring Intellectual Traditions* (ed. Richard Kearney, Wolfhound Press, Dublin / Humanities Press, New York, 1984) and in Berman's *Berkeley* (Oxford University Press, Oxford, 1994).

3 See H. Bracken, 'George Berkeley: The Irish Cartesian', p. 108.

4 See A.A. Luce (ed.) *Berkeley's Philosophical Commentaries* (Garland, New York, 1989).

5 See A.A. Luce, *Berkeley and Malebranche* (Oxford University Press, Oxford, 1934), p. 43.

6 See H. Bracken, 'George Berkeley: The Irish Cartesian', p. 107.

7 H. Bracken, *ibid.*, pp. 114, 117. Bracken provides the following useful summary of the above arguments: 'Berkeley's philosophy is best understood as a product of Cartesianism. As noted, Berkeley sees *esse est percipi* as (i) dissolving the very distinction between the being of things and their being perceived which constitute the source of scepticism; (ii) yielding a substantial self in which ideas inhered, not as a mere unfocused "cluster" of ideas derived from empirical sensations, and (iii) providing a solid basis for a simple awareness of God – who speaks to us in the language of our perceptions. In brief, the arguments Berkeley provides for this case, and the reactions of his contemporaries, suggest that Berkeley ought not to count as operating with Lockean notions. Since on a range of major points Berkeley stands with Descartes or Malebranche or Bayle, rather than with Locke, then the label "British empiricist" is inaccurate; it is the sort of inaccuracy that constitutes a hindrance to our understanding of a thinker. If anything, Berkeley should be labelled an Irish Cartesian working along the paths of continental philosophy and contributing to his own original insights particularly on the question of immaterialism and scepticism.'

8 J.-L. Borges, Interview in *The Crane Bag*, 6(2), 1982, pp. 75–76.

9 W.B. Yeats, *Selected Prose* (ed. N. Jeffares, Macmillan, New York, 1964), p. 131.

10 W.B. Yeats, *Essays and Introductions* (Macmillan, NewYork, 1961), p. 402. Cf. Thomas Bartlett, 'Protestant Nationalism in Eighteenth-Century Ireland', in *Nations and Nationalisms* (ed. K. Whelan and M. O'Dea, Voltaire Foundation, Oxford, 1996), pp. 79–88.

11 Seamus Deane, 'The Myths of the Literary Revival' in Deane's *Celtic Revivals* (Faber and Faber), 1985, pp. 28–38; see also my commentary on Deane's reading in the 'Introduction' to *The Irish Mind*, pp. 31–36.

12 *The Works of George Berkeley, Bishop of Cloyne* (eds A.A. Luce and T.E. Jessop, Nelson, London, 1948–57), p. 346 (quoted in Bracken, 'George Berkeley: the Irish Cartesian').

13 R. Houghton, *The World of George Berkeley* (The Irish Heritage Series 53,Dublin, 1985).

14 Quoted in H. Bracken, 'George Berkeley: The Irish Cartesian'.

15 Quoted in D. Berman, 'A Note on Berkeley and his Catholic Countrymen', *The Longroom*, 1978, p. 27.

16 Quoted in D. Berman, *ibid.*, p. 26.

17 Quoted in D. Berman, 'The Irish Counter-Enlightenment', p. 140.

18 D. Berman, *ibid.*, p. 139. David Berman offers the following illuminating account of the political and ideological background to the Irish Counter-Enlightenment philosophy of which Berkeley was perhaps the most

celebrated exponent: 'By 1691 the Glorious Revolution had been concluded. Irish Anglicans were thereby saved from the dominance of James II
and their Roman Catholic countrymen. The previous fifty years had been
stormy indeed. First the Irish Anglicans were buffeted by the Roman Catholics during the 1641 Rebellion, then by Cromwell and the Presbyterians, and
then by the Roman Catholics under Tyrconnell and James II. There was
now to be a period of political stability and calm, which would last for more
than a century. Initially, at least, the Irish Anglicans were in an insecure and
precarious position. They were faced with a hostile dispossessed majority,
and a Treaty that did not seem to go far enough in restricting the Catholic
majority. The Presbyterians also seemed a dangerous minority, as William
III was known to favour them. Yet from this insecure position the Irish
Anglicans developed a remarkably successful *modus operandi,* whose foundation was the Penal legislation against both Catholics and Presbyterians.
This legislation, which came into being in the 1690s and 1700s, established
the Ascendancy, just as it repressed the two other religious classes politically, economically and socially' (p. 137). See also D. Berman, *Berkeley*
(Oxford University Press, Oxford, 1994) and 'Irish Philosophy and Ideology', p. 159.
19 See Raymond Houghton, *The World of George Berkeley*.

10 JOHN TOLAND: AN IRISH PHILOSOPHER?

1 Robert Sullivan, *John Toland and the Deist Controversy* (Harvard University
 Press, Cambridge, Mass., 1982), p. 1.
2 *Ibid.*
3 *Ibid.*, p. 40. See also J. G. Simms, 'John Toland (1670–1722), A Donegal
 Heretic', *Irish Historical Studies*, XVI (63), 1969, pp. 304–320; P. des
 Maizeaux, *A Collection of Several Pieces of Mr. John Toland* (Montrose,
 London, 1814); S.H. Daniel, *John Toland: His Methods, Manners and Mind*
 (McGill–Queens University Press, Kingston and Montreal, 1984); Günter
 Gawlick, Introduction to critical bilingual (German–English) edition of
 Christianity not Mysterious (F. Frommann Verlag, Stuttgart-Bad
 Cannstatt, 1964), pp. 5–21; L. Stephen, *English Thought in the Eighteenth
 Century*, 2 vols (Smith and Elder, London, 1881), pp. 4–28; Pierre Lurbe,
 'John Toland, Cosmopolitanism and the Concept of Nation', and Desmond
 M. Clarke, 'Locke and Toland on Toleration', in *Nations and Nationalisms:
 France, Britain, Ireland and the Eighteenth Century*, ed. Michael O'Dea and
 Kevin Whelan (Voltaire Foundation, Oxford, 1996); my 'John Toland: An-
 cestor of Liberty but Follower of No Man' in *Fortnight*, no. 297, 1993, pp. 2–
 4; Sean Kearney, 'John Toland, 1670–1722: An Ulster Freethinker' in *The
 Humanist*, 3(6), 1996, pp. 10–14, where the author lays particular emphasis
 on Toland's cosmopolitan and European-republican thinking; and Alan
 Harrison's biography, *John Toland (1670–1722): Gael Eiricúil as Inis
 Eoghain* (Coiscéim, Dublin, 1994) which contributes new information on
 Toland's life but ultimately concedes that it remains an enigma.
4 Catholic Irish Colleges overseas acted as unofficial embassies for the di-
 asporic Irish in eighteenth-century continental Europe.
5 David Berman, 'The Irish Counter-Enlightenment' in *The Irish Mind*
 (ed. R. Kearney, Wolfhound Press, Dublin, 1984), pp. 119–140. See also

Berman's other articles, 'John Toland' in *The Encyclopedia of Unbelief* (ed. G. Stein, New York, 1985), pp. 669–670; 'Disclaimers as Offence Mechanisms in Charles Blount and John Toland' in *Atheism from the Reformation to the Enlightenment* (eds M. Hunter and D. Wootton, Clarendon Press, Oxford, 1992), pp. 255–272; and the selection from Toland in *The Field Day Anthology of Irish Writing*, vol. I (eds Seamus Deane, David Berman and Andrew Carpenter, Faber, London, 1991), pp. 760–768.

6 See Sullivan, *John Toland and the Deist Controversy*, pp. 16, 29.

7 Toland, *An Account of an Irish Manuscript of the Four Gospels* in *Nazarenus* (second edition, London, 1718), p. 2. See A. Harrison's analysis of this document in his article, 'John Toland and the discovery of an Irish Manuscript in Holland', *Irish University Review*, 22(1) 1992, pp. 33–39.

8 *Ibid.*, Toland, *An Account of an Irish Manuscript of the Four Gospels*, p. 18.

9 *Ibid.*, p. 23

10 *Ibid.*, p. 24

11 *Ibid.*, pp. 32–33

12 See *Irish Independent* report on Bishop Newman's address, 13 May 1985.

13 D. Berman, 'Irish Philosophy and Ideology' in *The Crane Bag*, 9(2), 1985, p. 159.

14 A. Harrison, 'John Toland and Celtic Studies' in *Celtic Languages and Celtic Peoples: Proceedings of the Second North American Congress of Celtic Studies* (eds C.G. Byrne, M. Harry and P. O' Siadhall, Halifax, Nova Scotia, 1991). See also A. Harrison, 'John Toland's Celtic Background' in *Christianity Not Mysterious* (eds A. Harrison, R. Kearney and P. McGuinness, Lilliput Press, Dublin, forthcoming).

15 Quoted in Sullivan, *John Toland and the Deist Controversy*, pp. 44–45 (p. iv of Preface to *Christianity not Mysterious* facsimile edition).

16 *Ibid.*, p. 39.

17 Harrison, 'John Toland and Celtic Studies', p. 562.

18 *Ibid.*, p. 555.

19 Stephen Daniel, 'The Subversive Philosophy of John Toland' in *Irish Writing, Exile and Subversion* (eds P. Hylland and N. Sammells, Macmillan, London, 1992), p. 5. Sean Kearney has much to say about Toland's dissident and iconoclastic freethinking particularly as it translates itself into a 'republican' suspicion of inherited authority and hierarchy, political or ecclesiastical. This is epitomized in Toland's support for republican figures like Ludlow, Milton and Harrington and his bold statement in favour of popular sovereignty as embodied in a commonwealth: 'I have always been, now am, and ever shall be persuaded that all sorts of magistrates are made for and by the people and not the people for or by the magistrates. . . . I am therefore and avowedly a Commonwealthman' (cited in Sean Kearney, 'John Toland, 1670–1722', p. 11).

20 Daniel, 'The Subversive Philosophy of John Toland', p. 5.

21 *Ibid.*

22 Berman, 'The Irish Counter-Enlightenment', p. 137: 'Consider now the birth of Irish philosophy in Toland. He was christened Janus Junius, and appropriately enough, for his background posed a two-faced threat to the ascendancy: born a Roman Catholic, he became a Dissenter at fifteen. But Toland's most threatening face was shown in *Christianity not Mysterious.* His attack on Christian mysteries and his defence of natural or deistic

religion represented a fundamental challenge to the ascendancy establish-ment. For if there were no Christian mysteries then there could be nothing to separate the rival Christian religions or sects. And then there could be no basis for the Penal Code. The success of deism or natural religion would be fatal to the ascendancy. Deism's belief in a few fundamental religious doctrines and little or no ritual, and its emphasis on morality and toler-ation, could hardly fail to soften or erode the Penal Code. At any rate, historians have agreed that this is what did happen, but that it happened late in the eighteenth century in Ireland. An attitude of scepticism was fatal to the Penal Code. If we allow that Toland's deistic thinking represented a threat to the material well-being of the ascendancy, then we can explain not only the fury unleashed against him (and Emlym and Clayton) but also the distinctively counter-enlightenment character of most of Irish philosophy'. For further discussion of this rationalist–irrationalist debate in Irish phil-osophy, see also Berman, *George Berkeley* (Oxford University Press, Oxford, 1994); and J.G. Simms's lament in 'John Toland (1670–1722)' that 'the prophet of rationalism [Toland] was without honour in his own country'.

23 Berman, 'Irish Philosophy and Ideology', p. 150.
24 *Ibid.* Kevin Whelan argues that Berman's dates for the 'Golden Age' run from the first passing of the Penal Laws (1696) to their first repeal (1757), thus betraying an equation of Irish philosophy with *protestant* thought.
25 Conor Cruise O'Brien, *The Great Melody* (Sinclair-Stevenson, London, 1992), p. 83.
26 *Ibid.*
27 Toland was, as mentioned at the outset, descended from the Ó Tuathalláin tribe of Inishowen in Donegal, a satellite family of the once powerful O'Neills and closely associated with the schools of traditional Irish learn-ing. See Harrison, 'John Toland and Celtic Studies', p. 557.
28 And, we might add, for Irish thinkers such as Berkeley and Swift who, as noted, also bear witness to countless divisions of fidelity – between resident country and foreign crown, between sympathy for their dispossessed com-patriots and loyalty to their own class, between colonized nation and colon-izing empire, powerlessness and power, poverty and privilege.
29 J.-J. Rousseau, *The Confessions* (Penguin, London, 1953), p. 300.

11 JOHN TYNDALL AND IRISH SCIENCE

1 See Gordon Herries Davies, 'Irish Thought in Science' in *The Irish Mind: Exploring Intellectual Traditions* (ed. R. Kearney, Wolfhound Press, Dublin, 1984), pp. 294–310. For a shorter version of the first part of this chapter see my 'Enlightenment and Counter-Enlightenment: Philosophy in Ireland' in *Proceedings of the International Tyndall School: Science, Green Issues and the Environment* (eds D. McMillan, C. O'Rourke, D. Frey and N. McMillan, Carlow, Ireland, September, 1993), pp. 6–10.
2 A. J. Slevin, 'The Case for Irish Science', Paper delivered at the Science and Communication Conference, Dublin City University, 24 November 1993, p. 5.
3 See Garret A. Fitzgerald, Director of the Centre for Cardiovascular Science and Professor of Medicine and Therapeutics in UCD, 'National Neglect of Science Must be Reversed' In *The Irish Times*, 28 December 1993, p. 14.
4 Quoted in the Introduction to *The Irish Mind*, p. 7.

5 Quoted in G.J. Watson, *Irish Identity and the Irish Literary Revival* (Croom Helm, London, 1979), pp. 16–17.

6 Cf. Roy Foster, *Paddy and Mr Punch* (Allan Lane, London, 1993).

7 Seamus Deane in *Two Decades of Irish Writing* (ed. D. Dunn, Carcanet, Cheadle, 1975), p. 8.

8 Garrett Barden, 'Image' in *The Crane Bag*, 1(1–2), pp. 140–141.

9 Quoted in 'Tyndall, John', *The Encyclopaedia of Philosophy* (Collier Macmillan, London, 1967), p. 167.

10 See *John the Scot. Periphyseon. On the Division of Nature* (eds J. Potter and M. Uhlfelder, Bobbs-Merrill, Indianapolis, 1976). For an excellent commentary on the Irish dimension of Eriugena's thought see Dermot Moran, 'Nature, Man and God in the Philosophy of John Scottus Eriugena' in *The Crane Bag,* 2(1–2), 1978, pp. 91–106.

11 See Norman McMillan's paper to the First International Tyndall Conference (Carlow, 1993) entitled 'John Tyndall the Philosopher'; see also N. McMillan, 'British Physics – The Irish Role in its Origin, Differentiation and Organisation as a Profession', *Phys. Educ.*, 1988, pp. 273–278. For the standard general text on Tyndall, see A.S. Eve and C.H. Creasey, *The Life and Work of John Tyndall* (Macmillan, London, 1945).

12 See. E. Frankland, 'Personal Reminiscences in the Life and Work of John Tyndall' in *The Westminster Gazette*, December 1893.

13 See N. McMillan, 'Tyndall the Philosopher'.

14 N. McMillan, 'British Physics – The Irish Role in its Origin, Differentiation and Organisation as a Profession'.

15 See F. Gregory, *Scientific Materialism in Nineteenth-Century Germany* (D. Reidel: Holland, 1976), p. 155.

POSTSCRIPT: TOWARDS A POSTNATIONALIST IRELAND

1 Raymond Williams, 'The Culture of Nations' in his *Towards 2000* (Chatto and Windus, London, 1983), p. 199. I am greately indebted to Simon Partridge, co-founder of the European Regionalist Network, for many of the arguments and sources cited in the discussion below.

2 John A. Murphy, 'Ireland: Identity and Relationships' in *National Identities* (ed. Bernard Crick, Blackwell, Oxford, 1991), pp. 88–90.

3 See Elie Kedourie's critique of political self-determination in *Nationalism* (Blackwell, Oxford, 1993), in particular Chapters 7 and 8.

4 Garrett Fitzgerald, 'Sovereignty-sharing Offers Most to Smaller States', *The Irish Times*, 30 September 1995, p. 12. It is significant, I think, that an *Irish Times*/MRBI Poll, June 1996, showed only 34 per cent of Irish citizens in favour of a united Ireland, while 'support for a solution linking the North to both the UK and the Republic, the political model underpinning the peace process, remains consistent' (*Irish Times*, 7 June 1996).

5 See Simon Partridge, 'Re-imagining These Islands: The Need for a Britannic Framework' in *New Times*, no. 92, 1995, pp. 6–7. In this paper, the author calls for a revision of the very notion of 'Britishness' in favour of new, more enabling narratives of identity. His critical sources for this view are Benedict Anderson's notion of nations as imagined constructs (*Imagined Communities – Reflections on the Origins and Spread of Nationalism*, Verso, London, 1983) and Hugh Kearney's inclusive definition of 'Britannic' as outlined in

The British Isles – A History of Four Nations (Canto, Cambridge, 1995). Partridge proposes a transinsular 'Britannic council', along Scandinavian lines, as an instrument of reconciliation between the British and Irish.

6 H. Kearney, *The British Isles – A History of Four Nations*, p. 4.

7 E. Hobsbawm, *Nations and Nationalism since 1780* (Cambridge University Press, Cambridge, 1990) pp. 182–183. See David Lloyd's critique of Hobsbawm, 'Nationalisms against the State', in *Gender and Colonialism* (ed. T. Foley *et al.*, Galway University Press, 1995).

8 S. Partridge, 'Re-imagining These Islands', p. 7.

9 V. Havel, Address to Harvard University, 8 June 1995. He continues: 'There is one great opportunity in the matter of co-existence between nations and spheres of civilisation, culture and region that should be grasped and exploited to the limit. This is the appearance of supranational or regional communities. By now, there are many such communities in the world, with diverse characteristics and differing degrees of integration. I believe in this approach. I believe in the importance of organisms that can be an important medium of global communication and co-operation' (p. 8–9). But Havel also issues the timely caveat that such transnational communities should 'rid themselves of fear that other like communities are directed against them. [Transnational] groupings in areas that have common traditions and a common political culture ought to be a natural part of the complex political architecture of the world. Co-operation between such regions ought to be a natural component of co-operation on a world-wide scale' (p. 9).

10 See the examples of the collapse of the USSR, Yugoslavia and the constitutional crisis in Canada caused by the virtual split decision of the October 1995 referendum on Quebec sovereignty. The Soviet and Yugoslav examples are self-evident, but the Canadian referendum of 1995 was a more complex situation in that democracy, economic prosperity and substantial concessions to Quebec identity (e.g. bilingualism) were already vouchsafed. Moreover, prior to the referendum, polls showed over 30 per cent of the Quebec 'sovereigntists' believing that sovereignty meant staying *within* Canada with permission for Quebec to pass its own laws, levy its taxes, conclude its treaties and enjoy dual citizenship (Canadian and Quebec). It is arguable, therefore, that many of those who voted for secession did so less for reasons of absolutist ethnic separatism than because they felt a need for greater regional identity and self-government – responding to a 'democratic deficit' of centralized government never adequately addressed in the 128 years of confederation, including the 1990 Lake Meese Accord and later compromises. A sovereignty-sharing, or post-sovereignty paradigm, along the lines of a European federation of regions might actually be more in keeping with the profound desire of francophone Quebec for a combination of distinctness and association, allowing for dual citizenship and 'multiple identity'. (This is close to what Charles Taylor suggests in his argument for the recognition of Quebec's distinctiveness within a reformed federal system, see *Reconciling the Solitudes: Essays on Canadian Federalism and Nationalism,* (McGill–Queen's University Press, Montreal, 1993).) We might note here that Quebec nationalism is in some respects a reaction against Canadian nationalism, understood in the sense of a single nation-state based on principles of indivisible sovereignty. Indeed, the Quebec demand for secession might –

from an identity-symbolic point of view – have been less acute if Canada had enjoyed its own historical 'declaration of independence' from the British Crown as the USA, Ireland or other former colonies did in establishing their respective 'republics'.

11 I. Kant, *Perpetual Peace: A Philosophical Sketch* in *Kant's Political Writings* (ed. H. Riess, Cambridge University Press, Cambridge, 1970), p. 104. I am indebted to my UCD colleague Attracta Ingram for this and several other quotations and discussions below. See in particular her illuminating papers, 'The European Federalist' (1994), 'Rawlsians, Pluralists and Cosmopolitans', and 'Constitutional Patriotism' (in *Philosophy and Social Criticism,* 22(6), 1996).

12 It was largely in response to this lingering 'democratic deficit' that Denmark voted no to the Maastricht Treaty and that Norway voted against EU membership.

13 See Vincent Geoghegan's argument for a 'post-nationalist citizenship' which allows for the separation of national identity from nationalism and its conjugation with a series of other subnational and supranational identities, 'Socialism, National Identities and Post-nationalist Citizenship', *Irish Political Studies*, 9, 1994, pp. 76–77 (see Note 4 of Chapter 4 above). On this question of 'multiple' identity see also C. Taylor, 'Nations and Federations: Living Among Others' in *States of Mind*, pp. 25–26 (see Note 29 below and Note 1 of Chapter 4); and *Reconciling the Solitudes: Essays on Canadian Federalism and Nationalism.* For a decidedly 'cosmopolitan' gloss on this extension of identities, expressing a postmodern variation on an Enlightenment theme, see J. Kristeva's commentary on Montesquieu's saying: 'If I knew something that would be useful to myself, but detrimental to my family, I would cast it from my mind. If I knew something that was useful to my family but detrimental to my country, I would consider it criminal. If I knew something useful to Europe, but detrimental to humankind, I would also consider it a crime' (See *Strangers to Ourselves*, Columbia University Press, New York, 1994). What interests Kristeva in this formula is that it recognizes the different levels of individual, family and national identity while pointing always to a wider frame. The ultimate horizon of such cosmopolitanism might, for some, be a form of world state, but this is certainly problematic and was opposed even by Kant who acknowledged the pitfalls of global uniformity. See A. Ingram, 'The European Federalist', p. 6: 'Matters of territorial distance, and feasible size from an administrative point of view, have always been recognized as placing practical limits on federal expansion, even by such ardent cosmopolitans as Kant. Indeed Kant insisted that world government is a wholly impractical and tyrannical idea. His idea of perpetual peace is a maxim to guide us to political principles and institutions of international right, *when the question of federation is on the cards.* The other point to make is that cosmopolitanism does not imply imposition of federal relations on unwilling partners. Federalism has always been thought of as a gradual, piecemeal type of change in international relations'.

14 N. Chomsky, 'The Politics of Language' in *States of Mind: Dialogues with Contemporary Thinkers on the European Mind* (ed. R. Kearney, Manchester University Press, Manchester / New York University Press, New York, 1995), pp. 48–49. It is interesting to note that the Reif analysis of

Eurobarometer data shows attachment to region and to nation to be broadly on a par (between 87–88 per cent): K. H. Reif, 'Cultural Convergence and Cultural Diversity as Factors in European Identity', in S. Garcia (ed.) *European Identity and the Search for Legitimacy* (Pinter, London, 1993). See also the critique of regionalist culture by George Steiner in 'Culture – The Price You Pay', *States of Mind*, p. 84: 'Differences and diversities, yes . . . but careful. Much of the regionalism has a cruel, dark atavism. It lives by hatred: Flammand against Walloon, the Basque situation, the Irish: the bombs in the pocket of the local, small, agricultural fanatical movement. Regions do tend too often to define themselves, not by remembering in joy, but in hatred. And I think we have to be very careful lest that flame burn again'.

15 J. Habermas, 'Citizenship and National Identity: Some Reflections on the Future of Europe', *Praxis International*, 12(1), 1992 and 'Citoyenneté et Identité Nationale' in *L'Europe au Soir du Siècle: Identité et Démocratie* (eds J. Lenoble and N. Dewandre, Paris, 1992). For good critical commentaries of the 'constitutional patriotism' position, see Attracta Ingram (Note 11 above) as well as Jean-Marc Ferry and André Berten, who defend Habermas's position, and Wayne Norman and Charles Taylor who challenge aspects of it on the grounds that a legal–rational set of abstract constitutional principles is not sufficient, in itself, to command the allegiance and communal solidarity of its many members. Though a committed federalist, Taylor has the complex experience of his native Quebec in mind, as articulated in *Reconciling the Solitudes: Essays on Canadian Federalism and Nationalism*. The motivation for such loyalty and consensus must come from the people themselves who make up the membership of whatever federal union is contractually agreed on (see Notes 23–28 below and Note 33 of the Introduction).

16 Attracta Ingram, 'The European Federalist', p. 4.

17 *Ibid.*, p. 8. As Ingram argues, 'The federal principle goes all the way down. I mean that the partners have internal federal structures wherever their situation calls for it. Subsidiarity is the reason of principle that justifies extension of the federal structure to territorial sub-units that can make a case for special status. What a people or a regional group can do best for themselves should not be committed to the authority of a wider political unit. Thus the claims of cultural and different internal nationalisms (Scots and Welsh and Basque, just to take some less controversial examples) to a range of powers to protect their special cultural interests could be accommodated. Non-territorially-based functional units (minorities living among majority populations, for example) might also be able to make a case under a generously interpreted subsidiarity principle for control over their own schools and hospitals'.

18 See the critiques of ideological nationalism upon which nation-state sovereignty is often predicated – i.e. *la nation une et indivisible* - by Hannah Arendt and Isaiah Berlin in Note 3 of Chapter 4 above. In 'The European Federalist', Ingram cites other proponents of federalism who believe that the nation-state in Europe has had its day and that it serves as a 'siren' for a wave of micronationalist claims with potentially regressive implications, e.g. J. Pindar, 'The new European Federalism: The Idea and the Achievements' in *Comparative Federalism and Federation: Competing Traditions and Future*

Directions (eds M. Burgess and A.-G. Gagnon, University of Toronto Press, Toronto, 1993), pp. 146–153. For those who argue for the consolidation of the nation-state within the European Union, see A.S. Milward and V. Sorenson, 'Interdependence or Integration? A National Choice' in *The Frontier of National Sovereignty: History and Theory 1945–1992* (London, 1993), in addition to the pro-nationalist apologists, R. Scruton, D. Miller and E. Renan cited in Note 33 of the Introduction. Finally, we could cite here the position of Edgar Morin who opposes abstract unitarian concepts of Europe, not in defence of nation-state nationalism, but in deference to a notion of Europe as a network of multiple differences, a *unitas multiplex* or 'cauldron of diversities'; see *Penser L'Europe* (Gallimard, Paris, 1987), p. 29. Morin resists all attempts to simplify Europe by way of idealization or reduction, arguing that Europe is a *complexus* woven out of contrasting threads and tensions, whose vocation it is to 'assemble the largest possible diversity without confounding it, to associate contraries while safeguarding their separateness. And this is why we need not only a just modesty but also a just thinking which may comprehend the gordian knot that makes up Europe with all its political, economic, social, cultural, religious and anti-religious histories intermixing and interconnecting in both conflict and solidarity'.

19 C. Taylor, 'Nations and Federations' in *States of Mind*, p. 25.

20 J. Kristeva, 'Strangers to Ourselves' in *States of Mind*, pp. 10–11. See the extension of her argument to include an acknowledgement of the 'death wish' embedded in several forms of modern nationalism (pp. 12–13): 'We have to take seriously the violence of identity desires. For instance, when somebody recognizes him or her self in an X or Y origin, it can appear very laudable, a very appealing need for identity. But one mustn't forget the violence behind this desire. This violence can be turned against oneself, and give rise to fratricidal wars. So what we learn is the relativeness of human fraternity and the interest, not only pedagogical but therapeutic, one should take in the death wish, in the violence within us. . . . Along with the care that one should give to the death wish, there is a need for a lot of finesse in the way one deals with individuals, but also with their relationship to nations. After the Enlightenment, the idea of the nation was for long considered a backward and archaic idea that one could brush away, do without. I believe that, at least on an economic level, the nation is here to stay; we will have it with us for at least another century. But it is not enough to realise its economic dimension; we have to measure the psychic violence of the adherence to this idea. This is a violence that can also be carried by religions, for religions can be another form of originary adhesion. The shapes of fundamentalism that spring up nowadays on all sides cannot be dissipated simply by fraternal good will. . . . We are faced with a death wish. So that great moral work which grapples with the problem of identity also grapples with this contemporary experience of death, violence and hate. Nationalisms, like fundamentalisms, are screens in front of this violence, fragile screens, see-through screens, because they only displace that hatred, sending it to the other, to the neighbour, to the rival ethnic group. The big work of our civilisation is trying to fight this hatred – without God'.

21 See the debate on the merits and demerits of 'constitutional patriotism' in Note 15 above and Note 33 of the Introduction.

22 C. Taylor, 'Nations and Federations' in *States of Mind*, p. 28. See the development of Taylor's argument in Note 1 of Chapter 4.

23 In contrast to the United States of America, which unites a melting pot of immigrants around a single language (English), the emerging European Union is composed of a multiplicity of languages, dialects, ethnicities and identities. Umberto Eco's proposed solution to this European multiplicity is to celebrate the possibility of radical *hybridization*: 'English became the unifying tongue in America. In Europe we are facing more and more a fragmentation of languages. . . . The Europe of tomorrow will have tens of different languages, each of them recognized in their own autonomy and dignity. And so the future of Europe is probably to acquire a sort of polylingual attitude. And there is in the universities at present an interesting prefiguration of this. I have always said that the most important feature of the Erasmus (education exchange) Project is the sexual one. Because, what does it mean if every student is supposed in the future to spend one year at least in another country? It means a lot of mixed marriages. It means that the next generation will be largely bilingual, with a father and mother from different countries. That's the best chance for Europe' ('Chaosmos' in *States of Mind*, p. 80). See, also, Edward Said's advocacy of a similar project of hybridization in response to the danger of Eurocentrism's becoming an exclusivist Euro-nationalism in its own right, 'Europe and its Others: An Arab Perspective' in *States of Mind*, p. 46: 'There has to be an understanding finally that no political or national grouping is homogeneous. Everything is mixed, we deal in a world of interdependent societies'. Hence the threat of an emerging 'rhetoric of purification . . . the Far Right, Le Pen, the idea that Europe is for the Europeans'. The fundamental question here, Said agrees with Eco, is education. 'Most systems of education today are still nationalist, that is to say, they promote the authority of the national identity in an idealised way and suggest that it is incapable of any criticism, it is virtue incarnate. There is nothing that lays the seed of conflict in the future more than what we educate our children and students in the universities to believe about themselves'. All of the above points, in my view, to a renewed sense of cosmopolitanism, as defined by Adriann Van der Staay, Professor of Cultural Policy at the Erasmus University of Rotterdam: 'Following the Enlightenment, cosmopolitanism became an essential word to reflect a general attitude of confidence towards different cultures, together with an optimistic belief that by encountering different solutions in different circumstances one may gain insight and competence. In this view, cultural growth is linked to the very encounters that tribalism fears' ('Cosmopolitanism' in *The European Cultural Foundation Newsletter*, xviii(2), 1995).

24 T. Nairn, *The Enchanted Glass: Britain and its Monarchy* (Radius, London, 1988), pp. 136–137. See Geoffrey Howe's remark on Margaret Thatcher: 'The insistence on the undivided sovereignty of her opinion, dressed up as the nation's sovereignty, was her undoing'. Cited by H. Gardiner, *Leading Minds* (HarperCollins, London, 1996), p. 24.

25 A. Ingram, 'The European Federalist', p. 9.

26 I. Kant, *Perpetual Peace*, p. 104. For critical discussion of this text see A. Ingram, 'The European Federalist' and Dick Howard, *From Kant to Marx* (State University of New York Press, Albany, 1985), especially Chapter 7 entitled 'The Modern Republic'. We might recall here the Preamble to the

Treaty of Paris, 1951, which resolved to ' substitute for age-old rivalries the merging of their essential interests: to create, by establishing an economic community, the basis for a broader and deeper community among peoples long divided by bloody conflicts'.

27 See, for example, A. Ingram's analysis of the communitarian principles contained in the Christian democratic tradition generally and the Catholic social philosophy of various Papal encyclicals in particular, 'The European Federalist', pp. 11–14.

28 For a more political assessment of the value motivations underlying the European regionalist project, see Brigid Laffan, 'The Politics of Identity and Political Order in Europe', in *The Journal of Common Market Studies*, 34 (1), March 1966, pp. 81–102. Laffan argues that the traditional congruity between shared identity, functional tasks and bounded territory, which provided the historic conditions for the development of the European nation-states, is no longer assured at national level. Hence the search for an alternative set of shared symbols and institutions – e.g. at regional and/or federal level. Laffan insists on the need to recognize the importance of 'affective attachment', in addition to the pragmatic measures of institution-building' and policy integration. The neo-functionalist strategy of the Monnet method is currently experiencing a 'legitimacy crisis' as national governance structures are increasingly challenged. Hence the requirement of a new 'identity politics' for the New Europe. Today the question as to what sort of community commands the allegiance and belonging of its members needs to look further than the traditional nation-states. Whence the search for alternative models of shared identity – myths, symbols, images, concepts, memories, dreams, visions – at subnational and trans-national levels. A return to revivalist nationalism, as witnessed in several EC member states, would be a recipe for national closure and a regression to old exclusivisms of 'them' and 'us' (accentuated by the rising hostility to immigrant communities). The movement for a Europe of Regions – known as the 'new regionalism' – seeks to provide a different response to the identity–legitimacy crisis. Laffan sketches the background thus:

> European integration has acted as a catalyst for a re-examination of relations between different levels of government in West European states and has led many regions, islands, cities and coastal areas to re-evaluate where they are in Europe's emerging political and economic order. In the 1960s, the resurgence of regional political and cultural movements took many European governments by surprise ... particularly in Scotland, Wales, Brittany, Corsica, Catalonia, the Basque country and in Belgium. The regionalist movements aim to radically restructure the balance be-tween central, regional and local power in the states to which they belong. The process of restructuring has gone furthest in Belgium which grad-ually assumed the traits of a federal system between 1980 and 1993. Post-Franco Spain granted considerable autonomy to the 'Autonomous Communities', especially those like Catalonia and the Basque country with long histories. In 1972, the post-war Italian constitutional provi-sions on regions were finally activated. This was followed in 1982 by the creation of directly elected regional councils in France, which represented a significant decentralization of the French state. The United Kingdom remains the only large unitary state left in Western Europe.

Laffan remarks on the telling fact that the regionalist movements see European integration–federation as an overarching roof under which to affirm local and regional identities unacknowledged by nation-states. Hence the call of the Scottish Nationalist Party for 'independence in Europe', a project reiterated by the Lega Lombarda and the Basques. These regionalist movements do not, generally, seek a sovereign nation-state of their own but a degree of local autonomy within a transnational federal network. Interestingly, the European Commission has actually encouraged these as-pirations by establishing direct links with regions in the member states (for example, the Leader project in Ireland) and by sponsoring the concept of 'partnership' across levels of government. The German *Länder* have taken the lead in this regard, insisting on direct representation to Brussels. Ac-cordingly, the number of regional representative offices has grown from 2 in 1985 to 50 in 1994; while the Euro-cities Association, founded in 1985 by 6 cities, represented 38 cities by 1995. In addition, we find organizations such as the Association of European Regions, the Council of European Municipalities and Regions, and the Atlantic Rim Association providing a transnational umbrella for regional and local communities. Laffan also recognizes that the inclusion of the Committee of the Regions in the Maas-tricht Treaty was an explicit acknowledgement of the growing significance of the regional dimension of European integration. But while she correctly identifies the aim of the Europe of Regions to be more 'democratic, efficient and economically dynamic' than the existing nation-states, she incorrectly (in my view) sees their underlying motivation to be the restoration of 'older ethnic regions'. The model of regionalism I have been advocating in this book is, as I mention on several occasions above, civic rather than ethnic, radical rather than conservative, cultural rather than territorial. In this sense, a region like Catalonia, with its cosmopolitan capital Barcelona, and its dynamic networking with its Mediterranean neighbours, offers a positive model. Regions, in the New Europe, should be ideally conceived as local democracies – something along the lines of the city-republics of Renais-sance Italy – which combine a sense of cultural identity and belonging with a sense of cultural self-invention as 'imagined communities': porous, inter-linked, open-ended. Indeed it is revealing how the EC regional policies have served not to isolate and insulate regions but to promote cross-border and transnational linkages between areas sharing similar environmental, agricultural, industrial and geographical interests –transcending or simply cutting across national borders. I agree, however, with Laffan's overall con-clusion that the integration project offers a frame for 'asserting new or submerged identities and is also bound up in the search for an overarching European identity'. What this amounts to, ultimately, is an attempt to re-construct a genuine politics at the heart of a European Community hitherto fragmented between rival nation-states. It operates, accordingly, on the pre-supposition that 'Europeanization' to date has, unfortunately, been far more pronounced at the level of 'policy-making than of politics', of market trade than of socio-cultural participation, of diplomatic compromise be-tween competing national units – orchestrated by 'expert' power – than of genuine democratic government. The task of the new Europe of regions, then, is to create a European network of active citizens, who participate and belong, rather than merely a brokered convenience treaty between consumers and producers. As Jacques Delors once remarked: 'You don't fall in love with the common market, you need something else'. This something else will be found, I submit, in a redressed sense of cultural allegiance to regional and European identity – recognizing that regions are not pre-existing entities but, in significant measure, imagined projects that are also 'talked and written into existence'. In the future one hopes that to be a *Cives Communitatis Europeae* (as the EC passport says) will be to define oneself not exclusively in terms of a nation-state but in terms of a multiple identity – at once regional, national and transnational. Where national identity may be said to appeal to an historical *past* and transnational-European identity to a projected *future*, regional identity represents a commitment to partici-patory democracy in the *present*. Indeed, I would go further and say that a real sense of regional participation is most likely to conjoin an economic to a political Europe via a genuine sense of a cultural Europe – albeit a *pluri-cultural* one.

I am additionally grateful to Brigid Laffan for bringing a number of recent discussions of the question of European regional identity to my attention – in particular, C. Harvie, *The Rise of Regional Europe*, Routledge, London, 1994; T. Wilson and E. Smith (eds), *Cultural Change and the New Europe: Perspectives on the European Community*, Westview Press, Boulder, 1993; N. Nye, *Peace in Parts: Integration and Conflict in Regional Organisa-tion*, University Press of America, New York, 1987; I. Neumann, 'A Region-Building Approach to Northern Europe', *Review of International Studies*, vol. 20, pp. 53–74; H. Miall, *Redefining Europe*, London, 1994; and R. O'Donnell, *Ireland and Europe: Challenges for a New Century*, ESRI, Dublin, 1993.

29 C. Taylor, 'Nations and Federations' in *States of Mind*, p. 24. See also here P. Ricoeur's suggestion that the question of *identity* – which easily degener-ates into definitions of sameness – be translated into the more negotiable position of *recognition* – which opens self-identity to the question of mutual relations with 'others' and 'otherness' (*La Critique et La Conviction*, Calmann-Lévy, Paris, 1995, pp. 94–106). As Ricoeur puts it: 'Dans la notion d'identité, il y a seulement l'idée du même; tandis que la reconnaissance est un concept qui intègre directement l'altérité, qui permet une dialectique du même et de l'autre. La revendication d'identité a toujours quelque chose de violent à l'égard d'autrui. Au contraire, la recherche de la reconnaissance implique la réciprocité' (p. 96) Ricoeur's basic point is that the need for identification-and-recognition cannot be adequately met at the level of individuals or states, but requires an 'intermediary' level which thinkers like Hannah Arendt and Jean-Marc Ferry locate in the civic life of com-munal 'association'. The basic question for such an 'intermediary' (postnationalist/post-individualist) position thus becomes one of *represen-tation:* how do we find appropriate forms of political 'representation' for these kinds of civic and social 'recognition'? The current crisis of represen-tation is a symptom of the 'political void' created in large part by the collapse of inherited models of sovereignty (God, Monarch, Nation-State, Individual). And this twin crisis of representation and sovereignty – which we have discussed in several of the chapters above – may best be resolved, Ricoeur suggests, in attempts to rethink the relation of historical par-ticularity and normative universality; his own proposed solution being a

combination of a 'regulative universal' (as promoted by Rawls and other neo-Kantian liberals) with an historically 'constitutive universal' (as promoted by Walzer, Thévenot and the communitarians). In the final analysis, the whole question of the 'limits' of representation and sovereignty amounts to a crisis of *legitimation*, perhaps nowhere more conspicuously evidenced than in the modern crisis of the nation-state.

30 As Simon Partridge rightly points out, the Irish and British are already substantially 'mongrelized' on both islands. The mix in Northern Ireland in particular speaks for itself, while the mix in Britain has been documented in a recent survey (1994–95) carried out by James O'Connell of the University of Bradford. In his survey on British attitudes towards 'Ireland and the Irish in Britain', he shows that in addition to the Irish-born population living in Britain and the several million explicitly claiming Irish descent, there are a quarter of Britons who have at least one Irish relative and over 60 per cent who have Irish friends or acquaintances. If one adds to this 'ethnic' evidence of hybridization, the pervasive cultural mixing between the two countries (music, media, cinema, literature, popular culture) one finds the mongrel dimension assuming even more significant proportions. As the Irish poet Thomas Kinsella remarks: 'We are what we are – mongrel pure'. Another Irish poet, Seamus Heaney, elaborates on this motif when he argues for an opening up of the 'symbolic ordering of Ireland', which may also admit 'a hope for the evolution of a political order, one tolerant of difference and capable of metamorphoses within all the multivalent possibilities of Irishness, Britishness, Europeanness, planetariness, creatureliness, whatever'. He then quotes the line from one of his poems that I have used in exergue to this book: 'Whatever is given / Can always be reimagined, however four-square, / . . . it happens to be' ('Frontiers of Writing' in *The Redress of Poetry*, Faber and Faber, London, 1995, p. 200).

Index